SOURCEBOOK ON PROBATION, PAROLE, AND PARDONS

— Second Edition —

Sourcebook on Probation, Parole and Pardons

By

CHARLES L. NEWMAN

Director
Correctional Training Program
Kent School of Social Work
University of Louisville

With an Introduction by

MILTON G. RECTOR

Director
National Council on Crime and Delinquency

CHARLES C THOMAS · PUBLISHER
Springfield · Illinois · U.S.A.

Published and Distributed Throughout the World by
CHARLES C THOMAS • PUBLISHER
BANNERSTONE HOUSE
301-327 East Lawrence Avenue, Springfield, Illinois, U.S.A.

Copyright 1958 and 1964, by CHARLES C THOMAS • PUBLISHER
Library of Congress Catalog Card Number: 64-11665

First Edition, 1958
Second Edition, 1964

Printed in the United States of America
N-1

DEDICATED TO THOSE
WHO SEEK TO IMPROVE
THE LOT OF THEIR
FELLOW MEN . . .

INTRODUCTION TO THE
SECOND EDITION

Since the first edition of this Sourcebook was published in 1958 developments have occurred which have had a significant impact on probation and parole. While these services are viewed and administered in many different ways, there are indications that they are increasingly viewed as integral parts of the total correctional process.

Probation and parole associations have in steadily increasing numbers changed their names to include "corrections" and to de-emphasize the past separateness of probation, parole, and institution personnel. The National Probation and Parole Association changed its name to the National Council on Crime and Delinquency to emphasize the problems with which we are all concerned rather than only two of the methods for dealing with these problems. The NCCD had in fact already extended its range of consultation, survey, standard setting and information service to all other phases of correction. The NCCD, however, continues to promote probation and parole as the two most effective and economical methods for dealing with the majority of offenders within the community and for identifying those offenders who require rehabilitation within the controls of an institution.

One of the most significant developments, spearheaded by federal legislation, the NCCD's Advisory Council of Judges, the National Conference of State Trial Judges, and the National Council of Juvenile Court Judges, has been the movement to provide training for judges. As federal, state, and local judges have gathered formally to examine the information and knowledge which must be available to them to make individualization fact rather than fiction in court decisions, the work of capable probation and parole officers and parole boards has found new respect in the minds of the judges.

A concomitant development has been the recognition that specialized training for probation and parole work is mandatory where common sense and an ability to work with people were not long ago considered sufficient by many employers in the court and correctional agencies. This recognition has increased the demands for short term institutes for personnel who have not had the benefit of professional training and more universities than ever before are offering such institutes. The accrediting agency for graduate schools of social work, the Council on Social Work Education, has made a special study of the social work training needs in corrections and has developed a project to give leadership in meeting these needs. This Sourcebook by Professor Charles L. Newman will continue to provide valuable information for the officer and professional-in-training, as well as for the professional in need of refreshing.

Hopefully the thirst for training in corrections and the movement toward professionalism in probation and parole will require another edition of this publication within a very few years. At that time we would hope to report more progress in the following where only a beginning has been made: New short term methods and techniques for probation and parole services for misdemeanants; increased application of group work and community organization methods in probation and parole; movement of the jail into the correctional complex as a short term treatment institution; the development of intake criteria and controls for adult detention; extension of diagnostic services to all juvenile, family, and criminal courts through regional detention-diagnostic centers to replace the old concepts of the local detention home and county jail; improved knowledge, techniques, and sentencing laws for dealing with dangerous offenders apart from those who are not dangerous; increased alternatives to institutional treatment with halfway houses and residential centers playing even more important roles in advance of confinement.

The millenium will have arrived when neither state nor federal agencies will increase the capacity of their institution systems until steps have been taken through standard setting, subsidy or direct operation to bring probation, parole, and other forms of community services up to the maximum level of use and performance.

MILTON G. RECTOR, *Director*
National Council on Crime and Delinquency

INTRODUCTION TO THE FIRST EDITION

T HE TERMS "probation," "parole," and "pardon" have meanings and usages which can be separately defined and identified. In the public eye, however, they are used inter-changeably, and unfortunately quite frequently with the connotation that the law-violator is being allowed to "get away" with "something."

It is difficult to say where the greatest confusion lies: in the differentiation between the usages of probation, parole, and pardons, or, in the appreciation of the underlying correctional philosophy involved in probation and parole, and the concept of social justice involved in the pardon.

Historically, pardon is by far the oldest. Absolute in its initial form, it later was transposed so that the focus included certain conditions, which in essence, changed pardon from the means of expunging guilt, to the recognition that guilt existed but that the penalty should be mitigated. From these roots, then, came the *conditional pardon,* and later, the parole.

The origin of probation remains in some dispute. It contains elements of the conditional pardon, in that requirements for incarceration are withheld conditional to the meeting of certain behavioral requirements, yet different because it does not involve imprisonment as may be the case in conditional pardon.

In this book, materials in the probation, parole, and pardons areas are surveyed. Although basically intended as a text for college courses in criminology and corrections, it should also have utility as a basic manual for in-service training of probation and parole workers. Moreover, it should provide basic material for the general reader who has more than a casual interest in the areas concerned.

No attempt has been made to make this volume an encyclopedia. There are many excellent books which have been devoted solely to counseling techniques, interviewing, case record preparation, and the like. Certainly the reader who wishes to have a more thorough knowledge of such materials will have to seek

beyond the confines of these covers. What I have attempted, however, is to prepare a volume, drawing materials from the most
authoritative sources, which will have practical, applied value to
the person who is or will be faced with the day to day function of
probation and parole supervision.

But man does not live by bread alone, and the probation or
parole officer needs to know that which is beyond his every day,
utilitarian needs. Thus, also are included materials which cover
the historical developments in probation, parole and pardons, as
well as a glimpse of these practices outside the United States.

We must recognize at the outset that this book has certain
biases and it is only fair that the reader be alerted before delving
into the contents. The assumption is carried throughout this book
that probation and parole are a part of the correctional cycle,
which begins with the arresting officer and ends with the final
release from prison or from parole, and the community.

The obvious conclusion is, then, that neither probation nor
parole will be any more effective than the weakest element in the
cycle. That is to say, where the court does not make proper dispositions in its assignment of probation, we cannot but assume
that the success of probation will be seriously handicapped. When
the prison does not prepare the inmate for community living,
then parole, by itself, is faced with a most difficult, and often
impossible task. When the community is unwilling to accept the
probationer or parolee after he has been "treated" and pronounced
"cured," then the task of these services are made immeasurably
more complex. When the police continue to "pick up" a parolee
on suspicion for every unsolved crime, regardless of the possibility
that he may not have been involved, because he has a "record,"
then the invitation is to repeated law violation.

Simply stated, the success of probation and parole can be
measured partly by the effectiveness of its personnel, and partly
by the quality of services rendered and attitudes maintained by
the auxiliary correctional services, law enforcement, and the
public.

Another bias refers to the professional identification of the
probation and parole officer. There are strong proponents for the
argument that probation and parole officers are, and *should be,*

social workers (and generally in the more restricted sense, case workers). Others argue with equal strength that this is not the case. We do not spend much time considering whether probation and parole are social work or something else. The duality between the aim of social control (expressed as the protection of society), and of social treatment (which is the necessity for rehabilitation of the law violator), is presented in a plaguing enigma in probation and parole work. Whatever methods are employed by the agent, whether they are labelled *case work, counseling, vocational rehabilitation* or something else, the dual aim must be met. And, insofar as society is concerned, the primacy of interest is directed to its own protection. It must be recognized, however, that the protection of society is vested in the rehabilitation of the offender as well as through strict, authoritarian surveillance.

Another bias is presented. Specifically, it states that the techniques of treatment involved in probation and parole work are basically the same, although the clientele may differ with the relation to their previous experience in anti-social behavior and/or institutionalization. The day may arrive when, on the basis of sound selective techniques, probation will be granted to only those individuals who would best profit from non-institutionalized re-education. The day may also arrive when all prisoners released from prison will be placed under parole supervision to assist in the process of readjustment from institution to community life. But until that time arrives, we can assume that there are a great many more likenesses between probationers and parolees than there are differences.

The selection of materials in this book represent, then, the foregoing orientation of the author. To the individual authors and publishers who graciously permitted the use of their materials in this volume, my grateful appreciation is expressed.

Bringing together these authoritative materials from their many sources form the design for this book. The responsibility for the choice and organization, as well as the introductory material is my own.

CHARLES L. NEWMAN
University of Louisville

CONTENTS

SOURCEBOOK ON
PROBATION, PAROLE,
AND PARDONS

Chapter One

CONDITIONAL PARDONS AND THE ORIGIN OF PAROLE

I N THE nineteenth century, the trend in penal philosophy shifted from one of punishment to that of reformation of the individual. The history of parole is inextricably a part of that movement. The reformers of the eighteenth and nineteenth centuries sowed the seeds from which sprang the reformatory idea. Subsequently, the parole movement was born.

The foundations of modern parole, then, are to be found in the progression from strict imprisonment, to freedom within limited areas, to liberation with conditions (either conditional pardon or ticket of leave), followed by restoration of liberty.

Parole, as it functions today, is difficult of definition in terms of a single precise concept. It is an integral part of the total correctional process. As such, it is a method of selectively releasing offenders from institutions, under supervision in the community, whereby the community is afforded continuing protection while the offender is making his adjustment and beginning his contribution to society.

Early parole practices, however, were closely tied to the colonizing of newly inhabited areas, as well as with the relocation of the offender in the community from which he came prior to imprisonment. In the beginning, supervision was limited to occasional surveillance. The concept of "treatment" developed slowly, and to this day has not received total public acceptance.

In this chapter, we consider the diverse roots from which parole has developed.

THE ORIGINS OF PAROLE*

A number of false beliefs exist regarding parole and its administration and at least two of these misconceptions which are current, have so little basis in fact that it is difficult to understand

---

* Reprinted in part by permission of the New York State Division of Parole. From, *Manual for Parole Officers*, 1953. p. 1-19 Footnotes omitted.

their widespread acceptance. There is, for example, the popular conception that parole developed from the Australian system of Ticket of Leave. The other equally fallacious belief is that rules and regulations of parole now in operation are those originated by members of boards of parole or administrators of parole.

Parole is the conditional release of an individual from a penal or correctional institution, after he has served part of the sentence imposed upon him. Parole did not develop from any specific source or experiment, but is an outgrowth of a number of independent measures, including the conditional pardon, apprenticeship by indenture, the transportation of criminals to America and Australia, the English and Irish experiences with the system of Ticket of Leave, and the work of American prison reformers during the Nineteenth Century.

Conditional Pardons and Transportation To America

The transportation of criminals to the American Colonies began early in the Seventeenth Century. The precedent for this removal of criminals from England can be found in a law passed in 1597 providing for the banishment "beyond the seas of rogues" who appeared to be dangerous. As early as 1617, the Privy Council passed an order granting reprieves and stays of execution to persons convicted of robbery, who were strong enough to be employed in service beyond the seas.

The transportation of criminals to America was backed and supported by the London, Virginia and Massachusetts companies, and similar organizations. At the time the plan was proposed, acute economic conditions prevailed in England. Unemployment was widespread. Taxes, particularly for the relief of the poor, were high and the English labor market was overcrowded. In spite of the existing situation, there were groups in England who opposed colonization, although the insistent demands for labor in the American Colonies could not be met. It was in an effort to avoid antagonizing these groups, and at the same time to satisfy the need for labor in the Colonies, that the Government devised the plan to transport convicted felons to America. The plan was presented to the King and he approved the proposal to grant reprieves and stays of execution to the convicted felons who were physically able to be employed in service.

The procedure developed to select individuals to be recommended to the King was somewhat similar to the present day methods followed by prison officials in recommending to the governor or parole boards in various states, the names of prisoners whose minimum terms are to be decreased by compensation or commutation allowance for good conduct and work willingly performed.

In England lists of names were compiled by court officials and signed by the judge or frequently by the mayor and recorder. The lists were then presented to the Secretary of State. In cases wherein a death sentence had been imposed, a stay of execution was automatically granted until the King had reviewed the recommendation made by the judge. The pardons granted by the King were written in Latin and accompanied by a docket in English, giving the name of the prisoner, his crime and, in some instances, a statement was added giving the reason why clemency had been granted.

In the beginning no specific conditions were imposed upon those receiving these pardons. However, a number of those pardoned had evaded transportation or had returned to England prior to the expiration of their term, it was found necessary to impose certain restrictions upon the individuals to whom these pardons were granted. It was about 1655 that the form of pardon was amended to include specific conditions and providing for the nullification of the pardon if the recipient failed to abide by the conditions imposed.

Transportation To America

During the early days of transportation, the Government paid to each contractor a fee of approximately five pounds for each prisoner transported. However, under the provisions of a law enacted in 1717, this procedure was discontinued and the contractor or shipmaster was given "property in the service" of the prisoner until the expiration of the full term. Once a prisoner was delivered to the contractor or shipmaster, the Government took no further interest in his welfare or behavior unless he violated the conditions of the pardon by returning to England prior to the expiration of his sentence.

Upon arrival of the pardoned felons in the Colonies, their services were sold to the highest bidder and the shipmaster then transferred the "property in service" agreement to the new master. The felon thereupon was no longer referred to as a criminal but became an indentured servant.

The system of indenture dates back to the Statute of Artifices enacted in 1562, and originally it had no relation to persons convicted of crime. Blackstone defined apprentices as "another species of servants who were usually bound out for a term of years by deed indenture." The contract of indenture was written on a large sheet of paper, the halves separated by a wavy or jagged line called an indent. The master and the apprentice or his guardian signed the form thereby agreeing to conform with the conditions specified. Van Doren in his biography of Benjamin Franklin quotes the conditions imposed upon Franklin in 1718, when at the age of twelve, he became indentured to his brother:

> ". . . During which term the said apprentice his master faithfully shall or will serve, his secrets keep, his lawful demands everywhere gladly do. He shall do no damage to his said master nor see it done to others, but to his power shall let or forthwith give notice to his said master of the same. The goods of his said master he shall not waste, nor the same without license of him to give or lend. Hurt to his said master he shall not do, cause or procure to be done. He shall neither buy nor sell without his master's license. Taverns, inns or alehouses he shall not haunt. At cards or dice tables or any other unlawful game he shall not play. Matrimony he shall not contract nor from the services of his master day or night absent himself but in all things as an honest faithful apprentice shall and will demean and behave himself toward said master all during said term."

This indenture bears a similarity to the procedure now followed by parole boards in this country. Like the indentured servant, a prisoner conditionally released on parole agrees in writing to accept certain conditions included on the release form which is signed by the members of the parole board and the prisoner. Even some of the conditions imposed today on conditionally released prisoners are similar to those included on the indenture agreement.

Transportation was, of course, terminated by the Revolutionary War, but for some time before this, the Colonists had vigorously protested against the importation of criminals. A tax was levied on each poor, disabled individual or felon received in the Colonies but even the imposition of the tax did not end the practice.

Bentham in reviewing criminal laws, comments that transportation had all the defects punishment can have and none of the qualities it might have; that under the transportation system, bondage was added to banishment but the convict who was able to offer the shipmaster a sum larger than that offered by an American Colonist could procure his liberty at the first port of call en route to America.

Transportation To Australia

The termination of the Revolutionary War ended transportation to America but England did not repeal her transportation law. Judges continued to impose sentences of transportation and the places of detention for prisoners awaiting transportation became overcrowded. Some attempt was made to relieve the situation by granting pardons freely but when a serious outbreak of crime occurred, the public demanded that the transportation law be enforced.

The Pitt Government had no interest in the rehabilitation of criminals. However, faced with a crime wave and the unsanitary conditions and overcrowding in the criminal detention quarters, the Government recognized the need for some immediate action. Australia had been discovered by Captain Cook in 1770 and the Government deliberated whether to use this land as a refuge for the thousands of American Royalists who had returned to England and were starving, or to establish Australia as a new colony for the reception of transported felons.

In 1787, the King announced that Australia was to be used for convict settlement and in May, 1787 the first fleet sailed, arriving at Botany Bay on January 18, 1788.

A different procedure was followed by the Government in dealing with prisoners transported to Australia than had previously been followed in transporting prisoners to America. All the expense incurred was met by the Government and the criminals transported did not become indentured servants but remained prisoners under the control of the Government which assumed responsibility for their behavior and welfare.

More conservative writers like Ives admit that the system of transportation had some value. He stated he believed transportation was to some extent "the wisest method of dealing with major criminals." O'Brien asserts: "It afforded an army of more than one hundred thousand persons a fresh start with real possibilities of rehabilitation."

No unbiased account of the history of transportation to Australia has been published. Authors who have dealt with this subject have dilated upon the primitive conditions which prevailed and the horrors which existed at Norfolk Island, Port Arthur, and the other penal settlements. The murders resulting from the sadistic treatment accorded to prisoners have been stressed and there are even accounts of prisoners who escaped and later practiced cannibalism.

The first governor of the penal settlement was given "property in service" for all felons under his supervision. He inaugurated the plan of assigning prisoners to the free settlers and when this transfer became effective, the settler or new custodian took over the "property in service" agreement.

From the days of Henry VIII, power to pardon felons could not be delegated to any individual without statutory authority. In 1790 a special enabling act gave to the governors of the penal settlements, power to remit sentences of transported prisoners. The first governor of Australia received instructions from the Government regarding the emancipation and discharge from servitude of prisoners whose conduct and work records indicated they were worthy to receive a grant of land. At first, these prisoners received an absolute pardon but later a new form of conditional pardon was instituted which became known as "Ticket-of-Leave." This Ticket-of-Leave was merely a declaration signed by the governor or his secretary, dispensing a convict from attendance at government work and enabling him, on condition of supporting himself, to seek employment within a specified district. No provision was made for his supervision by the government, the Ticket merely stating:

> "It is His Excellency, the Governor's pleasure to dispense with the government work of . . . . . . tried at . . . . . . convicted of . . . . . . and to permit . . . . . . to employ . . . . . . (off government stores) in any lawful occupation with the district of . . . . . . for his own advantage during good behavior or until His Excellency's further pleasure shall be made known."

This type of permit also took its origin from the Statute Artifices which provided that a servant, having lawfully terminated his employment, must be given a testimonial by his master. This testimonial gave the servant license to depart from the master and liberty to work elsewhere. No employer could legally accept anyone for service unless this testimonial or certificate of availability was produced.

Until 1811, Tickets-of-Leave were freely granted to prisoners for good conduct, meritorious service, or for the purpose of marriage. In 1811 a policy was adopted requiring that prisoners serve specific periods of time before being eligible to receive Tickets-of-Leave. This procedure, however, was not strictly adhered to until 1821, when a regular scale was formulated. Those who had a sentence of seven years could obtain a Ticket-of-Leave after serving four years; those with sentences of fourteen years, after serving six years, and those with life sentences, after serving eight years.

Great stress has been placed upon the experience of Alexander Maconochie, who was assigned as Governor of Norfolk Island in 1840. He devised new methods of treating prisoners but his experiments were limited to the prisoners confined in Norfolk and the success he achieved can hardly be attributed to the entire Australian system.

Maconochie said that in Van Dieman's Island he had "witnessed the dreadful state of depravity" to which the men in the public gangs had sunk, and the idea occurred to him that these conditions arose from the state of slavery to which the prisoners had been reduced. He originated the experiment of granting marks as a form of wages by which the state of slavery might be obviated and whereby the act of punishment would not be eliminated. He brought his proposed plan to the attention of the House of Commons in 1837, three years prior to his appointment as Governor of Norfolk.

He proposed that the duration of the sentence be measured by labor and good conduct within a minimum of time; that the labor thus required be represented by marks proportional to the original sentence, the prisoner to earn these marks in penal servitude before discharge. Marks were to be credited day by day to the convict, according to the amount of work accomplished. Maconochie, however, remained at Norfolk Island for a period of only four years and while his ideas were progressive and his experiments successful, his term of office was so limited that his achievements did not have any revolutionary effect on the system of transportation.

With the increase of free settlers, Australian Colonists began to protest the Government's use of the land for what they termed "a dumping ground for criminals." Although there were other reasons, the contributing factor in the decision of the Government to terminate transportation to Australia, was the threat of the Colonists to revolt.

Prior to the decision to terminate transportation, some effort had been made to alleviate some of the caustic criticism of the system by careful selection of the prisoners to be transported to Australia. The proposal was made that prisoners would first have to undergo a period of training and discipline in penal servitude in England, before transportation was effected. It was planned that this training period would cover a period of eighteen months. However, the experiment of selection was a failure, but it did mark the beginning of the utilization of trained and experienced individuals who were made responsible for the selection of the prisoners who had profited by the training program.

Three prison commissioners were appointed to accomplish the selection. The membership of this group may have established the precedent followed by American prison reformers in creating boards of parole consisting of three members.

The final termination of transportation to Australia did not occur until 1867, although opposition to the plan had been expressed as early as 1812.

England's Experience With Ticket-of-Leave

In America, as early as 1817, provisions had been made for the reduction of sentences by allowances for satisfactory work and conduct. The English Penal Servitude Act of 1853, governing prisoners convicted in England and Ireland, substituted imprisonment for transportation. By this Act, prisoners who received sentences of fourteen years or less were committed to prison, but the judge was granted permissive power to order the transportation or imprisonment of individuals who had received terms of more than fourteen years. This law also specified the length of time prisoners were required to serve before becoming eligible for conditional release on Ticket-of-Leave.

Those who had sentences exceeding seven years but not more than ten years, became eligible for Ticket-of-Leave after they had served four years and not more than six years. Prisoners who had sentences of more than ten years but less than fifteen, were required to serve at least six but not more than eight years, and those with sentences of fifteen years or more were required to serve not less than six nor more than ten years. America did not develop the use of the indeterminate sentence until nearly a quarter of a century after the enactment of the English Act of 1853.

The Act of 1853 related to conditional release and gave legal status to the system of Ticket-of-Leave. It provided:

"It shall be lawful for her Majesty by an order in writing under the hand and seal of one of Her Majesty's principal secretaries of State, to grant to any convict now under sentence of transportation, or who may hereafter be sentenced to transportation, or to any punishment substituted for transportation, by this Act, a license to be at large in the United Kingdom and the Channel Islands, or in such part thereof respectively as in such license shall be expressed, during such portions of his or her term of transportation or imprisonment, and upon such conditions in all respects as to Her Majesty shall deem fit; and that it shall be lawful for Her Majesty to revoke or alter such license by a like order at Her Majesty's pleasure.

"So long as such license shall continue in force and unrevoked, such convict shall not be liable to be imprisoned or transported by reason of his or her sentence, but shall be allowed to go and remain at large according to the terms of such license.

"Provided always, that if it shall please Her Majesty to revoke any such license as aforesaid, it shall be lawful for one of Her Majesty's principal secretaries of State, by warrant under his hand and seal, to signify to anyone of the Police Magistrates of the Metropolis that such license has been revoked, and to require such Magistrate to issue his warrant under his hand and seal for the apprehension of the convict to whom such license was granted, and such Magistrate shall issue his warrant accordingly and such warrant shall and may be executed by the constable to whom the same shall be delivered, for that purpose in any part of the United Kingdom or in the Isles of Jersey, Guernsey, Alderney or Sark, and shall have the same force and effect in all the said places as if the same had been originally issued or subsequently endorsed by a Justice of the Peace or Magistrate or other lawful authority having jurisdiction in the place where the same shall be executed, and such convict, when apprehended under such warrant, shall be brought, as soon as he conveniently may be, before the Magistrate by whom the said warrant shall have been issued or some other Magistrate of the same Court, and such Magistrate shall thereupon make out his warrant under his hand and seal, for the recommitment of such convict to the prison or place of confinement from which he was released by virtue of the said license, and such convict shall be so recommitted accordingly, and shall thereupon be remitted to his or her original sentence, and shall undergo the residue thereof as if no such license had been granted."

The following conditions were endorsed on the license of every convict liberated on a Ticket-of-Leave in England:

"1. The power of revoking or altering the license of a convict will most certainly be exercised in the case of misconduct.

2. If, therefore, he wishes to retain the privilege, which by his good behavior under penal discipline he has obtained, he must prove by his subsequent conduct that he is really worthy of Her Majesty's clemency.

3. To produce a forfeiture of the license, it is by no means necessary that the holder should be convicted of any new offense. If he associates with notoriously bad characters, leads an idle or dissolute life, or has no visible means of ob-

taining an honest livelihood etc., it will be assumed that he is about to relapse into crime, and he will be at once apprehended and recommitted to prison under his original sentence."

The British public accepted that in compliance with the provisions of the law, the programs followed in the prisons would be reformative and that prisoners selected for release on Ticket-of-Leave represented definite proof of having profited by the training and, therefore, their conditional release would not be incompatible with the welfare of society.

Long before the termination of transportation, it had been recognized that the experiment followed in Australia of releasing prisoners on Ticket-of-Leave without further supervision, was a serious mistake. However, this knowledge did not prevent a repetition of the procedure. The public had assumed that the Home Office planned to enforce the conditions imposed upon prisoners on Ticket-of-Leave during the first two years after the enactment of the Servitude Act of 1853. The outbreak of serious crimes which occurred within the next three years was attributed to the lack of supervision accorded the released prisoners. A campaign of criticism was carried on and Ticket-of-Leave men were blamed for most of the crimes committed. The public became convinced that the Ticket-of-Leave system was not only a menace to public safety but was an absolute failure.

The public was vociferous in its demands for action to correct the misuse of Tickets-of-Leave. A select committee was appointed to hold hearings and at one of the meetings a representative of the Home Office testified that no efforts had been made to develop any plan for the supervision of Ticket-of-Leave men after release. The Home Office had merely accepted that Ticket-of-Leave men were prisoners who had completed their sentences. The head of the London Police admitted that he had also misinterpreted the Provisions of the Act of 1853 and had, in fact, issued orders to the police that they were not to interfere with Ticket-of-Leave men.

Representatives of other law enforcing agencies asserted that it was not possible to identify Ticket-of-Leave men because no report on the convicts was furnished them by the officials granting the

Ticket and they learned that Ticket-of-Leave men had destroyed their licenses to be at large as a means of avoiding apprehension and identification. The only result of these hearings was the adoption of a Resolution by the Select Committee:

1. That the system of license to be at large, or Ticket-of-Leave, has been in operation too short a time to enable the committee to form a clear and decided opinion either as to the effect which it had already produced or to its probable ultimate workings.

2. That the system appears to be founded upon a principle, wise and just in itself, viz., that of enabling a convict to obtain by continued good conduct, while undergoing punishment, the remission of a portion of his sentence upon the expressed condition, however, that in case of subsequent misconduct, he should serve the residue of the original term specified in the original sentence.

3. That to render this system of Ticket-of-Leave, adopted both for the reformation of offenders and the interest of the public, the conditions endorsed on the Ticket-of-Leave ought to be enforced more strongly than appears to have been hitherto the case.

4. That every convict on his release with a Ticket-of-Leave ought to be reported to the Police of the town or district to which he is sent.

A series of prison riots occurred in the English prisons in 1862. Coupled with another serious crime wave, this again focussed attention on the administration of prisons and the Ticket-of-Leave system. The public again demanded that effective measures be taken to change the administration of prisons and correct the weaknesses of the Ticket-of-Leave system. Although the intent of the Act of 1853 had been to make prisons reformative in character, this objective had not been achieved. No real labor was performed in the prisons, discipline was lax, and the prison officials, apprehensive of the dangerous convicts, freely granted credit for good conduct to make prisoners eligible for release at the earliest possible date.

The House of Commons was petitioned to bring the situation to the attention of the Queen, who appointed a Royal Commission. At the public hearings held by the Commission, it was discovered that during the seven years which had elapsed since 1856, when the Select Committee had adopted its resolution, no system had been put into operation to supervise prisoners after their release. The fact that no understanding or cooperative agreement existed between the Home Office and the law enforcing agencies was also brought out. The head of the London Police openly admitted that until a few minutes prior to his appearance before the Royal Commission he had never seen a Ticket-of-Leave and had no knowledge of the conditions endorsed thereon.

Individuals who favored supervision by the police and those who opposed it, appeared before the Commission. Ticket-of-Leave men testified that they objected to reporting to the police because the latter were considered their "special enemies who dogged them and informed their employers of their criminal status." These criminals stated that they would be forced to steal or starve if supervised by the police, as no employer would hire them if aware of their criminal record. The police testified that if a Ticket-of-Leave man were required to report to the police in each community he visited, the need for watching would cease. They urged that the system of irregular supervision be abolished and that some uniform procedure with prescribed rules and regulations be established.

The Royal Commission in its report stressed the unreformative programs in operation in the prisons which rendered the prisoners unprepared for freedom. They also expressed the opinion that a large proportion of the prisoners released on Ticket-of-Leave had given no reliable proof of their reformation prior to release. The Commission strongly urged that England adopt the system followed in the prisons of Ireland.

As a result of the report of the Royal Commission, the services of the police were used for supervision and later a number of Prisoner's Aid Societies, supported partly by the Government, were established. These agencies followed the methods of supervising prisoners which had proven effective in Ireland.

The Irish System of Ticket-of-Leave

Sir William Crofton became head of the Irish prison system in 1854, one year after the enactment of the Servitude Act. He accepted the idea that the intent of the law was to make penal institutions something more than places of safe keeping, and that the programs in the prisons should be designed toward reformation and Tickets-of-Leave granted only to prisoners who gave visible evidence of definite achievement and change of attitude.

The Irish convict system under Crofton's administration, became famous for its three stages of penal servitude, particularly the second stage where classification was governed by marks obtained for good conduct and achievement in education and industry. So-called "indeterminate prisons" were also utilized, where conditions were made as nearly normal as possible and no more restraint was exercised over the inmates than was necessary to maintain order.

The administrators of the Irish System maintained that its success was due to the cooperation extended by the convict toward his own amendment and his conviction sooner or later that the system, however penal in its character, was designed for his benefit and that stringent regulations imposed for his supervision after release rendered a vocation of crime unprofitable and hazardous to follow. The form of Ticket-of-Leave issued in Ireland was slightly different than the one used in England. Known as Form E, it reads:

"Number of Convict's Book . . . . Order of License to be a convict made under Statute 27 and 28 Victoria, Chapter 47, Dublin Castle . . . . day of . . . . 18. . . . Her Majesty is graciously pleased to grant to . . . . of . . . . who was convicted of burglary first degree, at . . . . the . . . . thereupon sentenced to be kept in penal servitude for the term of . . . . and is now confined in the . . . . Convict Prison, Her Royal license to be at large from the day of his liberation under this order, during the remaining portion of said time of penal servitude, unless the said . . . . shall before the expiration of the said time be convicted of some indictable offense within the United Kingdom, in which case such license will be immediately forfeited by law, or unless it shall please Her Majesty sooner, to revoke or alter such license. This license is given subject to the conditions endorsed upon the same. Upon the breach of any of which it will be liable to be revoked whether such breach is followed by conviction or not, and Her

Majesty hereby orders that the said .... be set at liberty within thirty days from the date of this order."

The Ticket-of-Leave was signed by the Chief Secretary of the Lord Lieutenant of Ireland, and imposed the following conditions:

"1. The holder shall preserve this license and produce it when called upon to do so by a magistrate or police officer.
2. He shall abstain from any violation of the law.
3. He shall not habitually associate with notoriously bad characters, such as reported thieves and prostitutes.
4. He shall not lead an idle and dissolute life, without means of obtaining an honest livelihood."

"If the license is forfeited or revoked in consequence of a conviction of any felony, he will be liable to undergo a term of penal servitude equal to that portion of his term of . . . . years, which remains unexpired when his license was granted, viz., the term of . . . . years . . . . months."

Each Ticket-of-Leave man was further instructed as follows:

"Each convict coming to reside in Dublin City or in the County of Dublin will, within three days after his arrival, report himself at the Police Office, Exchange Court, Dublin, where he will receive instructions as to his further reporting himself.

"Each convict, residing in the provinces, will report himself to the constabulary station of his locality within three days after his arrival and subsequently on the first of each month.

"A convict must not change his locality without notifying the change to his constabulary in order that his registration may be changed to the locality to which he is about to proceed.

"Any infringement of these rules by the convict will cause to be assumed that he is leading an idle, irregular life and thereby entail a revocation of his license."

A description of the convicted man granted a Ticket-of-Leave was fully outlined on the back of the form.

Ticket-of-Leave men residing in rural districts were supervised entirely by the police, but those residing in Dublin were supervised by a civilian employee who had the title of Inspector of Released Prisoners. He worked cooperatively with the police but it was his responsibility to secure employment for the Ticket-of-Leave men. He required them to report at stated intervals and visited their homes every two weeks and also verified their employment. The problem of hounding by the police, which had been stressed at the hearings before the Select Committee and the Royal Commission in London, did not arise in Ireland. It was accepted that conditionally released prisoners would inform their employers of their criminal record and if they failed to do so, the head of the police was responsible for this action. Many of the problems being discussed by present day parole executives were confronted by the administrators of the Irish System and they adopted their policies to meet the needs. Contrary to the experience in England, the Irish System of Ticket-of-Leave had the confidence and support of both the public and the convicted criminal.

Prisoners Aid Societies

In England and Ireland after 1864, Prisoners Aid Societies were established, the Government contributing a share of funds equal to the sum raised by the Society for its work. These Societies employed agents who devoted their full time to the supervision of released prisoners, and whose duties were outlined as follows:

1. To visit the local prisoners weekly or oftener, if ordered by the Honorable Secretary and to take his instruction as to dealing with the cases selected for aid.
2. To visit local employers of labor taking every opportunity of seeing and becoming personally acquainted with foreman and other officials explaining to them the objectives of the Society and endeavoring to secure their cooperation.
3. To see the prisoner at the jail and accompany him to the railway station when needed, and to provide board and lodging for him for a limited time.
4. To visit constantly all persons under the care of the Society so long as they were unemployed and after employment is found.
5. To enter daily in a journal all parties seen and places visited and to submit the journal to the Committee at the monthly meeting.
6. To expend, under the direction of the Honorable Secretary, the money of all Ticket-of-Leave men under his supervision and to lose no opportunity of procuring suitable employment for them.

Developments in the United States

By 1865, the Crofton System had been widely publicized in America and prison reformers who were critical of the conditions existing in our prisons, suggested the adoption of new methods based on the Crofton plan. Although there were some critics of the Irish System, little attention was given to their opposition and American reformers continuously enunciated the need for new types of prison programs to provide for the grading of criminals, according to the degree of their reformation, and the use of the mark system as a check on their progress and restraint against disorder.

Propagandists for the Crofton System, however, did not believe in the adoption of the Ticket-of-Leave and specifically stated that "no Ticket-of-Leave system will ever be made acceptable and proper in the United States." Their attitude was apparently based on the conception that it would be un-American to place any individual under police supervision and they did not believe that any form of supervision would be effective. A letter written by Crofton in 1874, in reply to an inquiry sent him by the Secretary of the New York Prison Association, may have been responsible for a change in their viewpoint. In his communication, Crofton stressed that the police of Ireland were permitted to delegate competent individuals in the community to act as custodians for Ticket-of-Leave men. He suggested that America follow the practice of having prisoners about to be released name a "next friend" to whom they would be willing to make their reports, a person "likely to befriend them" and then to arrange with competent persons for supervision of a friendly character to the well-doer, but at the same time of a nature which will restrain the evil disposed by compelling them to observe the conditions upon which they have been liberated.

At the time the propaganda was being carried on for the adoption of the Crofton plan, the Elmira Reformatory in New York State was being constructed. Because of the widespread interest in prison programs, it would logically be assumed that before the new institution was opened, a suitable plan or organization would have been developed and necessary legislation enacted, or at least suggested by the Board of Managers of the State Government.

Elmira Reformatory was formally opened in July 1876, and had been operating for almost a year before its first Superintendent, Z. E. Brockway drafted a measure establishing a definite policy.

Prior to his appointment to Elmira Reformatory, Mr. Brockway had been head of the House of Correction in Detroit and while there, had drafted an indeterminate sentence law. His proposed measure outlined the following special features for the Elmira System:

1. An indeterminate or indefinite sentence, the length of time served to be dependent upon the behavior and capacity of the prisoner, within statutory limitation.
2. The status and privileges accorded to the prisoner, as in the Crofton plan, were to be determined by his behavior and progress.
3. Education was to be compulsory.
4. Provision was made for the release on parole of carefully selected prisoners.

Although no novel idea was included in the organization and administrative plan for Elmira, in its operation the system combined principles, the validity of which had been recognized separately.

The acceptance of the indeterminate sentence is so general today that it is difficult to comprehend why it should have become a serious controversial issue. The movement to substitute the indeterminate or reformative sentence for the fixed or definite term, began in England early in the Nineteenth Century.

As early as 1839 George Combs, a Scotch philosopher, visited America to lecture and it was he who suggested the idea of a sentencing board, the indeterminate sentence, parole, and what later became the basis for the system under which modern boards of parole function. In one of his lectures he said:

"If the principles which I advocate shall ever be adopted, the sentence of the criminal judge, on conviction of a crime, would simply be one of finding the individual has committed a certain offense and is not fit to live in society, and therefore granting warrant for his transmission to a penitentiary to be there confined, instructed, and employed until liberated in due course of law.

"The process of liberation would then become one of the greatest importance. There should be official inspectors of penitentiaries invested with some of the powers of a court, sitting at regular intervals and proceeding according to fixed rules. They should be authorized to receive applications for liberation at all their sessions and to grant the prayer of them on being satisfied that such a thorough change had been effected in the mental condition of the prisoner that he might safely be permitted to resume his place in society.

"Until this conviction was produced upon examination of his disposition, of his attainment, in knowledge of his acquired skills or some useful employment, of his habits of industry, and, in short, of his general qualifications to provide for his own support, to restrain his criminal propensities from committing abuses and to act the part of a useful citizen, he should be retained as an inmate of a penitentiary."

The vital principle of the indeterminate sentence was that no prisoner would be paroled until he was fit for freedom. Those who campaigned for the adoption of the indeterminate sentence recognized that in itself it had no mystic power but that its real strength was in the reformatory agencies—labor, education, and religion. It was also recognized that the indeterminate sentence placed in the hands of competent prison officials a tool which could be effectively used.

The main opposition to the enactment of indeterminate sentence laws came from the judges who were unwilling to relinquish their traditional privilege of fixing the time prisoners must serve. Despite their opposition, however, the law was enacted and provisions were also made for the parole of prisoners. At the beginning of the Twentieth Century, twenty-six states had adopted these measures.

The Elmira Reformatory and the Inception of Parole

Parole originated at the Elmira Reformatory and hence the procedures as they were initiated, may have some historical interest. Before being considered for parole, each inmate was required to maintain a good record of conduct for a period of twelve months. He was expected to have gained the confidence of the superintendent and the managers and before being released, he was required to present suitable plans for permanent employment. When his release had been approved, he was given a new suit of clothing and sufficient funds to reach his destination and to pay his immediate expenses. The superintendent then interviewed him on the day of his release and instructed him to proceed to his employment and remain there, if practicable, for at least six months. He was required to report to a guardian on his arrival and write directly to the superintendent notifying him that he had done so.

One of the conditions of his parole was that he must report on the first of every month to his guardian and report his situation and conduct. The guardian's report and certification by the parolee's employer as to his wages, were transmitted to the superintendent of Elmira. A record was kept of all paroled men who were required to report for a minimum period of six months. It was the belief that a longer period under supervision would be discouraging to the average paroled man.

→ According to the philosophy of the Reformatory officials it was considered preferable to have the paroled prisoner return to the place from which he was committed or the place of his usual habitation, on the basis that "recuperation from a damaged reputation and recovery of public confidence are easiest in the community where the misconduct occurred." The employer and the parole supervisor were "always made fully acquainted with all the facts, this for the sake of honesty, safety, and for the salutary mutuality of the confidential relations involved." Paroled prisoners were not permitted to conceal or deny their history. Monthly reports certified by the employer and supervisor were required. The officials considered the chief of the local police—"not the average policeman in the great cities, nor indeed a religious or philanthropical organization or private individual" the most satisfactory individual to supervise paroled prisoners.

→ American prison reformers were aware of the conditions under which prisoners conditionally released from institutions in England and Ireland were granted their liberation. Although for the most part, the same restrictions were enforced, certain new procedures were developed in the supervision of released prisoners in this country.

One of the first institutions for juvenile delinquents was established in New York State in 1820. An Indenturing Committee of three members was appointed and they adopted the policy of requiring written reports from the sponsors and the children who were released from the institution.

Early in the history of prisons in the United States, public interest and one of the major considerations of the penologists was centered in the problems presented by discharged prisoners. Prisoners Aid Societies were established early in the Nineteenth Century to give needed relief to prisoners discharged from the institutions and to aid them in securing employment. Each prisoner who was given assistance by the Society was required to submit written reports to the Society covering his progress, behavior, earnings, and savings. This policy of requiring written reports from prisoners was later adopted by the officials at the Elmira Reformatory.

With the great stress placed upon reformation, and the knowledge of England's experience with Ticket-of-Leave men, it should have been obvious that if the new system was to be given a fair trial, prison programs would have to be revolutionized. Ignoring this important factor in the treatment of criminals, state after state proceeded to enact indeterminate sentence and parole laws and the abuse of them became widespread.

No thought was given to the training of prisoners toward their future adjustment in the community and both prison administrators and inmates soon accepted the idea that reformed or unreformed, allowance of time for good behavior was automatic and release at the earliest possible date was a right, rather than a privilege. After release, supervision was either non-existent or totally inadequate if it was required. The result was a duplication of the English experience.

Every charge that had been made against the operation of the early English system of Ticket-of-Leave was leveled against the administration of parole in the United States.

It has been only within the past two decades that drastic action has been taken by a number of states to render prison reform and parole effective parts of the state system of correctional care. It is now recognized that parole can be an effective method of community protection and at the same time offer constructive aid to released prisoners. To achieve these objectives, however, the system must be adequately financed, non-political in operation, and supported by public trust and confidence.

Chapter Two

ORIGIN AND DEVELOPMENT OF THE PARDONING POWER

THE INSTITUTION of pardon and the practice of pardoning long antedates the prison system. Evidences of it appear in Mosaic law, the Vedic Law of India, and elsewhere. In England, the use of executive clemency seems to have grown out of the conflict between the King and the nobles who threatened his power. Although loosely recognized among his predecessors, it was William the Conqueror who brought to England the view that the pardoning power was the exclusive prerogative of the king. The main exception to this practice was the "benefit of clergy" which had been built up by the church in its system of canon law.

Many of the early English legal writers admitted the necessity of pardons as long as justice was exercised as it was. Recall that in the seventeenth century there were some three hundred crimes which were designated as felonies and that as felonies, where "clergy" could not be pleaded, the punishment was death. The judge had no alternative: he could condemn to death, or he could reprieve. Beccaria argued that as punishments became more mild, there would be less necessity for pardons. And so it has been.

The English practice of pardon was followed by the American colonies. In the establishment of colonial charters, the pardoning power was vested in the royal representative.

Following the liberation of the colonies from England, the pardoning power was vested in different officials in the various States.

The administration of the machinery of pardons in the United States today continues to be confused and not infrequently inequitably maintained. The major study of pardons continues to be among the Attorney General's *Survey of Release Procedures* (5 volumes) 1939-1940. Over two decades later, the report, insofar as pardons are concerned, remains substantially correct.

Are pardons being abused? The true functions of pardons are still misunderstood in many quarters. Pardon as a legal device for tempering justice with mercy and for righting the wrongs of justice should be forever preserved. It is not, however, a substitute for parole, nor a reward for exemplary conduct while under penal servitude.

Closely associated with the pardon is the topic of the legal rights of prisoners. Strangely, the statutes of many states are silent on the matter of rights of convicted felons. Needless to say, the general public is even more confused by many of the popular misconceptions regarding the "loss of citizenship" and "civil rights."

LEGAL RIGHTS OF PRISONERS*

No asset in our cultural heritage has been more precious than the sense of justice and the methods by which we have traditionally sought to fulfill it. We have accepted as a rudimentary necessity of social control the fair testing of man's legal guilt of crime. The struggles of democratic revolution in England and on the Continent have erected a bulwark of procedures to assure a full protection against wrongful conviction, so that innocent suspects might not be accursed as criminals. In this country, the legal rights with which history has endowed the accused have persevered more or less intact through the vicissitudes of recurrent emergencies and hysteria.

The critical observer of our culture is confronted with a strikingly different picture in our methods of dealing with convicted criminals. For the accused, there is regularity and uniformity assured through the rule of law, but once convicted, offenders are handled under a veritable chaos of procedures, philosophies, and objectives. In sentencing and treatment, one finds an administrative hegemony little restrained by legal or due process conceptions. This contrast between a well-defined legal ordering of trial and a poorly defined administrative system of sentencing and treatment appears to be rooted largely in the differing historical evolution of each. The modern correctional sanctions, together with their supporting theories and procedures, have developed in the main subsequent to that renaissance of criminal law in which our basic ideals of justice were molded.

---

* Reprinted by permission of the American Academy of Political and Social Science. Paul W. Tappan: The Legal Rights of Prisoners, The *Annals,* Vol. 293, May 1954. p. 99-111. Footnotes are omitted.

The old retributive penology was predicated on the view that the proven criminal was an "outlaw" without legal rights. Not only might he be subjected to the crudest penalties, but he lost his citizenship (if not his life), his identity of person, and his property. The historical development of a legal due process to protect those accused of crime did not substantially alter the nature of punishments inflicted on those convicted. Religious, moral, and political conceptions established little refuge for the criminal, once his guilt was established. However, humanistic influences, particularly during the nineteenth century, came to alleviate some of the barbarism in the treatment of offenders, to provide extenuations, exceptions, and escapes from the full rigor of punishment. There has been a gradual and considerable change in modern penology under the impact of social humanitarianism, of behavior sciences and permissive philosophy, and of diverse other cultural influences. Correctional treatment has been swayed by new and often conflicting ideologies of individualization, rehabilitation, social protection, and social reform. But the changes have occurred for the most part administratively, with little relation to conceptions of due process and the rule of law that had developed during the eighteenth century and before. In an age of reliance upon administrative judgment and process, we have deprecated the restriction of executive authority by law. As in other areas of governance, we have looked, often with dewy-eyed expectancy, to the expert, though with great uncertainty in the field of corrections as to what constitutes expertness. We have sought abstract, loosely defined goals, with a minimum of direction or control by law over the authorities charged with the treatment of the criminal.

Thus it is that as we look to the legal rights of prisoners in the United States we find, in vivid contrast to the substantive law of crimes and to the law of evidence and procedure, that there are broad penumbra of vague legal specifications and areas of deep shade, where the law is wholly silent. Rights of citizenship and of person and property attaching to the criminal have not been clearly defined by constitution or statute. The convict generally has the right to appeal from conviction and to protection against cruel and unusual punishments but, as we shall note in more detail below, even these protections are limited and vary in practice. Certain other rights and restrictions are established by law in some jurisdictions, but there is no consistency in the matter.

Loss of Rights

There are four main ways in which ordinary political or civil rights of the individual may be taken away as a direct or indirect consequence of criminal conviction.

Civil-death Statutes

1. Special statutes may attach the status of civil death to the offender, usually on the basis of a sentence to life imprisonment or to death. Civil-death statutes survive today in some seventeen jurisdictions, though the meaning of the term is far from uniform in these states. It has been held that the convict who is civilly dead cannot sue to enforce his rights in court. The seriousness of this restriction is discussed briefly at a later point. In several of these states, offenders under life sentence are specifically prohibited from exercising rights to contract or to sell or inherit property. In some, their property is distributed after conviction as though they were actually dead. In others, it may pass at once under a will, though it is unlikely that this could result in the absence of a statute specifically so providing. Ordinary political rights to vote, hold office, testify, or act as juror are extinguished.

Civil-death statutes are among the most primitive survivals in our system of penalties. It appears clear that where certain rights should be taken from the felon, this ought to be done in specific terms rather than under a civil-death law.

Suspended Rights

2. Rights may be suspended during a term of imprisonment less than life. Nine of the states with civil-death statutes and one other provide for the general suspension of rights during imprisonment short of a life term. Where no such statutes exist, it appears that convicts can sue but that where rights are suspended, they cannot, though they may be sued and can defend against an action. The right to hold public office or positions of honor or trust is sus-

pended during imprisonment in several states, though a majority of jurisdictions provide for actual forfeiture persisting after incarceration rather than mere suspension. The right to testify is suspended as a matter of convenience in most jurisdictions, but a number of states provide that the offender's deposition may be taken in prison.

Permanent Deprivations

3. Conviction of a felony, generally, or of specified crimes involving "moral turpitude" may result in the absolute loss of certain rights. Commonly, these statutory provisions establish the deprivations on conviction coupled with imprisonment, and one must look to the provisions on restoration of rights to determine whether the conviction terminates rights or whether imprisonment merely suspends them. The laws are neither consistent nor clear in this matter. It appears from the statutes that there is not mere suspension but full deprivation (unless and until there is a subsequent restoration by pardon or other means) of the right to vote in at least thirty-five states. In a majority of states, there is also actual forfeiture of public office and positions of trust. A few states disqualify the felon for jury duty.

Marital rights and status present a somewhat peculiar problem. Rights of cohabitation are suspended universally. In other respects, policy varies extensively. In several jurisdictions, life imprisonment involving civil death automatically terminates the marriage, without the necessity for any legal action. In others, the spouse must secure a decree even though the prisoner is civilly dead. In thirty-six states, conviction of a felony, coupled with imprisonment, is a ground for divorce, and if a divorce is granted pardon does not restore conjugal rights. In some jurisdictions, the felon's children can be given to adoption without his consent.

Deprivation by Commissions or Boards

4. Conviction may be the basis of action by a licensing agency or professional board to deprive the offender of certain rights, usually those of employment. This is an indirect method of determining his rights. In the fields of civil service regulations for gov-

ernmental employment, licensing and revocation of license for certain professions and other occupations, and rights of compensation for injury or other wrongs and of residence within the United States, deprivations may often be determined by commissions or boards rather than by courts of criminal law.

State statutes commonly list some of the following who may be deprived of their occupations as a result of their conviction of an infamous crime: accountants, barbers, civil engineers, detectives, automobile operators, embalmers, hairdressers, junk dealers, real estate brokers, liquor store owners, pawnbrokers, pharmacists, midwives, naturopaths, nurses, veterinarians, chiropodists, chiropractors, dentists, physicians, surgeons, and lawyers. It is the general rule that a licensing agency, court, or governmental department may refuse to issue or may revoke a license or permit in such occupations where it is shown that the offender has been convicted of a felony, a crime involving moral turpitude, or an offense specifically designated as a basis of exclusion. Where revocation has occurred, the offender generally has a right to appeal to a court for review, as provided by statute. He may have a similar right to appeal if a license is denied him. The power to issue or revoke is a specialized administrative one, however, and the courts will not generally overrule the decision of an agency without a clear showing of gross abuse of discretion.

It may be noted that there is some provision limiting or postponing the exercise of civil or personal rights directly or indirectly (as, for example, by tolling the statutes of limitations) in every state. Since the deprivations that we have mentioned are derived to a large extent from the common law, it is probable that some losses of rights are drawn from tradition in jurisdictions where there are no express statutory provisions therefor.

Restoration of Rights

We have summarized briefly the general patterns relating to the suspension or deprivation of rights entailed by criminal conviction. It is apparent that the existing structures have developed crescively and differentially throughout the country over a period of time. There has been nothing uniform or systematic in the philosophy or objectives by which the rules have developed. And there has been little effort to assure a regulatory due process of law to protect either the offender or the public. In practice, two or more of the methods described above are employed in most jurisdictions in denying or limiting offenders' rights, and the restrictions differ considerably in nature, as we have noted. Commonly it is impossible to determine from the statutes alone whether particular rights are lost, suspended, or retained by the offender.

Further confusion arises from the variation in practice as to the restoration of rights forfeited or suspended. There appear to be several patterns by which rights may be restored. (1) Restoration may occur automatically, by operation of law, upon discharge from imprisonment or from parole. (2) An ordinary executive pardon may restore some or all rights automatically or particular rights may need to be specified in the pardon. (3) Some form of special action of certification, as provided by statute, may be required.

State Pardon

The most generally prevailing method of restoring civil rights that have been denied as a consequence of conviction is through pardon by the state. Some or all rights removed may be restored either by pardon or by some similar form of executive or legislative clemency in thirty-seven states. In ten of those noted, only the suffrage is restored by pardon, but in one of these (Rhode Island) the voting privilege may not be restored where conviction was for perjury or an infamous crime. Two others (Nevada and Virginia) prohibit the subsequent holding of office or positions of trust. A minority rule, prevailing in at least five jurisdictions, requires that the pardon must provide specifically for the restoration of any rights that the executive may wish to return. It should be noted, moreover, that in certain situations, rights lost may not be restored even by a full and unconditional pardon. Thus, property interests that have been vested in others cannot be returned. Pardoned offenders who have been rendered civilly dead are most likely to have suffered permanent loss of property rights, of course. Also, where a spouse has exercised the privilege of divorce from the offender, the convict cannot regain connubial rights through a pardon. The writer has noted elsewhere his opinion that pardon is a poor device for restoring civil or other rights.*

Enforcement of Franchise Loss

Enforcement of provisions for the deprivation of the franchise and other political rights, when they are not automatically restored upon release from imprisonment, is generally of a quite superficial nature. Unless a special investigation is made into voting frauds, for example, the police and FBI files are not ordinarily consulted to determine whether men have been convicted of crimes. There are laws in most if not all jurisdictions, however, making illegal registration or voting and the usurping of office crimes, and such laws undoubtedly act as some deterrent. When an offender moves into a jurisdiction where his prior conviction or incarceration raises a bar to certain civil rights he may wrongfully but unknowingly exercise the rights that he has lost without being discovered. It has been held that where the defendant honestly believed that his rights had been restored by a pardon, he was improperly convicted of willful and knowing violation.

Automatic Restoration

The most liberal, least discriminating method of restoring lost rights is to return them automatically upon completion of sentence. Wisconsin provides for automatic restoration when the offender serves out his term, or otherwise satisfies the sentence of the court. Somewhat similarly, Ohio law restores forfeited rights to all prisoners who have served their maximum terms or who are granted final release by the Pardon and Parole Commission. In

---

* "While in theory pardon is an act of executive clemency, to be used sparingly in instances where innocence has been shown subsequent to conviction or where some other injustice has been worked, actually in many jurisdictions the pardoning power is often used by the chief executive of the state as a substitute for parole and in this connection may be badly misused. It does not make sense or justice to grant restoration of civil rights either generally or by specific provision through the governor's pardon and to withhold these rights from those released on parole or discharged at the expiration of sentence. The effect is to make restoration a matter of gubernatorial leniency rather than a considered policy of correctional rehabilitation. Other methods, therefore, are desirable to restore the offender to the normal rights and duties of the citizen in the community."

Colorado, rights may be restored either by pardon or service of a full term, and in Kansas "citizenship" is restored where the governor commutes sentence or where prisoners are discharged from supervision. In several jurisdictions, a time factor or some other element is introduced into this sort of provision. Thus, Missouri law releases from disabilities prisoners who have received good time allowances, and who have lived in the community without further offense for a period of two years. In South Dakota the criminal discharged from the penitentiary with a clear record of good conduct is restored to full rights. Tennessee restores rights automatically after six months or three years, depending on the offense involved, except for infamous crimes, where a court action is required. Several states apply a rule of restoration to probationers comparable to the principle recommended by the Model Act of the National Probation and Parole Association. Delaware allows the striking of the verdict or plea of guilty from the record, when a probationer has complied with all conditions of his probation. Idaho and Illinois provide, somewhat less liberally, for the restoration of civil rights upon completion of the probation period. In Oregon, the probationer or parolee may exercise all civil rights that are not "political," presumably voting and holding office.

Certification

A more selective approach to restoration has been established in several jurisdictions where some form of certification is required for the purpose. A California law of 1944 provides that any felon released from a state institution may apply for a certificate of rehabilitation and a pardon after completing his sentence or parole period with satisfactory behavior. The certificate restores most civil rights. In New York a certificate of good conduct may be granted by the Parole Board, upon application of the offender, after he has conducted himself satisfactorily for five years after suspension of sentence, release on parole, or termination of sentence. This certificate ends disabilities that were created by conviction. Certificates of good conduct are also issued in Colorado, Minnesota, Ohio (at the Women's Reformatory), and Wyoming. In these states, however, certification is by the warden of the institution and on the basis of that action the governor will restore civil rights in Minnesota and Ohio and may do so in Colorado and Wyoming.

Restoration of Licenses

Finally, where licenses or permits to practice certain occupations or professions are taken away by special boards or commissions, such privilege is ordinarily not restored merely by pardon or by certification of the sort noted above. These deprivations represent the effort of an occupational group to protect itself and the general public against dangers that may be threatened by the criminal. Once an agency has withdrawn a privilege, it must itself act positively to restore it and may refuse to do so, depending on the law and the rules under which it operates. In order to force its favorable action, it must generally be shown in court that the agency has abused its discretion.

Rights Generally Retained

We have discussed above some of the rights that are lost as a consequence of criminal conviction or imprisonment and how these rights may be regained. Our penal system also provides specifically for the prisoner's retention of some rights of person and property, generally so that he may be protected from excessive abuses. As we have noted, the tendency has been to avoid or mitigate the harsh consequences that historically have attached to civil death and to imprisonment. There are serious problems involved, however, in the lack of consistent policy and even more in finding means by which to make these rights real in practice.

As to property rights it is the general rule that the prisoner may sue. However, as indicated above, where rights are generally suspended, the inmate cannot sue. This is a serious restriction on his power to secure remedy for injuries or wrongs that may have been done him during imprisonment. It is generally held, however, that the prisoner may be sued and can, therefore, defend such action. Moreover, except where statutes specifically provide to the contrary it appears to be the rule that the prisoner may contract and may take, hold, convey, or inherit property. In several jurisdictions, provision is made for the appointment of trustees to care for the prisoner's property until after his release. And in thirty states there are provisions suspending the statutes of limitations during imprisonment, so that where inmates cannot sue while imprisoned, they may have their action after release. In at least twenty-eight states the laws make some provisions against forfeitures, so that the historical consequences of attainder and corruption of blood may be avoided.

Protections and Remedies for the Offender

One form of protection for the convicted offended is the provision against cruel and unusual punishments that may be found in the Eighth Amendment of the federal Constitution and in those of all states except Connecticut and Vermont. Presumably, the infliction of cruel punishments would also be in violation of the due process clause of the Fourteenth Amendment. Seven of the states establish in their constitutions the principle that punishment should be proportioned to the offense. Unfortunately these general provisions do not inform at all concretely as to what should be considered cruel. They are generally interpreted to refer to the kind rather than the amount of punishment, but conceptions of excessive cruelty vary. In nine states, specific laws prohibit corporal punishment, and in some others restrictions are imposed on the forms or conditions of its employment. Such practices as whipping and striking, showering, tying up, and using the strait jacket, gag, or thumbscrew are prohibited in a few states. Only one jurisdiction (Louisiana) prohibits solitary confinement and many provide specifically for its use, some with severe dietary restrictions to accompany it. The Attorney General's Survey in 1939 observed that solitary segregation was being used in all but four prisons of the United States. That report also noted that at least twenty-six prisons were employing some form of corporal punishment; probably many more were, since it is difficult to secure valid information on this sort of question. It appears that constitutional and statutory provisions are of limited utility in protecting the committing offender, mainly because we have found it difficult to define what is improper and because enforcement of a good policy is extremely difficult. Perhaps sound practice depends more on the good sense and humaneness of individual wardens than anything else.

Legal Remedies

The legal remedies available to the prisoner against wrongs occurring to him during confinement are injunctions, habeas corpus writs, and civil suits for damages. Unfortunately, these are by no means always adequate. As Samuel Widdifield has noted:

> ... it has been held that disciplinary punishment is peremptory and not subject to review except where there has been gross excess. The problem of proof may be a difficult one to surmount. In states where the prisoner has been declared civilly dead or has had his civil rights suspended access to the courts may be impossible. Further, the prisoner may not be permitted to see a lawyer, or may not be able to afford one, in order to be made aware of his rights. Most objectionable, the prison officials may do everything they can to prevent a prisoner from asserting his rights.

The remedy of injunction is ordinarily not allowed unless it can be clearly shown that irremediable injury to property or personal rights is threatened. The writ of habeas corpus, however, may be used to rectify mistreatment under both state and federal practice. Its effectiveness has been limited by the holding that recourse to federal process can only be had after state remedies are exhausted. The record in Illinois reveals that the state courts can effectively prevent such remedies over an extended period of time, and it has recently been held that the federal courts will provide remedy where the state has failed to do so.

A civil suit for damages sustained is a somewhat inadequate remedy, not only because it is not designed to prevent injury initially, but because in a number of jurisdictions, as we have seen, the prisoner cannot sue until after discharge from incarceration. The difficulties of proof are greatly increased, of course, when this is the case. There is a federal civil rights statute that may be invoked for wrongs sustained, either under state or federal imprisonment. A few states have similar laws. Actions brought under such statutes must be taken against the warden or his staff, however, since state governments are protected from suit. The courts have generally held that it is the duty of prison officials to exercise reasonable care to protect the life and health of the prisoner. There have been very few such suits successfully pursued, however.

Criminal action may be directed against those responsible for prison mistreatment or neglect of duty under the federal civil rights law and special criminal statutes in some thirty-four states. These provide generally for fines or jail terms. Difficulty of access to the courts and of mustering proof may account for the small number of such cases successfully prosecuted.

Rights as Affected by Federal Law

Some special comment must be made on civil rights as they are affected by federal law. For the most part, United States statutes do not provide for the loss of either citizenship or civil rights. Most such rights derive from state constitutions and laws rather than federal, and their deprivation occurs, therefore, through the jurisdictional power of the state. Hence, a federal conviction of a crime or imprisonment in a federal institution may result in loss of political and other rights by reason of the specific legal provisions for the deprivation of such rights in the particular state, even though the conviction was not had in a state court. Restoration of rights also depends upon state law, but it too may be affected by federal action: Presidential pardon, while it does not itself confer or restore any rights, generally removes the effect of conviction and imprisonment, so that the individual may regain his privileges either with or without further action by the state, depending upon its legal provisions on restoration. As under state practice, federal actions of clemency may be specifically denominated as "pardons to restore civil rights" where they are not based upon innocence. Naturally, only federal pardons may be granted for federal offenses, state pardons for state crimes. It should be noted that, in accordance with the principle involved here, civil and other deprivations that are auxiliary to the conviction are quite different in effect than are the major penalties imposed by the courts: a conviction or imprisonment in *any* state or in the federal courts may result in loss of rights in another jurisdiction in accordance with its laws. Similarly a pardon or other device of clemency employed by an appropriate executive has effects elsewhere that depend upon the laws of the jurisdiction where the offender attempts to assert his rights.

As a partial exception to the generalizations made above, it should be noted that there are some limited provisions in the laws of the United States for a direct denial of rights. Loss of citizenship or nationality may result from a court martial conviction for desertion in time of war or from a charge of treason, of attempting to overthrow the government by force, or of bearing arms against the United States.

Beyond these provisions, the law disqualifies from holding federal office or position of trust individuals convicted of treason, inciting rebellion, conspiracy to violate civil rights of any citizen, bribery, mutilation, or falsification of public records, and government employees who receive compensation for rendering service to any person in relation to a matter, in which the United States is interested before any government department.

Deportation and Loss of Citizenship

On a somewhat different footing are the provisions for deportation of aliens on the basis of criminal conviction: the deprivation of the privilege of domicile. The Immigration Act of 1917 makes provision for the deportation of undesirable aliens upon the directive of the Attorney General where it can be shown that they have been convicted of crimes involving moral turpitude. An order of deportation may be appealed to the Board of Immigration Appeals or attacked by a writ of habeas corpus, if the alien is in custody and can show that his hearing was not fair, that the evidence was not substantial, that the order exceeded the Attorney General's authority, or that he has been held unreasonably long. Also, in accordance with provisions of law in the jurisdiction where such convictions occurred, as unconditional pardon may preclude deportation by blotting out guilt. In at least one jurisdiction (Pennsylvania) completion of the prison term is sufficient to accomplish this result. In one recent year, a governor of New York

State granted forty-eight pardons to aliens whose prison terms had expired but who had remained liable to deportation, some of them for a number of years.

Save for the exceptional offenses we have noted, the native does not lose his citizenship through law violations. When he does sustain such loss he becomes a stateless person, but this does not necessitate his deportation. However, it has been held that when a native here has become a citizen of another country, though he did not intend to abandon his United States citizenship, he may be deprived of the latter and refused admission to the United States as an alien, even if no crime was involved. Under our immigration laws the criminal alien may be excluded or deported for fraudulent admission. The noncriminal alien who is admitted may be deported for the subsequent commission of crimes involving moral turpitude and, if he has been issued a certificate of citizenship, may be deprived thereof.

A Reasonable Approach

It is not proposed in this paper to deal elaborately with solutions to the problems of civil rights. Our purpose was merely to describe summarily the present confused condition of these matters. In conclusion, however, it may not be inappropriate to comment on the principles involved and what may be a reasonable social and penological approach. The deprivation of "civil rights" may be conceived to be either an auxiliary punishment in itself or the incidental consequence of conviction and sentence, not intended to be specifically punitive but merely protective of public interests and of official convenience. Such a distinction as this appears unimportant to the offender: he may well consider these losses to be a part of the vindictive punishments that society exacts. And, in fact, they do appear very frequently to reflect retributive sentiments rather than any real need for community protection. The risk of repeated crime to which society is continuously subject from released offenders is patently greater than the possible consequences of their exercise of the rights that are generally removed.

Deprivation of the right to vote, to hold public office, or to act as juror during a period of incarceration is quite clearly a matter of convenience, if not necessity. Loss of the right to practice one's business or profession or to assume a position of trust, even after release from imprisonment, may often be more largely a matter of public protection than of retribution. However, when the right to vote, to act as juror or to testify, to hold office or trust, to practice in an occupation of one's training and choice is denied to probationers, to parolees, to those who have completed their sentences and been discharged, and even to those who have been pardoned, the gratuitously punitive element is great. In such instances, it appears that more mischief than benefit may commonly be worked, for the restrictions imposed do more to prevent rehabilitation than they do to protect the public.

The customary forms of deprivations of civil rights, it is submitted, are not for the most part sound as auxiliary punishments. Except for the deprivation of occupational privileges (including the holding of public office), they do little or nothing to repress crime. This is not to deny that auxiliary punishments—such as restitution, for example—may serve an obviously useful purpose, but the losses of civil rights are not, for the most part, of comparable utility.

Some General Principles

In the light of what we have written, the following principles are submitted:

1. The ordinary forms of deprivations that we have discussed are not appropriate as auxiliary punishments, for they serve little purpose in deterring crime or incapacitating criminals. Put differently, they are not appropriate measures under a penology that would eschew punishments exacted for their own sake or designed to brand the offender as infamous or outlaw.

2. As a matter of public and official convenience, it is desirable during imprisonment to limit the criminal's freedom to act as juror or serve in public office, perhaps to vote (though no great harm would result, it seems, from prisoners' use of "absentee ballots"). This principle of convenience is restricted, obviously, to the period of actual incarceration. Moreover, though some considerable inconvenience may be involved, it is desirable to *permit* the exercise of certain important privileges, such as the right to

sue and to receive and convey property, real and personal. The right to sue for wrongs done to the prisoner or his property is of special importance. If the offender is not allowed direct access to the courts for such purposes, he should at least be permitted to enjoy these rights through a representative.

3. Aside from periods of incarceration, it may be desirable to protect public interests by prohibiting the exercise of certain ordinary rights for some period of time, such as the privileges of occupation and office. It appears, however, that a finer discrimination should be employed in serving this objective. Some balance must be struck between the measures of threat to community welfare, on the one side, and on the other both the intrinsic value of maximizing personal freedom under a system of democratic justice and the utility of encouraging the sound exercise of rights in helping individuals to become responsible citizens. For the most part, aside from exceptions that have been noted, the civil and property rights lost through conviction raise small problem of social danger. It appears that the law should not provide flatly for denial of civil and political rights to those who are on probation or parole. Limited and special provisions might well be made, however, for the denial during the period of their sentences of certain political rights (particularly the holding of office) to those who have committed atrocious political offenses and of certain occupational privileges to those who have exploited their occupations in seriously illegal ways. There appears to be no excessive hazard, however, in the English rule that leaves full rights with those who are selected for probation. And there is merit in assisting the rehabilitation of the parolee by restoring all rights to him. There is also some danger, of course, but prison release must involve risk in any event.

4. Justice demands an end to penalties. So does rehabilitation. No principle is more clear, perhaps, than this: upon completion of his sentence, if not before, the offender should be fully restored to his rights. If any of these deprivations are so significant penologically that they should persist beyond the court's sentence to prison or probation, they should be elevated to the status of primary and independent sanctions, specifically designed to accomplish appropriate correctional goals of deterrence, incapacitation, or re-

habilitation. In that way, they would receive the special focus of attention required in adjusting penalty both to the offense and the offender. Possibly the grafting politician, the corrupt judge, or the purveyor of illicit medication, for example, should not be permitted ever again to ply his trade. Restrictions of this sort have major impact on the offender, however, comparable to that of imprisonment, and often of even greater seriousness to the individual involved. The employment of a permanent or long-persistent sanction of this sort should be based on quite specific categories of offense and on judicial discrimination as to those individual offenders for whom the sanction appears to be necessary as a matter of public protection. Unfortunately, it has not been possible under our system to control the actions of licensing agencies in accordance with sound principles of justice, but so far as legal deprivations and the behavior of courts are concerned we can eradicate from current practice such obsolete residuals as civil death and blanket deprivations based on conviction or sentence, and such unnecessarily complicated forms of restoration as pardon and certificates of good conduct.

In this entire area of the incidental deprivation of rights and their restoration, we can liberalize practice greatly with very little threat to the public and with considerable advantage in maintaining a legitimate measure of self-respect on the part of the offender. Wisconsin law seems reasonable in this respect.

THE PARDONING POWER*

The substantive criminal law—concerning itself with the technical problem of what act combined with what mental state is necessary to constitute any of the various crimes in our criminal jurisprudence—has been aptly described as "an island of technicality in a sea of discretion." Thus, before trial, the police have broad discretion as to whether to arrest, and the prosecutor as to whether to prosecute, and if so, for what crime. After conviction, the trial judge (or, less frequently, the trial jury) has discretion as

* Reprinted by permission of the American Academy of Political and Social Science. Austin W. Scott, Jr.: The Pardoning Power, The *Annals*, Vol. 284, Nov. 1952. p. 95-100. Footnotes are omitted.

to what sentence, within limits, to impose or whether to suspend sentence and place on probation; the parole board has discretion as to the duration of penal treatment; and the pardoning authorities have discretion as to the use of the pardon power.

The technical and inflexible nature of the problem of guilt or innocence of crime (inherited largely from the historical fact that in England, when the criminal law was being developed, so many crimes were punishable by death) makes desirable the placing of a good deal of discretion in the groups concerned with criminal law enforcement—police, prosecutors, judges, juries, parole boards, and pardon authorities. If this discretion is taken away from any one of these groups, the burden becomes correspondingly greater on the others to make wise use of their discretionary powers.

Thus in capital cases it has in the past been not uncommon to deprive judges or juries of their normal discretion as to sentence, by making the death sentence mandatory. The trend in recent years has been, if not to abolish capital punishment, at least to abolish the mandatory death sentence. Accompanying this movement has been something of a decline in the importance of the pardon power in capital cases. But as long as capital punishment continues, power to pardon in capital cases is bound to remain an important element in the administration of criminal justice.

The broad power vested in pardon officials to pardon, to commute sentences, and to grant reprieves, applies, of course, to many crimes other than capital crimes. In this section, however, we shall limit ourselves to a consideration of these powers in relation to capital cases where the death penalty has been imposed.

Who May Exercise Pardon Powers

All civilized countries make use of some form of the pardon power to give flexibility to the administration of justice in criminal cases. In England this power historically is vested in the Crown. But in the United States it is vested in the People, who can delegate the power to whomever they please. As a matter of practice, the People have found it most convenient to give the power to the executive branch of the government. Thus, under the United States Constitution the pardon power in federal cases has been delegated to the President; and practically all the state constitutions have delegated this power in state criminal cases to the governor, either alone or in conjunction with advisers.

A large majority of state constitutions originally gave the power to pardon to the governor alone. The more recent trend has been toward putting more power in the hands of a board. Simplifying matters somewhat, we find that today there are in general three different arrangements among the states. First, in about one-quarter of the states, the executive pardon power is vested in the governor alone; some of these states, however, furnish a pardon attorney to aid the governor in these cases. Second, about half the states have provided for advisory boards whose function is to hold hearings on pardon applications and make recommendations to the governor, who alone may make the final decision; in practice, the governor usually adopts the recommendations of the board. Third, in about a quarter of the states there are boards which, instead of acting simply in an advisory capacity, have the final decision about pardons; in all these states, however, the governor is a member of the board.

Types of Pardon in Capital Cases

In discussing the power to pardon in cases where the death penalty has been imposed, it will be well to consider separately three different types of executive clemency: (1) full pardon; (2) commutation of sentence to imprisonment for life or a term of years; and (3) reprieve, or stay of execution.

Full Pardon

In only a rare case does one sentenced to death for crime receive a full pardon. Usually the best he can hope for is a commutation of his sentence to life imprisonment. But there is one type of case, fortunately quite rare in capital cases, where justice demands a full pardon—namely, where subsequent events prove that the convicted person is innocent.

There is some dispute as to how often innocent persons are convicted of serious crimes. Some enthusiasts assert that the many procedural safeguards which are afforded criminal defendants in this country—the right to a jury trial, to counsel, to be informed of the charge, to call witnesses, the privilege against self-incrimination, for instance—make it impossible to convict an innocent person. The District Attorney for New York County reports that only three out of 27,288 persons convicted in that county of felony during the years 1938-49 were later shown to be innocent.

On the other hand, Professor Edwin M. Borchard, in his book, *Convicting the Innocent,* has collected and discussed at length sixty-five cases of innocent persons convicted of crime, mostly in this country, of which twenty-nine are murder cases. He says that these sixty-five were chosen from a much larger number.

Borchard's cases show that innocent persons are sometimes convicted of crime in mistaken identification by the victim, who is often emotionally disturbed by his experience; sometimes on erroneous inferences drawn from circumstantial evidence; sometimes on the basis of perjured testimony of hostile witnesses. Prosecutors, expected by the public to produce convictions, are seldom as impartial as they are ideally supposed to be, although they do not often stoop so low as intentionally to use perjured testimony against the defendant or to suppress evidence favorable to him. Public pressure for revenge sometimes leads juries to convict innocent persons. If the jury learns that an accused person has previously been convicted of an earlier crime, his chances of being convicted of this later crime are considerably enhanced, so much so that he often refuses to testify in his own behalf for fear the jury will learn of his former conviction.

Thus it is clear that for one reason or another an innocent defendant is sometimes convicted and sentenced to death, a fact which obviously constitutes one of the strongest reasons for abolishing capital punishment. In such a case it is only right that the defendant should be given a full pardon. It seems odd, but in most cases of innocence established some time after conviction, a pardon is the only effective way to rectify the wrong, since courts generally have no power to grant new trials because of newly discovered evidence after a relatively short period of time following conviction.

Commutation of Sentence

Commutation is the substitution of a lighter for a heavier punishment. Unlike pardon, it does not mean forgiveness, and does not effect a restoration of civil rights. Most state constitutions specifically include in the pardoning power the power to grant commutations. In those states whose constitutions do not specifically so provide, it is held that such a power is included in the grant of the pardoning power, for the reason that the greater power (to pardon) necessarily includes the lesser power (to commute).

The power to commute sentences is exercised in a great many cases other than death cases, usually to make eligible for parole a prisoner whose term has not expired. Here we shall consider the power only as used to avoid the death sentence, an important but far less common use of commutation. In practice, the power is generally exercised by commuting death sentences to life imprisonment, although occasionally the sentence is reduced to imprisonment of a term of years.

To prevent the arbitrary or dishonest exercise of the pardoning power by pardon authorities, most of the states require regular annual or biennial reports to the legislature by pardon authorities concerning the granting of pardons, commutations, and reprieves. A study of these reports give us some indication as to the reasons why commutations are granted in practice. Often the recommendation of the judge who tried the case, the district attorney who prosecuted it, or the state supreme court which reviewed it, is emphasized. Frequently the fact that, of several joint participants in the crime, only one received the death sentence (particularly if this one was not the moving spirit behind the commission of the crime) is given as a reason for commuting the sentence to life imprisonment.

Sometimes the evidence against the defendant, although sufficient to sustain a conviction, is conflicting or is based on circumstantial evidence alone, in which cases the pardon authorities may decide to commute the death sentence. Commutations (or even occasionally full pardons) are sometimes granted because of prior promises made by prosecutors, which the state feels bound to honor, of lighter punishment or immunity in return for turning state's evidence. Sometimes there are extenuating circumstances which do not affect the technical legal question of guilt or innocence of a capital crime but which do call for the exercise of mercy.

A variety of other reasons have been given as well, including such matters as the youth of the condemned person, the evil influence exercised over him by his stronger or older companions, his good prison record, or the fact that this was his first offense. At times the reasons are suggested very vaguely: "because of the peculiar circumstances of the crime" or "because it is considered that justice will be satisfied without the taking of this man's life."

Factors Influencing Pardon Officials

Without doubt there are motivating forces which lead pardon officials to grant pardons or commutations but which are not given as reasons for acting. At times the condemned man is a member of a group which exercises great pressure on pardon officials to grant clemency; conversely, the victim of the crime may be a member of a group which just as vigorously opposes clemency. Politics is an important factor, too, especially where the governor alone exercises the pardoning power without being insulated by a board of pardons. As an elected official, he is not impervious to the display of public opinion for or against a condemned prisoner.

An interesting question arises as to how the governor's private views of capital punishment affect his commutation of death sentences. We may expect, for instance, that one who strongly disapproves of such punishment would be more prone to commute death sentences than would others. A number of years ago, the Governor of Oklahoma announced his view that the death penalty was legalized murder and stated that he would commute all death sentences to life imprisonment. The Oklahoma Criminal Court of Appeals thereupon denounced the Governor's position in angry tones, stating that the law forbade him to "allow his scruples to influence him in the least." But since it is uniformly held that the exercise of discretion by pardon officials is a matter not to be reviewed or interfered with by the courts, it is difficult to see how, as a practical matter, there can be any effective way of preventing pardon authorities from letting their views on capital punishment influence their decisions on commutations of death sentences.

Extent of Commutation

One last problem is the extent to which pardoning officials have in fact exercised their power to commute death sentences. Figures are not directly available on a national basis as to the number of cases where the death penalty was imposed but sentence was commuted. However, we can learn something by comparing the number of prisoners received by federal and state prisons each year under sentence of death with the number of prisoners executed at these same prisons during the same period. Those not executed must have either received commutation, died (either naturally or by suicide), escaped, or had their cases reversed by a higher court. The latter three possibilities are not very common, however.

For the seven years 1940-46 inclusive, 771 condemned prisoners were received, of which number 587 were executed. Most of the 184 unaccounted for undoubtedly received commutations. It would seem, then, that, taking the country as a whole, commutations are granted in about 20 to 25 per cent of the cases where the penalty is imposed. This statement is somewhat confirmed by the earlier assertion of the Select Committee on Capital Punishment that "over a given period, the percentage of death sentences carried out to execution is 71.9 in the United States."

Statistics are available in some of the individual states as to the numerical relationship between those executed and those whose sentences were commuted. Thus in New York from 1920 to 1936 there were 252 executions and 83 commutations. In New Jersey from 1907 to 1937 there were 119 persons electrocuted and 27 granted commutation. Texas granted 7 commutations out of 64 cases in the four years 1947-51.

It seems safe to say that of the many persons who are convicted of crimes whose maximum punishment is death, comparatively few receive a death sentence. Of those who are sentenced to die, most are executed, but about one in four or five obtains a commutation to life imprisonment.

Reprieve

A reprieve in the case of one sentenced to death is merely a postponement of excution. In general, the power to pardon carries with it the power to reprieve, whether or not the reprieve is expressly mentioned in the constitution among the other forms of clemency. While reprieves are sometimes granted in noncapital cases, they are most important in capital cases, to stay execution of death.

The reports of pardon authorities indicate a variety of different reasons for granting reprieves in capital cases. They are often granted—as of course they should be if the law does not provide for an automatic stay of execution—pending the appeal of the case to a higher court or to allow the condemned man to apply to the United States Supreme Court for certiorari or to allow him to pursue other procedural remedies in the courts. If newly discovered evidence bearing on the case is found, reprieve should be granted a woman prisoner who is pregnant. It is a well-settled rule of law that an insane person cannot be executed, so reprieves are often granted to determine the question of insanity; and, if insanity is found, to postpone execution until sanity is regained. Reprieves are sometimes granted for less important reasons, such as the fact that the date of execution is a holiday or a Sunday or the prisoner's birthday.

Conclusion

Pardon authorities are given broad and almost unrestricted discretion over pardons, commutations, and reprieves. This fact is one of the elements of strength in the proper administration of criminal justice. But it has sometimes led to abuse, especially in those states where one man has the final determination over clemency. Unscrupulous governors may build up their political careers by using the pardoning power to please people with political influence. Others, more honest, are influenced by the effect of their decisions on the electorate, rather than by the merits of the particular case.

While the discretion of pardon authorities is so broad that there exists no definite standard by which to determine whether the discretion is being abused or not, yet some situations have arisen which clearly show an abuse of discretion. The most notorious of these cases is that of a former Governor of Oklahoma, who was impeached because he frequently exercised his power to pardon, not on the merits of the case, but rather as an accommodation for friends or for financial rewards for himself.

In spite of occasional abuse, however, it seems obvious that the power to pardon is a necessary part of American criminal jurisprudence, in capital as well as noncapital cases. As long as a conviction cannot be reversed after a period of time for newly discovered evidence proving the defendant's innocence, we need the power to pardon for innocence. There will always be cases of technical guilt but, because of extenuating circumstances, comparatively little moral fault. The pardon power, in other words, is necessary in cases where the strict legal rules of guilt and innocence have produced harsh or unjust results. Doubtless the administration of the pardoning power can be improved, as the Attorney General's Survey of Release Procedures, including Pardon has concluded. But the power to pardon will continue to play an important part in the ultimate disposition of capital cases as long as capital punishment remains with us.

WHY PARDON? A RE-EXAMINATION*

The question may even be raised whether the ancient institution has not outlived its usefulness. Is there any valid reason why pardon should be retained? Are not judicial review and modern release procedures like parole sufficient to do all that pardon ever did—and do it better?

To a large extent, the answer must be yes. Much, and in some States most, of what is being done under the Governor's pardoning power could and should be done either by the courts or by a parole board. There remains a valid field for the pardoning power to occupy, but it is a much more restricted field than it occupies today.

This is perhaps the most important conclusion this survey of

---

* Reprinted in part by permission. United States Attorney-General, *Survey of Release Procedures*, Vol. 3, 1940, p. 296-300. Footnotes are omitted.

pardon has to offer. Let us therefore state it emphatically and in detail:

The exercise of the pardoning power should be restricted from two sides:

1. *Criminal procedure should be liberalized so as to permit reversal of a conviction where new evidence is found indicating that the defendant was innocent.*—A pardon granted on the ground of innocence is an anomaly at best. Anglo-American law has been peculiarly indifferent to this problem. Continental law has gone much further in permitting judicial reconsideration of such cases. Obviously, this is the only logical and satisfactory way to handle the problem. An innocent man who has been wrongly convicted is entitled to vindication, by reversal of the erroneous conviction. To pardon him for being innocent is irony. What is more, it creates confusion in determining the proper effect to be given to a pardon.

The objection to permitting such reversal, of course, is that it would render the law uncertain if there were not a time after which a case was closed and the judgment final. It may be conceded that some limits must be drawn, but the fact remains that the right of appellate review is much more restricted in this regard in most American states than it is restricted in most continental countries.

2. *All releases on condition of good behavior and under supervision should be under the parole law, and not by conditional pardon.*—This is the legitimate field of parole. There is no reason for having similar types of releases granted by two different agencies. Furthermore, the parole organization has better facilities for determining when a prisoner should be so released and for supervising him thereafter. Even where the parole law is inadequate, the proper approach is to strengthen it, rather than to handle the problem by conditional pardon or other forms of executive clemency.

This would mean the almost total elimination of conditional pardons. Special situations may arise from time to time when certain conditions may properly be attached to a pardon, but the use of conditional pardon as a regular procedure, in lieu of parole, should be abandoned. Even the states having no separate parole system, and where parole rests legally upon the Governor's clemency power, should enact a parole law resting upon the state's power to punish criminals and rehabilitate socially dangerous persons, wholly divorced from the Governor's power to grant clemency.

To the same end, the parole laws should be liberalized so as to give the parole board full discretion to parole any prisoner it deems worthy. This means repealing all restrictions in the parole statutes making certain classes of prisoners ineligible for parole. The primary reason why conditional pardon, commutation, reprieve, and other forms of executive clemency have been so extensively used to effect conditionally release has been to cover cases noc eligible for parole. The big mistake made by those who think we should be "hard boiled" about parole is in forgetting that while they may bar the door against release on parole, the back door of executive clemency always remains open. The result is that restrictions written into the parole laws by those who do not think that certain kinds of criminals should be turned loose on parole—murderers, rapists, second offenders, or those who have not served a certain portion of their sentences—too often defeat their own object. The convicts we refuse to release on parole are released on indefinite furloughs, on conditional pardons, or other types of release under which there is much less actual supervision and control than under parole.

Of course, taking all restrictions out of the parole law and vesting the parole board with unrestricted power to determine when and to whom parole should be granted means giving the board a degree of power which could be easily abused. The answer, however, must be to safeguard the capability and honesty of the board rather than to cut down its power by arbitrary restrictions. Granting parole is necessarily a matter of individualized consideration of each case. The board should be so constituted as to guarantee that its decisions will be based upon careful, scientific, investigation and capable and honest judgement. In short, the answer to defects in the parole system is a better parole system, not less parole.

If such reforms were adopted, what would be left for executive clemency? Enough. It would still be needed for the same general purposes for which it has historically always been used—to take care of cases where the legal rules have produced a harsh, unjust, or popularly unacceptable result, or where for politic reasons the rule of law should be set aside. Such cases will continue to arise under any legal system. A criminal code can only define antisocial conduct in general terms. It can never take into account all the special circumstances which may be involved in a given case. The safety valve will remain necessary. To imagine that the reforms we have suggested would remove all necessity for the intervention of a pardoning power would be as naive as the notion of the French Revolutionists that the introduction of the jury system would make justice perfect and pardon unnecessary.

We may enumerate some of the situations which will continue to arise, in which pardon may be proper:

a. Political upheavals and emergencies, wherein pardon may be necessary to pacify a revolution-torn country or unite a country for war.

b. Calm second judgment after a period of war hysteria, during which persons were given very severe sentences for political offenses later realized to have been very minor or upon evidence later felt to be insufficient.

c. Similarly, changed public opinion after a period of severe penalties against certain conduct which is later looked upon as much less criminal, or as no crime at all. Prohibition is a recent example. The present severity against kidnappers may give rise to cases which future judgment may recommend for clemency.

d. Cases "where punishment would do more harm than good," to quote Bentham, as in certain cases of sedition, conspiracy, or acts of public disorder.

e. Technical violations leading to hard results. We can mention at least one example—where the legal "principal" in a crime may be only a comparatively innocent hireling, while the brains of the plot is legally guilty only as an accessory.

f. Cases where pardon is necessary to uphold the good faith of the State, as where a criminal has been promised immunity for turning State's evidence.

g. Cases of later proved innocence or of mitigating circumstances. Although we have recommended liberalizing judicial procedure so that most of these cases could be handled by proceedings to reverse the conviction, probably some restrictions will necessarily be retained upon the right to such judicial review, and cases may still arise in which such review is impossible, though innocence is clearly probable.

h. Applications for reprieve or commutation, especially in death sentence cases. Here, too, liberalization of judicial procedure should permit reprieves to be granted by the courts. But while there is somewhat less logical reason for retaining this power in the executive than can be found for most of the other examples listed above, this last recourse to the Governor in these cases is a benevolent power, which we shall probably want to retain and it will no doubt continue to be a major part of the pardoning power.

ORGANIZATION OF PARDON ADMINISTRATION*

The obvious political implications and considerations involved in most of the valid grounds for pardon indicate the propriety of retaining this power in the hands of the chief executive. The objection that this takes too much of the Governor's time from more important matters of state is true today, when executive clemency is used in so many states as a regular and normal release procedure, handling cases which should be left to a competent parole board, but it should not be true if pardon were restricted to the exceptional cases as we have recommended. In the Federal Government, where this distinction is observed, there is no undue press of pardon cases burdening the President.

This does not mean that it would not be helpful to have a pardon official or board to assist the Governor in this function. A board would seem preferable to one official, for the determination of whether or not clemency should be granted would usually involve considerations of policy upon which it would be well for the Governor to have the views of other executive officials of his administration, rather than a pardon attorney or other official who too often may be merely a kind of secretary.

* Reprinted in part by permission. United States Attorney-General, *Survey of Release Procedures*, Vol. 3, 1940, p. 302-308. Footnotes are omitted.

In most states the board might properly be composed of such other executive officers as the attorney general and the secretary of state. The attorney general should be included because many of the cases will probably involve legal implications.

Prison and parole officials should not be members of this board. Considerations relevant in ordinary release procedures should not be interpolated into the deliberations, and if the viewpoint of penal authorities were introduced into clemency hearings, it would promote exactly the situation we have tried to rectify—the usurpation by the executive clemency power of the field belonging to parole and penology generally. Even such major penal officials as the head of a department of correction or of public welfare should therefore have no place on the pardon board.

It would be helpful for the board to have a secretary or pardon attorney devoting all or a substantial part of his time to his duties as such. Certainly in the larger states this would be necessary. His duties might be patterned after those of the pardon attorney of the United States.

The board may or may not be given some power beyond merely advising the Governor. Three main alternatives suggest themselves:

1. All applications must be brought before the board, but the Governor may, after obtaining the board's views, take any action he wishes.

2. The Governor must obtain the board's consent, and cannot grant a pardon over the unfavorable action of the board.

3. The ultimate pardoning power is in the board itself, of which the Governor is only one member. The Governor may have only one vote, as any other member, or he may have a veto power.

It seems unnecessary to go beyond the first method. This subjects the Governor's action to control which is sufficient to exert powerful pressure against abuse, and yet is respectful and leaves full responsibility resting very directly upon his own shoulders.

Vesting the pardoning power in a board, of which the Governor is only one member with one vote scatters responsibility so that it may be difficult for the public to place the blame for abuse of the pardon power.

Of course it should be mandatory for the Governor to report regularly to the legislature all cases of clemency granted. This publicity, together with the requirement that he first submit all cases to the board, would seem to place sufficient checks upon the Governor to make abuse unlikely.

Procedure

Pardon procedure should be (1) simple, (2) thorough, (3) public, (4) free of charge, and (5) adversary rather than *ex parte* in nature.

By a simple procedure is meant one which the average prisoner is able to handle without the aid of a lawyer. Of course, important or difficult cases probably will require a lawyer and certainly the right to counsel in all cases should be allowed.

By a thorough procedure is meant one in which the final decision is reached not merely upon allegations stated in the prisoner's petition, or in court records, or upon recommendations of the trial judge, prosecutor, or interested citizens, but upon a careful investigation of the case. The pardoning authorities should have available at least one officer to make such investigations.

Not every phase of the procedure can be public, but it is proper that a right to a public hearing be granted, in which the whole case may be subjected to the full light of publicity.

The granting of clemency in proper cases is a matter of public interest, and not of interest to the prisoner alone. There is, therefore, no reason for charging the cost to him. The right to apply should be free of charge. The practice of one state of charging $10 for the privilege of applying for clemency is not to be commended.

By adversary proceedings is meant a procedure in which the State is regularly represented at any public hearings.

Application

The regulations found in most states concerning the manner in which executive clemency may be applied for are usually designed to accomplish two aims:

1. To bring applications before the pardoning authorities in

an orderly manner, with at least a minimum of the necessary facts in the case to permit intelligent disposition; and (2) to provide notice to the prosecuting officials and to the public generally of the fact that clemency is being applied for.

While the first of these is a wholly proper purpose, in many states too much reliance seems to be placed upon it. It is proper to demand that the petitioner state the grounds upon which he asks for clemency, but such statements can never be sufficient to decide the case. The elaborate requirements found in some States, therefore, of affidavits of the trial judge and prosecutor and others, transcripts of the evidence in the criminal trial, and even copies of the indictment, verdict and judgment, prison records, statements of the prosecuting witness and members of the jury—all these are still inadequate and unreliable. No multiplication of such documents will enable the board to reach a sound result merely upon the papers in the case. A personal investigation by the board itself is necessary, and for this reason it is indispensable that the board have at its command the services of an investigator to assemble the facts.

Public notice of the fact that application has been made is a wholesome requirement. Unfortunately, no method of accomplishing this purpose adequate for modern society has been devised. The requirement still found in some States that such notice be posted in the courthouse was effective in the horse-and-buggy days, but it is practically negligible in effect today. Not much better is the usual requirement of publication in a newspaper. This problem of official public notice is, of course, not peculiar to pardon cases; it arises in numerous other situations. It is, however, probably somewhat more acute here than in other connections. Building contractors have a business interest in keeping themselves informed of advertisements for bids for public work; the same is more or less true of tax sales, etc. But no one has any specific interest in contesting pardon applications. The victim of the crime may feel an interest, but he will probably not make it a point to read newspaper advertisements of pardon applications for years after the crime.

Perhaps the laggard law will eventually adopt modern publicity devices like the radio to replace outmoded methods like posting in the courthouse or publishing a small notice in an obscure journal.

One aid to publicity is to have pardon hearings held at regular stated times. This, in itself, does not give notice of the specific cases to be heard, but it is of some value.

Limitations on Repeated Applications

Surprisingly few States have placed any restrictions on the right to petition for clemency again and again. In New Jersey a convict whose petition for clemency has once been refused must wait two years before petitioning again; and in Florida, Georgia, Nebraska, and Utah he must wait one year. In all other States he can petition every six months or even oftener.

Apparently, pardon boards in most States have not felt that this privilege was being abused, even though many of them hear applications for parole as well as for pardon, and may have a high percentage of all the prison inmates applying for one or the other at a single session.

Investigation

As already said, in all too many States, the pardoning authorities do not have the benefit of any personal investigation of the cases coming before them, but rely entirely upon the papers in their files. Only a few States have an investigator available. In States where pardon and parole administration is combined, the parole staff is available for pardon cases. The catch is that parole investigations are often inadequate, too. Moreover, as we have pointed out, pardon should be restricted to cases requiring a different sort of investigation from that used in parole.

Hearings

A formal, public hearing should be a prerequisite to the granting of any pardon or commutation. This is granted in most of the states where a pardon board exists.

Applicants should not only be permitted but requested to be present, and should have the right to present any relevant evidence. The pardon board should have power to subpoena witnesses and take testimony under oath. If cases which should be handled by parole are excluded from executive clemency, the remaining cases are likely to be of greater importance than is now generally the case, and so will probably require more elaborate consideration.

Attorneys should be permitted to appear before the board on behalf of an applicant, as is true now in about half the States where formal pardon hearings are held. However, it seems undesirable to permit attorneys to appear without the prisoner himself. The objections sometimes made that permitting prisoners to appear before the pardon board disrupts prison discipline, and unduly influences the board members in his favor, are without foundation. Very often the prisoner's personal appearance is unfavorable and influences the board to refuse clemency.

It is most important that the State be made a party to all pardon cases, and that it be represented at the hearings by the attorney general or a member of his staff, who should oppose the granting of the petition where that course seems proper. Merely notifying the prosecutor who tried the criminal case and permitting him to be present if he wishes is not sufficient to protect the public's interest. What is needed is a statutory provision providing for the presence of the attorney general or a member of his staff. The mere knowledge that the State will be thus represented should contribute considerably to reduce unfounded applications.

Function of the Board

It is vain to insist, that the board should in no case undertake to act as a court of review, but should confine itself to a consideration only of matters which "properly bear upon the propriety of extending clemency." Necessarily the board will act more or less as a court of review, not only in cases where the claim is innocence, but in most other cases as well. Of course the sort of cross-examining of the witnesses about the facts of the crime in which lawyer members of the board are prone to indulge are usually rather irrelevant, especially where there is no claim that the applicant is innocent. We have pointed out that the rigidity of the law or the fallibility of evidence sometimes demands the complement of the pardoning power to achieve justice. Pardon is a corrective measure in such cases, and the board in determining whether the penalty should be dispensed with or mitigated is necessarily performing a function which is quasi judicial at least.

Decisions

While hearings should be public, decisions obviously should be arrived at in closed session. In some states, such session is held immediately after the hearing; in others several days later. Where a great mass of cases is handled at one session, it is almost compulsory to dispose of them at once lest the members forget the facts and circumstances involved. If cases properly belonging to parole were excluded, a plethora of pardon cases would be unlikely, and it would probably be better to allow some days for reflection between the hearing and the board's decision.

Chapter Three

HISTORY OF THE DEVELOPMENT
OF PROBATION

T HE EMERGENCE of a method called probation during the last half of the nineteenth century marked a definite advance in the disposition and treatment of law violators. As a system, it began as a legal device for alleviating the harshness of punishment and preventing the contamination of the criminal novice in the unsavory atmosphere of the prison. Over the years, the concept has been expanded far beyond that envisioned by its founders.

But in parts of the country, probation has grown without sound guidance or definite direction, with resultant inadequacies and abuse. Since its administration has remained primarily with the trial courts, it is essentially local in character.

In this chapter, we trace the development of probation. What are the precursors of probation? Is it a social invention of American design, or are its roots in English common law? In the following selections, two opposing points of view are presented. The reader can then make up his own mind, based on the respective arguments presented.

THE ORIGINS OF PROBATION: FROM
COMMON LAW ROOTS*

Several attempts have been made to trace back the legal origins of probation to medieval and early modern European law. The precedents found in this period of legal history, however, generally relate to the suspension of punishment subject to good behavior rather than to probation as such, that is, a *combination* of the conditional suspension of punishment and the personal supervision of the released offender during a trial period. There can be little doubt that there has not been any continuous process of historical development linking early Continental instances of the use of the conditional suspension of punishment with contemporary proba-

* Reprinted in part by permission of the United Nations. Department of Social Affairs, *Probation and Related Measures*, 1951, p. 16-26. Footnotes are omitted.

tion. Probation as it is known today has been derived from the practical extension of the English common law, and an analysis of the legal origins of probation must therefore be principally concerned with England and America.

In England and in the United States of America probation developed out of various methods for the conditional suspension of punishment. Generally speaking, the court practices in question were inaugurated, or adopted from previously existing practices, as attempts to avoid the mechanical application of the harsh and cruel precepts of a rigorous, repressive criminal law. Among these Anglo-American judicial expedients which have been mentioned as direct precursors of probation, are the so-called benefit of clergy, the judicial reprieve, the release of an offender on his own recognizance, provisional "filing" of a case, and other legal devices for the suspension of either the imposition or the execution of sentence. With a view to a full understanding of the legal origins of probation, it is necessary to review briefly the nature of these practices.

The Benefit of Clergy

The so-called benefit of clergy was a special plea of devious origin by virtue of which certain categories of offenders could, after conviction, but before judgment, claim exemption from, or mitigation of, punishment. In practice it was primarily a device to avoid capital punishment. The importance of this plea in the criminal proceedings of the eigtheenth and early nineteenth century is beyond any doubt: "according to the common practice in England of working out modern improvements through antiquated forms, this exemption was made the means of modifying the severity of the criminal law." It is, however, extremely doubtful whether this device had any direct influence on the later development of the suspension of sentence or of any other immediate precursor of probation.

The Judicial Reprieve

The judicial reprieve was a temporary suspension by the court of either the imposition or the execution of a sentence. It was used for specific purposes such as to permit a convicted person to apply for a pardon, or under circumstances such as where the judge was not satisfied with the verdict or where the evidence was suspicious. Although this measure involved only a temporary stay of imposition or execution of sentence, it did lead, in some cases, to an abandonment of prosecution. It does not appear, however, that in England this device was ever extended to embrace what is now termed an indefinite suspension of sentence, particularly in cases which presented no peculiar reason, arising out the lack of or limitations on procedure, for withholding execution of sentence. On the other hand, there is, no doubt, more than a modicum of good reason in tracing the later pretensions of American courts to a power of indefinite suspension of sentence back to this early practice of reprieve in the English courts.

The Recognizance

The recognizance is a legal device deeply embeded in English law. It originated as a measure of preventive justice, and as such it consists in obliging those persons, whom there is a probable ground to suspect of future misbehavior, to stipulate with and to give full assurance to the public, that such offense as is apprehended shall not happen. . . . This "assurance to the public" is given by entering into a recognizance or bond (with or without sureties) creating a debt to the State which becomes enforceable, however, only when the specified conditions are not observed. The recognizance is entered into for a specified period of time.

At an early date the use of the principle of the recognizance (or binding-over) was also extended to actual offenders arraigned before the criminal courts. The device came to be used both to ensure the appearance of an offender before the court at a future date when called upon, and as a disposition (or part thereof) in the case of convicted offenders. With the passing of time, the recognizance came to be used almost exclusively with reference to criminal proceedings rather than as a measure of preventive justice. It should be noted, however, that the recognizance, when used in connection with persons arraigned before criminal courts, does not lose its character as a measure of preventive justice but is actually designed to ensure the future lawful behaviour of the offender or, as Blackstone said, "must be understood rather as a caution against the repetition of the offence, than (as) any immediate pain or punishment."

For centuries the courts of England on occasion bound over and released minor offenders on their own recognizance, *with* or *without sureties.* Similarly, instances of this practice can be found in the records of the American colonies. During the first half of the nineteenth century this device was adopted with increasing frequency, particularly in the case of youthful and petty offenders, the imprisonment of whom did not appear to be warranted. The practice seems to have been common in New England (particularly Massachusetts) at the time, and was to be found also in other jurisdictions of the United States of America.

The device of binding-over was used extensively and imaginatively by Judge Peter Oxenbridge Thacher during his term of office (1823-1843) in the Municipal Court of Boston, and the practices developed by him were of particular significance in the later development of probation in Massachusetts. The earliest recorded case in this connection is the case of *Commonwealth* vs. *Chase* (1830). In Judge Thacher's opinion we find in this case a clear statement of the nature of the practice of binding-over as employed by him:

> "The indictment against Jerusha Chase was found at the January term of this court, 1830. She pleaded guilty to the same, and sentence would have been pronounced at that time, but upon the application of her friends, and with the consent of the attorney of the commonwealth, she was permitted, upon her recognizance for her appearance in this court whenever she should be called for, to go at large. It has sometimes been practiced in this court, in cases of peculiar interest, and in the hope that the party would avoid the commission of any offense afterwards, to discharge him on a recognizance of this description. The effect is, that no sentence will ever be pronounced against him, if he shall behave himself well afterwards, and avoid any further violation of the law. . . ."

In 1836, the State of Massachusetts, as part of a general revision of its statutory law, gave legislative recognition to the practice of release upon recognizance, *with sureties,* at any stage of the proceedings, in so far as it applied to petty offenders in the lower courts. In the report of the commissioners charged with the revision of the statutory law of the State, the commissioners formulated the theoretical basis of this alteration in the law relating to the punishment of petty offenders, as follows:

> "This alteration consists in the discretionary power proposed to be given to the courts and magistrates, before whom this class of offenders may be brought, to discharge them, if they have any friends who will give satisfactory security for their future good behavior, for a reasonable time. When such sureties can be obtained, it can hardly fail to operate as powerful check upon the conduct of the party, who is thus put upon his good behavior. And if his character and habits are such that no one will consent to be sponsor for him, it must forcibly impress on his mind the value of a good character, while it deprives him of all ground of just complaint of the severity of the law, or the magistrate."

It is significant to compare this formulation of the theory underlying the use of release on recognizance, with a British formulation of the second half of the nineteenth century. In a book published in 1877, Edward William Cox, Recorder of Portsmouth, specifically described the release of offenders on their own recognizance, with sureties, as a "substitute for punishment," and he noted that, while the conduct of the released offenders was proper, no further action was taken. In particular, he was strongly motivated by the desire to avoid the demoralizing and contaminating influence of short terms of imprisonment, especially in the case of first and juvenile offenders. As for the *rationale* of the use of the recognizances, with sureties, he says, "The suspension only of the judgment, the knowledge that if he (the offender) offends he may yet be punished—the hold which his bail thus has upon him, to a great extent guarantee that if there is in him an inclination to redeem himself he will return to a life of honesty."

Provisional Release on Bail

It has been noted in the preceding paragraphs that the device of releasing an offender on his own recognizance (binding-over) may be used *with,* or, *without, sureties.* Conversely, the device of sureties (or bail) may be employed with or without simultaneously binding over the defendant on his own recognizance. The significance of the device of sureties, when combined with the recognizance, as a precursor of probation, has already been discussed; it remains to be pointed out, however, that both in England and in the United States of America the device of bail as such (that is, when not used in conjunction with the recognizance) has similarly been of major historical significance in the evolution of probation, namely, as a device for the provisional suspension of punishment in relation to rudimentary probation practices.

Binding-Over, Bail and the Origins of Probation

It has been noted above, that the recognizance is essentially a preventive rather than a punitive measure of dealing with actual or potential offenders. In the early nineteenth century the increased use of this device was motivated, no doubt, to a considerable extent by considerations of mercy and in this respect the device was one of the measures employed to reduce the hardships involved in the mechanical application of a rigorous criminal law. The rehabilitative object of the measure—i.e., the prevention of crime by the restoration of the offender as a law-abiding member of society—was, however, always present. Nevertheless, during this era the device came to be applied with an increasing realization of its rehabilitative potentialities, and same to be accompanied by increasingly effective safeguards and aids in the form of the personal supervision of, and assistance to the released offender during the trial period. It should further be noted that the recognizance has always contained the germs of supervision—it involves the conditional suspension of punishment, and some vigilance is required to ascertain whether the conditions concerned are being complied with.

It is clear that the provisional release of offenders in the charge of sureties similarly contained the germs of probationary supervision (irrespective of whether this device was combined with the recognizance or not). In view of their financial interest in the conduct of the provisionally released offender, sureties are bound to try to ensure the good behavior of the offender through personal supervision, assistance or influence. The deliberate use, by the courts, of the salutory influence of sureties on offenders released conditionally, either on their own recognizance or on bail, indeed seems to have been in a very real sense the first, rudimentary stage in the development of probation.

The Provisional "Filing" of Cases

The practice of provisionally "filing" a case seems to have been peculiar to Massachusetts. This device consisted of the suspension of the imposition of sentence when, "after verdict of guilty in a criminal case . . . the Court is satisfied that, by reason of extenuating circumstances, or of the pendency of a question of law in a like case before a higher court, or other sufficient reason, public justice does not require an immediate sentence. . . ." The use of this procedure was subject to the consent of the defendant and of the prosecuting attorney, and the suspension was made subject to such conditions as the court in its discretion might impose. The order that a case be laid on file was not equivalent to a final judgment, but left it within the power of the court to take action on the case at any time, upon motion of either party.

The Suspension of Sentences at Common Law

By way of summary, it may be noted that there existed, during the nineteenth century and earlier, several legal devices which enabled the English and the American courts to suspend either the imposition of sentence (recognizance to keep the peace or to be of good behavior and to appear for judgment when called upon, provisional release on bail, the provisional "filing of a case," and the judicial reprieve) or the execution of sentence (also the judicial reprieve). That these devices existed, and allowed *at least* for the temporary suspension of sentence for *specific purposes,* is beyond any doubt. The question whether the English and American courts possess, at common law, an inherent power to suspend sentence *indefinitely* is, however, more problematic.

In analysing the question of an inherent judicial power to suspend sentence *indefinitely,* it is necessary to distinguish clearly between the use of the special devices of the recognizance and bail, on the one hand, and other devices used for the provisional suspension of punishment, on the other hand. Prior to statutory provisions to this effect, the courts both in England and in the

United States of America *did*, in fact, engage in the suspension of the imposition of sentence when releasing offenders on their own recognizances, and took no further action with regard to the infliction of punishment if the condition of good behavior was complied with. Similarly, this procedure was followed, prior to statutory authorization, in at least two of the other countries of the British Commonwealth, viz., New England and Canada. Both in England and in certain jurisdictions of the United States of America (notably Massachusetts), the conditional suspension of the imposition of sentence, with the ultimate release of the offender from all punishment in case of good behavior, was practiced (without statutory authorization) also in relation to the provisional release of offenders on bail.

For all practical purposes it may be said that—beyond the relatively circumscribed practice of suspending the imposition of a sentence by means of releasing an offender on a recognizance and/or bail—the English courts *did not* assume the existence of an inherent common law power to suspend sentence indefinitely. In the United States of America, however, a variety of practices developed, with a tendency to extend the suspension of sentence beyond the employment of the recognizance and/or bail. In particular, this involved the suspension of the imposition or of the execution of sentence on the basis of the common law precedent of the judicial reprieve. With the increasing use of the conditional suspension of punishment, with or without some sort of probationary supervision, courts in different jurisdictions adopted contradictory points of view on the question of the existence, at common law, of an inherent judicial power of indefinite suspension of sentence. While some held that the courts had such a power, others rejected this view arguing either that the conditions justifying the recognition of such a power in England did not obtain in the United States, or that the indefinite suspension of sentence by the court constituted an encroachment on the executive prerogative of pardon and reprieve, and thus infringes upon the doctrine of the separation of powers.

The United States Supreme Court finally expressed itself on the issue in question in the so-called *Killits* case. In his opinion in this case, the late Chief Justice White decided that the English common law did not give the Federal courts the power to suspend sentence indefinitely.

"It is true that, owing to the want of power in common law courts to grant new trials and to the absence of a right to review convictions in a higher court, it is we think, to be conceded: (a) that both suspensions of sentence and suspensions of the enforcement of sentence, temporary in character, were often resorted to on grounds of error or miscarriage of justice which under our system would be corrected either by new trials or by the exercise of the power to review; (b) that not infrequently, where the suspension either of the imposition of a sentence or of its execution was made for the purpose of enabling a pardon to be sought or bestowed, by a failure to further proceed in the criminal cause in the future, although no pardon had been sought or obtained, the punishment fixed by law was escaped. But neither of these conditions serves to convert the mere exercise of a judicial discretion to temporarily suspend for the accomplishment of a purpose contemplated by law into the existence of an arbitrary judicial power to permanently refuse to enforce the law."

With reference to the decision in the *Killits* case, the Attorney General's Survey concludes as follows:

"For practical purposes it may be said that this decision served to explode the erroneous belief that had grown up in some States. . . . It may be concluded, therefore, that there is no historical warrant in the English common law for the claim that American courts have an inherent power to suspend sentence indefinitely. Where this power has been asserted, it has been based on a misconception of English authorities or recognized because it tempered the criminal law with mercy and had grown as a local practice."

It should be noted that the Court's decision in the *Killits* case did not seek to invalidate the practice of releasing offenders on their own recognizances, but referred to "the fact that common law courts possessed the power by recognizances to secure good behavior, that is, to enforce the law. . . ." This fact did not, however, afford support for "the proposition that those courts possessed the arbitrary discretion to permanently decline to enforce the law."

From the point of view of the development of probation as a distinct method for the treatment of offenders, the extent to which the judicial devices in which it had its historical origins, were, in fact, extra-legal and not warranted by the English common law, is of small significance. The important point is that these devices developed, and could in fact only develop, in a system of common law jurisdiction which is flexible enough to allow for the gradual adjustment of existing practices to new needs and new objectives. In England this process of adjustment was more conservative and it is probable that the courts stayed within their common law powers, in any case, the legality of the devices used for the conditional suspension of punishment, in relation to early pre-statutory probation practices, was never challenged in England, in Canada, or in New Zealand. In the United States of America, the courts overstepped their common law powers, and the resulting diversity and confusion of principles and authorities necessitated the authoritative revision of the legal bases of the practices that have developed. Nevertheless, the definitive explosion of the doctrine of an inherent judicial power to suspend any part of the administration of criminal justice, and when public opinion had already been fully prepared for this new method for the treatment of offenders. Consequently, the final rejection by the Supreme Court of the doctrine of a common law judicial power of indefinite suspension of sentence actually served as a stimulus for the enactment of statutes expressly authorizing the suspension of sentence and probation.

THE ORIGIN OF PROBATION: STATUTORY ROOTS*

Probation, both in conception and development, is America's distinctive contribution to progressive penology. I would like to make a point of this phrase "distinctively American," because some of the textbooks go to great lengths to trace its origins back to British common law and to what Dean Roscoe Pound calls "the received ideals" of Continental legal systems. In this they are wrong. The development of probation has been entirely statu-

* Reprinted in part by permission of the National Probation and Parole Association. Edmond Fitzgerald: The Presentence Investigation, NPPA Journal, Vol. 2, No. 4, Oct. 1956, p. 321-323. Footnotes are omitted.

tory, certainly so insofar as the system is an expression of *planned state policy*. Probation in America is characterized principally not by affinities with, but by deliberate divergences from, the common law and European precedents in general.

One of the interesting things to observe over the span of the century is the degree to which our entire philosophy of criminal law—and not merely that phase of it represented by probation—is moving farther and farther away from old-world antecedents as the years go on. In the older countries, when there still was some political and economic stability, the identifying hallmark of the legal philosophy could be described as reverence for precedent and for time honored institutions and resistance to radical change. In England the historical record is one of a legal system slowly and cautiously—adapting itself to the changing needs and talents of the people. It took them a long time, for example, to relax the lengthy syllabus of excessively punitive sanctions which were applied even to minor offenders up to comparatively recent times. The death penalty or mutilation was provided until well into the nineteenth century for some offenses that would today be considered trivial. It is typical of the British that the moderation of the penal statutes, when this finally came about, resulted from the slow momentum of unfolding history rather than from the initiative or Parliament or of any specific man or movement.

It is true that the momentum has been helped along here and there by the venalities of rules (e.g., Bentham's *Principles of Morals and Legislation*); or by the barbs of satirists (e.g., Jonathan Swift's *Drapier's Letters* and its influence on the repeal of a whole series of penal laws aimed not so much at crime control as at suppression of civil liberties). But in the main the record shows that, for the Englishman, the pragmatic test sufficed: if his laws worked somehow and if they did not bother him personally, he was not interested in seeing how they worked and he was not disposed to tamper with them overmuch. And similarly on the Continent.

In America, by contrast, the tendency was—and is—not to regard tradition as necessarily sacred. We have never been interested in preserving the *status quo,* except to maintain our "inalienable rights" and our constitutional freedoms. This is perhaps inevitable in a policy which has grown as rapidly as ours has. The pace of economic expansion, of receding frontiers, of polyglot population increase, of proliferating technology, has made it difficult for governmental forms to keep abreast. It is not surprising, therefore, that legislative policy, in penal no less than in other spheres, has been determined more by the utilitarian needs of the growing community than by precedent or tradition. And probation is nothing if not utilitarian.

The generally accepted definition of probation, as applied to adult offenders at any rate, is about as follows: a form of disposition under which a court suspends either the sentence or execution of the judgment of sentence on selected offenders, releasing them conditionally on good behavior, under prescribed terms and rules and subject to the control, guidance, and assistance of the court as exercised through officers appointed to supervise them. The essence of the system is the conditional suspension of sentence *plus* supervision of all the activities of the defendant (probationer) for the period of the suspension. It was in America that the combination was first set in motion, by the judges of the Boston Municipal Court in cooperation with John Augustus. It was accomplished, in the beginning, not in any continuous process of historical development arising out of early British or Continental use of the conditional suspension, but rather in an ingenious departure from, or distortion of, the precedents.

For many years and in several jurisdictions in the United States, the courts proceeded on the theory that there was an inherent power at common law to suspend sentences on convicted criminals indefinitely. The fact is, however, that apart from a relatively circumscribed practice of invoking the procedures known as "benefit of clergy" and "judicial reprieve," the British courts had never assumed or claimed any such inherent power. In actuality, both benefit of clergy and judicial reprieve were little more than artifices to avoid imposition of full legal process; they were employed principally to delay or avert punishment in cases where the courts felt the prescribed penalty for the given offense to be either "out of order" or excessive for the particular individual convicted. In that sense, the devices were negative rather than positive. Both were used in the colonies for some years but were found to be of uneven or unsatisfactory application. They were later practically abandoned as the American courts began to confer upon themselves the right to make positive suspensions for fixed periods, by which is meant purposeful suspensions with the stated or implicit objective of regeneration and with definite or determinate time limits. They fell into complete disuse after probation emerged as an accepted legal system.

This acceptance of probation did not come about quietly or automatically. Throughout the latter part of the nineteenth century and well into the twentieth, judges and lawyers had considerable difficulty in reconciling the system with the existing scheme of things, mainly because of the absence of established legal and procedural precedents. A number of appeals arose, for instance, in various states out of the question as to whether placements on probation represented a judicial invasion of the executives's pardoning prerogative under the "separation of powers" doctrine. The New York Court of Appeals, in ruling on an appeal from a suspension of sentence and grant of probation in 1894, upheld the trail court's action over the prosecutor's appeal but stated that its opinion "must not be understood as conferring any new power, because the power to suspend was inherent in all Superior Courts of criminal jurisdiction at common law." This decision was later discovered to be based largely on a misconstruction, if not indeed misquotation, of a famous passage in Lord Hale's *Pleas of the Crown* describing a practice which had grown up under British law. Chief Justice White, of the United States Supreme Court, commenting on the decision, referred to the misquotation from Lord Hale as "complete error," stating that in a diligent examination of *Pleas of the Crown* he found no passage containing the clauses cited by the New York Court of Appeals.

Chief Justice White thus demolished any lingering theory of common law antecedents for probation. As a consequence, its further development had to be entirely statutory; in the past fifty years hundreds of enabling laws have been passed, providing for probation service of either statewide or local coverage.

One by-product of what might be called the "illegitimate" origins of probation is that while its philosophy and objectives have always met with ready acceptance, its methods have not, at any rate not to the same extent. Notwithstanding that broad definitions of rules and procedures have often been enunciated, legislatively and other-wise, their testing and refinement was a long, difficult, and not always completely understood experimental process. Not until the Supreme Court review of probation's policies and practices in the momentous Williams decision did these finally achieve constitutional acceptability, so to speak. The Williams case, then, is epochal in the sense that it became the agent through which the husky hundred-year-old probation infant was "legitimatized."

Chapter Four

EDUCATION AND TRAINING FOR PROBATION AND PAROLE PERSONNEL

T HE IDEA that probation and parole officers are not merely agents of surveillance, but in large measure should be responsible for the rehabilitation of offenders, raises questions of qualifications and training for such personnel.

The issue has been raised frequently and argued heatedly by some that probation and parole are *social work practice,* and as such, require the specialized *professional* training offered by scores of social work schools across the country. Others, with equal conviction, have pointed out the vast differences which prevail between corrections and social work.

Correctional work is a highly specialized occupation, calling for special training and experience. The weight of opinion today seems to favor training of the probation counselor in case work with a psychiatric focus. Yet, it stands to reason that preparation in criminology, corrections, and social psychology are vital underpinnings of probation and parole work.

Educational requirements now vary considerably but probation departments should insist on the probation officer-applicant having completed as the minimum requirement four years of undergraduate training in a college or university leading to a bachelor's degree with a major in corrections, pre-social work, social welfare, or social science sequence. Such training, however, is no substitute for such personal characteristics as integrity, tolerance, emotional maturity, initiative, tact, and the ability to work cooperatively and unselfishly with others.

The success of probation is in no small measure determined by the quality of the supervision rendered. Unquestionably much of the current criticism of probation should be confined to the inadequacies and inaptitudes of its practitioners rather than to the principles upon which probation is based. It is only with enhanced skill which comes through training and supervised experience that we can hope to raise the performance level, and the success rate of probation practice.

THE PROBATION OFFICER AND HIS PERSONALITY*

We hold that the probation officer's personality and the use he makes of it in helping his clients is his most potent therapeutic tool. Those who agree with this proposition will necessarily include probation work among the helping arts. Its kinship with psychiatric and casework help will be assumed. Furthermore, those who agree with this proposition will see important implications for probation service in a statement on interpersonal relations recently appearing in the *Menninger Clinic Bulletin:* "The physician's personality is one of, if not *the* most potent therapeutic tool he can use." And they will appreciate a paraphrase of Somerset Maugham's insight as to the core problem of writing: "All the probation officer has to offer, when you come down to brass tacks, is himself."

We are not considering here such elements of probation work as procedures, practices, and regulations, but rather the more subjective elements—the intangibles, personal attributes, qualities of character—which are at the heart of a probation officer's service. The impatient or the overly scientific may turn away from this approach. For them it may seem too elusive, not susceptible of scientific proof. Admittedly, discussion of qualifications for practicing an art partakes of the emotional, of imponderables. These are qualities that refuse to lend themselves to precise measurement or to yield to impatient urgings. We gladly admit the inconclusiveness and the uncertainties. But we believe that even though there are no precise formulae nor systems of measurements for the development of healing personalities, the professionals who operate in our courts have, through the years, acquired a certain wisdom. While they cannot make silk purses out of sow's ears, they can make pretty good probation officers out of those who at first appear not too promising.

---

* Reprinted by permission of *Federal Probation*. Edmund G. Burbank and Ernest W. Goldsborough: The Probation Officer's Personality: A Key Factor in Rehabilitation, *Federal Probation*, Vol. 18, No. 2, June, 1954, p. 11-14. Footnotes are omitted.

In the preceding paragraphs we already have made some assumptions. The first is that personalities are capable of change,
that is, probation officers are made and not born. The second is
that knowledge and skill are available to help bring out the best
in the personality of a probation officer. If there is agreement on
these two assumptions, then it seems to us that the first problem
confronting the court is to decide what it wants the probation
officer to become and, second, how the office should be set up to
achieve that end. We are concerned here with a discussion of
those two problems. We suspect it is easier to catalogue an acceptable list of personality attributes of a probation officer than
to spell out how such attributes are developed. Always, in the
field of rehabilitation, the important point is *how do you do it?*

Some Cardinal Qualities of Personality

Probation work, in common with the other healing arts, requires a pretty mature and well-integrated personality. The over-
riding motive, the wider purpose, and the deepest plan of the
probation officer will be reflected in his day-to-day achievements.
Those achievements of the task, if properly done, will reflect an
implicit faith in the capacity of his probationer to grow. The
demands on an officer are great, for he is working with persons
who almost always are playing a dangerous game. Yet, even while
affirming the ultimate value of genuine personal integrity, we are
bound to recognize that each officer will have weaknesses. The
better part of integrity, as of wisdom, is to acknowledge weakness
—to recognize and acknowledge our particular prejudices, defenses, blind spots, and where we do not have full knowledge.
Conceal or rationalize them as we will, they are bound to affect
our job performance in one way or another. It is no sin to possess
such weaknesses and limitations; the sin is denying them, un-
repentantly inflicting them on others, and in continuing to work
with other human beings and not trying to discipline ourselves.

More specifically, by maturity and integrity we mean these
things:

1. *The ability to form and sustain wholesome interpersonal
relationships.*—In probation work, the officer needs the capacity
to identify with a wide range of people. He will work with the

"white collar" criminal and the defective delinquent, the addict and the alcoholic, the homosexual and the homicidal. The degree to which the officer cares for what happens to his client, whatever the offense and whatever the cultural background, will be reflected in a thousand ways as he proceeds with his daily tasks. "The outer trend confirms the inner pattern." If the inner pattern of the probation officer is to confuse the delinquent deed with the whole life of the man committing it, the outer trend, the achieved result, will show a judgmental, intolerant probation officer. If the inner pattern of the officer is devotion to the cause of helping the offender to summon up his own vision of the better life, to muster his own strength to achieve that better life, then the outer trend, the achieved result, will show a probation officer with a healing personality.

2. *The ability to accept responsibility for the authority he carries.*—This ability is not easily won. Many an adult is unwilling to face his infantile attitudes toward authority. He will not willingly yield to the rightful and inevitable demands which life with other people compels. Nor will he always give proper consideration to the impact his own authority has upon those subject to it. The probation officer who is an adult accepts authority as a condition of everyday living—a process of disciplining our individual impulses and desires for the mutual benefit of all. Probation signifies the offender is out of tune with the social demands of the community. The probation officer who represents authority must use it firmly but tempered with judgment and understanding. If he has the proper measure of his own adequacy, he will not yield to his own need to superimpose his power and control over one who is in his care. He will view his essential task as helping the probationer decide on a course of action.

Long ago Galileo wrote: "You cannot teach a man anything; you can only help him to find it within himself." In keeping with this sage advice, the probation officer can help the probationer to find within himself the power and readiness to decide on a course of action, the power and readiness to use relationships constructively. The probationer will never accept a condition—or an officer—he cannot respect. He may kowtow and conform, but he will inwardly despise and rebel and will not grow in responsibility. We are aware of no more trenchant thinking on the conditions of personality change, whether applied to probation or parole officer, probationer or parolee, than is contained in the following excerpt:

> . . . the individual personality and behavior pattern invariably and inevitably changes, if it changes at all, from the individual's own motivations, from his own choices, from his own efforts to attain his own satisfactions. No decisions made under duress or by somebody else are binding upon the individual when he is free. No behavior based upon fear is maintained when danger is past. The one absolutely indispensable foundation of any effort to correct unacceptable patterns of behavior, or to sustain new, acceptable patterns—which is the basic aim of (parole)—is that the responsibility for that behavior shall remain, always and throughout, with the individual. And the one essential skill required in the administration of a helping service directed to this end is the disciplined ability to develop and maintain a helping relationship in which the individual remains always free, and always obliged to accept and discharge—never to evade—his own responsibility for his own choices and judgements and their consequences. The only help which anyone can give to another person toward accepting new patterns of behavior is to afford the opportunity for clearly facing and steadily clarifying the available alternatives of action and their potential consequences, and to sustain the individual's strength to face the realities and to accept responsibility for the choices he does and must make.

3. Ability to work with aggressive persons.—The probation officer, as has been well said, must have "strength and some immunity in facing extreme aggression and hostility because some responsibilities in this field include ability to meet hazardous situations where the awareness of the need as well as the ability to take calculated risks is essential."

The probation officer will not always find his charges obviously aggressive. Their hostility is revealed in more subtle ways. Real tears must be distinguished from crocodile tears. Scenes of rage or despair are often admirably staged. To acknowledge this does not in itself make it easier for the probation officer to do his job, but somehow he must learn to work with all types of aggression with a high degree of objectivity and poise.

4. *Ability to work with other agencies and people.*—The type of person who must be the star of the show is out of place in a probation office. This is true, first of all, because the key person is the probationer. It is in his power to use or abuse the proffered service. Secondly, probation work is too complicated and difficult to provide space for a prima donna. Those of us responsible for helping human beings need all of the assistance we can get. The diversity and perversity of human personality are so extensive that no one person and no one discipline has a cure-all. We can operate more effectively by pooling our resources of information and talent for the good of the probationer and the community.

5. *Ability to improve in performance.*—This, of course, implies change for the probation officer as he works on the job. It is surely not unreasonable to expect and require this for the person who expects and requires change in his probationer. It is altogether too easy to see and stress the probationer's faults and shortcomings; not so easy to see or to discipline one's own. Yet it is elementary that there is no helping possible if the helper cannot distinguish his own emotions from those of the client. It is of great importance to be sure that rightful insistence upon the offender assuming responsibility for his own conduct is not the product of an officer's own laziness; not an attempt to justify an officer's own indifference or unwillingness to reach out; not a community rationalization for niggardly supply of legitimate, essential probation services.

The great Roman writer Juvenal once asked a profound question which has echoed down the corridors of the history of government for 2,000 years: "Who shall guard the guards themselves?" His question rephrased we would ask: Who shall help the helpers themselves? That question takes us to the second part of our inquiry. We have stated what in general the probation officer should become. Now we will look at how we might set up the office so that the probation officer has the best chance of becoming that kind of a person.

There is no need here to detail widely known and accepted principles which, when taken together, comprise a sound code of personnel practices. Standards and procedures for recruitment and for the payment of personnel are readily available. Optimum case load and the proper allocation of time between presentence investigations and supervision of probationers are subjects of frequent discussion and written analysis. While these are aids to good performance on the job, in our judgment, there is need to dwell on questions which are too often begged. *Who helps the helper and how is it done?* Probation officers are not born with helping skill nor is it thrust upon them. It is acquired. It is acquired either in a professional school of social work or in inservice training. In any event, it is acquired in a probation office.

Atmosphere of the Court and Probation Office

The most important thing about a probation office is its spirit, its atmosphere, the morale of its staff. Its tone is set, above all, by the judge or the board of judges. We do not mean to be in contempt of court when we suggest, therefore, that the five cardinal qualities of a probation officer's personality apply equally to the judges. When the probation office, as an arm of the court, is viewed as a setting in which growth of skill and development of adult responsibility take place, no special wisdom is required to appreciate the importance of the breezes which blow from the judge's chambers. The memories of too many probation officers are filled with cross-currents of unjudicial, antisocial attitudes of some judges. They recall vividly that Judge X had confidence in his probation officers, discussed cases with them freely, and, most important of all, relied on the probation officer's judgment. They recall Judge Y, a martinet, with contempt of probation and those who came within the jurisdiction of the court. Multiply Judge X and Judge Y two or three times to account for the larger board of judges and let your imagination paint the picture of the chaotic atmosphere of the probation office and the frustration of its officers.

The atmosphere of the probation office cannot be overstressed, because it sets the condition in which a job is done by many people. A healthy court atmosphere implies high standards of probation performance. New officers, and old, in such a setting are expected to carry the type of responsibility which demonstrates increasingly their integrity and maturity. What we are saying is this: The atmosphere of a probation office reveals the degree of integration of purpose and, in the last analysis, the level of performance and effectiveness in discharging its responsibility to clientele and community. Who more than the judges are in a position to set the spirit of the court and its office? If they want it to be subject to improper political influences, it will be. If they want loyal, creative, competent personnel, the judges can do more than anyone else to insure it. Who helps the helper? Part of our answer is that the judges do.

The Probation Officer Can Always Learn

Mindful that an administrative chain is no stronger than its weakest links, the chief probation officer and supervisory staff are other links in the chain of those who help the helper. The function of supervisory staff is to assist the probation officer in evaluating the assets and liabilities of *his* personality as it relates to his role in helping his charges achieve acceptable changes in their behavior. The focus of supervision should be on the officer's learning and performance on the job.

What must he be required to learn? At the very least these five abilities which we have already characterized as the mark of maturity and integrity of the probation officer.

First, he must move substantially beyond his former prejudices, defenses, blind spots, and limitations in order to enhance his ability to sustain wholesome interpersonal relationships.

Second, how he has used supervision should reveal his unmistakable attitude toward authority and dependency. The very attitudes which inhibit his use of supervision will invariably limit his capacity to help his charges.

Third, as with the probationer, an officer's attempt to examine his own weak spots are met with varying degrees of aggressive and subtle resistance. The probation officer must demonstrate his ability to understand and discipline his own aggression and resistance.

Fourth, no probation officer possesses the key which unlocks the door to any one man's problem. It is, therefore, essential to make use of all available knowledge and insights which other agencies in the community may possess from their contacts with the probationer.

Fifth, if the probation officer is not concerned about his level of performance and is unwilling or unable to make a different and more constructive use of supervision, then he is not the man for the job. Is the probation officer not concerned with helping a probationer begin to make constructive use of supervision? Does he not have to help him understand the problem with which he is struggling to accept and to conform to community standards? Is he not concerned with helping the probationer find a different and more satisfying solution to his way of life? Acceptable standards of performance are a rightful expectation of the court and the community. To demand acceptable performance from probation officers without helping them to achieve this end is just as false as placing a man on probation and allowing him to go it alone. We affirm there should be no probation without supervision for the probation officer. One needs help to achieve the degree of objectivity, maturity, and self-discipline necessary to help probationers.

It is in this spirit, we think, that Judge Elwood Melson is writing when he defines the responsibility of the court in these words:

> It is, I believe, to create those conditions and that atmosphere which, within the court's limitations, are most conducive to the production of change.
>
> Again, experience has taught me, and I believe will teach any other judge who is able and willing to learn, that there is nothing, absolutely nothing, which will better create the conditions and atmosphere most conducive to change, than the employment and the complete integration within the authority of his court, of a technically trained staff of skilled and thoroughly understanding probation officers working under trained, skilled supervision.
>
> Not until this has been done, will the court have discharged its responsibility to the community.

For centuries, the western world has known that man can be free only through mastery of himself; free, that is, to assume his inescapable responsibility for meeting the obligations of community living. Part of the challenge of our era is to provide the proper atmosphere and setting for probation officers to develop the kind of skill to become the persons who really help probationers to achieve more responsible behavior.

SOCIAL WORK AND CORRECTIONS*

The present scene is part of an historical process in which, after an early close association, schools of social work and corrections drifted apart from each other. The reasons why this happened are complex: It is probably an oversimplification to say, as many do, that this was partly because social work theory became increasingly dependent upon psychoanalytic concepts, with emphasis on a-rational, unconscious motivation; as well as because of an increased emphasis on the right of the client to self-determination. And that these taken together resulted in doubts about the effective use of social work in an authoritarian setting. These concepts undoubtedly seemed incompatible with some of the assumptions of the criminal law and the ways in which many courts were conducted. Moreover, the penal system was either punitive or else relied upon efforts at individual reform based upon environmental manipulation, moral exhortation and arbitrarily imposed controls on behavior. In short, it punished or undertook custodial care of the offender in order to protect the community, or else sought to reform him by means which social workers had long since discovered to be ineffective, in that change forced upon the individual does not change his inner motivation.

At present, movement from both sides is altering this apparent deadlock. The growth of knowledge in the social and behavioral sciences, the very substantial research in this country into the causation and treatment of delinquency, together with more humane attitudes toward the offender, have all contributed toward provision of increased facilities for diagnosis and treatment in correctional institutions and as a basic element in probation and parole. Psychologists, psychiatrists, sociologists, social workers and teachers work together on the professional staffs of correc-

*Reprinted in part by permission of the Council on Social Work Education, Eileen L. Younghusband: Report on a Survey of Social Work in the Field of Corrections, *Social Work Education Bimonthly News Publication*, Vol. VIII, No. 4, Supplement, August, 1960, p. 1-11.

tional agencies, with varying degrees of clarification of their appropriate roles. There is also emphasis on a broader orientation for judges, of more psycho-social content in the training of law enforcement officers, and on in-service training for house parents, detention home counselors and custodial staff in prisons and other correctional institutions.

The range and extent of single or multi-discipline research in delinquency or closely related fields is exceedingly impressive, whether undertaken by universities, correctional agencies, various national organizations or independent groups. The problems of making these research findings known and of embodying them in operational programs is, however, acute. The field of corrections in the United States is generally characterized by inadequate exchange of information and, often, by ignorance of significant current developments.

So far as the correctional services themselves are concerned, the most fruitful growing points often seem to be in treatment-oriented correctional institutions rather than through probation and parole services to the offender in the community. This is somewhat out of line with the general trend toward rehabilitation of the individual in his social milieu, rather than removal from it; though in the most enlightened institutions an attempt is made to create a therapeutic community.

Juvenile probation appears to have a higher status than adult probation though in a few states or localities the latter service may be more highly developed. This was said to be related to feeling in the United States about constructive help to young people, their greater ability to profit from it and their importance as future citizens. This argument is potent in itself but it ignores the fact that the adult offender is often a member of a family in which there are children. It is rare to find work being undertaken with the families of offenders in correctional institutions, whether for juvenile or adults, or close cooperation with other agencies which may—or should—be helping them. The quantity and quality of help available to parolees may also be insufficient to support treatment achievements in the best institutions. It is, of course, well known that in any country the percentage of women offenders is small compared with that of men. All the same, the low number of women in prison or on probation in this country suggests that other factors may well be at work. The social adjustment of women offenders not given the "help" of probation or a prison sentence and parole may have been studied already. If not, it would well repay this. From the point of view of the present enquiry, this situation and the fact that in the United States women are commonly put on probation or parole to men helps to cast light on the very small number of openings for women social workers in corrections. In a few instances women graduate social workers are supervising men probation officers while in several departments of corrections there were plans to appoint a few more women, whether in prison, probation or parole services.

Treatment services in correctional institutions, which sometimes started with a small and possibly isolated psychiatric clinic team, are now, where they exist, becoming well integrated as part of the total service. The role of social workers is commonly exercised at key points in connection with reception, diagnosis and classification, family visits, community contacts, reading selected mail (as a means of identifying inmates' problems and offering help with them), work and group assignments, case conferences, group services, and reports for parole board reviews and decisions. Both employed social workers and students are involved in group services which are a significant development in correctional institutions. These groups seem to be of three kinds: discussion groups conducted by custodial or other untrained staff, group counseling undertaken by social workers, and group therapy undertaken by psychologists or occasionally by psychiatrists. Some important aims seem to be to modify the individual's attitudes as a result of peer group discussion, to arouse anxiety and motivation for a change, or conversely to allay it in relation to family and community problems; and to lessen the distance between the staff and the inmate system. Possibly the most important single purpose is to enable the individual to learn through group participation the A. B. C. of social living.

The schools of social work are less concerned than formerly about the incompatibility between authority and social work. It is now generally recognized that use of authority is inherent in the operation of various agencies, that authority may be used positively and that social controls are necessary. The discussion thus shifts from whether it should be used to how it should be used. This shift of emphasis is in part attributed to the development of work with "hard-to-reach" clients, multi-problem families and street gangs; to increased psychiatric knowledge in relation to character disorders and sociopaths; as well as to the growth and application of knowledge from social psychology and sociology, especially in relation to gangs, social deviance, delinquent subcultures, lower and middle class social values and the effects of social structure, roles and status on individual behavior. In the new possibilities thus opening up for treatment of the involuntary and unmotivated, acting-out, impulse-ridden, hostile or inadequate client the correctional agency begins to be seen as a significant setting for such treatment, or at least as capable of becoming so, because it is the only agency which can hold the involuntary client long enough for treatment to take effect. Much work yet remains to be done on the use of limit setting and controls as a means to increase the client's capacity for socially mature self-determination rather than to motive him to conform to accepted standards.

There is a general shortage of case records for teaching purposes in corrections. A few casework records exist, notably the Council's *Casebook in Correctional Casework*. There appear, however, to be practically no group work (except of work with street gangs) or community organization records in this field. This is a serious gap in view of the heavy emphasis on group methods in treatment-oriented correctional institutions and in some non-institutional settings. Relations within correctional agencies and between them and the community are also capable of providing a significant source of community organization records. In addition, the rich sociological and psychiatric material in this field is in marked contrast to the paucity of basic studies of social work findings and problems. The writings of Elliot Studt indeed stand out as the biggest single contribution to the much needed attempt to relate sociological, psychological and psychiatric knowledge in the field to social work theory and practice, and in so doing to enrich both education and practice.

Some ideas that correctional material is "specialized" whereas that from settings more traditionally associated with social work is "generic" seemed on further analysis to spring from insufficient study of the material in relation to a generic program. For example, the fact that certain great social issues like the use of coercion, or the necessity both to use social controls and to impose democratic limitations on their use, appear at their zenith in corrections does not mean that they can realistically be ignored elsewhere.

The general trends already noted are either actually or potentially bringing about a rapprochement between the schools of social work and correctional agencies. To say this is not to suggest that all courts or other correctional agencies are treatment-oriented; while those who wish to improve practices often struggle with problems of untrained staffs, heavy caseloads and lack of financial resources. In any event, they do not necessarily want to employ or know how to use graduate social workers.

Probation and parole are regarded by some as a skilled casework service but by others as a means to force upon the offender the observance of a series of restrictions on his behavior. Similarly, correctional institutions may be thought of primarily as a means to punish the offender and protect the community or as a controlled situation in which, by individual diagnosis and treatment, group services and planned milieu therapy, lasting attitude changes may be brought about. Some of the failure of social workers to function effectively in corrections is due to their inability to adapt their professional practice in the setting. But rehabilitation is not simply the outcome of a professional skill exercised in isolation from the whole operation of the agency. Correctional agencies are social structures and systems in which old attitudes may be congealed in out-of-date buildings, legal enactments and practices. And social workers, like others who seek to bring new ideas to birth, must be able to work within the agency in such a way as to provide the dynamic for change, and to demonstrate better results as an outcome of change.

There is also acute conflict throughout the field of corrections as to whether it is desirable to employ professional personnel whose identification would be both with their profession and with corrections or whether it would be preferable to develop a profession of corrections. Some university programs prepare students specifically for work in corrections, and proposals for a 1-2 year specialized training find favor because this would be closely related to perceived requirements in this field; moreover, those so trained would be less likely to leave for other jobs. From another angle, there are also those who believe that the untrained or in-service trained worker from a working class background is closer to the client, speaks his language, and is thus able both to understand and control him more effectively than the professionally qualified social worker.

It is also suggested that social workers, psychiatrists, and psychologists often do not consult with house parents, custodial staff and law enforcement officers, or else force their professional viewpoint upon them in jargon which they do not understand. These approaches tend to make these staffs feel devalued and frustrated; whereas in fact they may have acquired considerable experience of practice in relation to deviant behavior which would repay study and discussion sessions to clarify the concepts underlying their empirical knowledge and working methods.

Some schools of social work already have a long connection with the correctional field or else are seeking to establish this connection or to expand and improve field placements. On the other hand, it must be recognized that deans and other faculty members have their hands full with existing commitments, that they are often not familiar with and may have mixed feelings about corrections, that there is no dearth of jobs in other agencies for graduates of schools of social work and that training grants are readily available in certain other fields but scarce in corrections.

In the schools visited, a number of faculty members had had or were having substantial experience in the correctional field. This was primarily among those responsible for coordinating field practice or for teaching social services courses or social process or research. A considerable volume of research was being undertaken by faculty members in various parts of the correctional field. There were, however, comparatively few methods course teachers with direct experience in corrections, though some had improved their understanding of this field through teaching institutes for correctional personnel. This meant that the real grass roots knowledge of the field was mainly found among research staffs and faculty members in charge of field instruction.

The overall impression left upon an enquirer from another country is that schools of social work and correctional agencies are becoming aware that they have much to gain from and give to each other. There are, however, still uncertainties and reservations about this; moreover, each is both proud and sensitive, fearful of criticism, of being told what "ought" to be done, or of having new ways of thought or action imposed upon them. In short, the schools may think that correctional agencies do not understand social work nor the educational standards required in graduate study, and correctional agencies are sometimes equally convinced that the schools are by and large unfamiliar with or unrealistic about the needs of the correctional situation. Nonetheless, many bridges, some old and some new, exist. Joint discussion, exploration, experimentation and research are needed in order to give each a better understanding of the other and to modify attitudes which hinder the development of better service and closer cooperation.

It is common to find job classifications in corrections for "social workers," "caseworkers," "group workers," "group counselors," or else that an M.S.W. is a preferred or even required qualification for appointment as a probation or parole officer or to some specific post in a correctional institution. Even though many people in corrections still have mixed feelings about graduate social workers, it is significant that there are vastly most jobs open to social workers in this field than there are qualified people to fill them. It must, of course, be remembered that the majority of students in schools of social work are women and that probably 80-90 per cent of the jobs in corrections are only open to men. One result is that many jobs which by definition require social work skill are in fact filled by persons with at most a Bachelor's degree, who have not subsequently received any in-service training, and who may have no opportunity for educational leave or to qualify through a work-study program. It is now beginning to be accepted that this may not be a temporary phenomenon and serious thought must be given to devising forms of training for them.

There are, of course, a number of individual examples of

juvenile or family courts substantially staffed with graduate social workers (largely women) as probation officers; of adult probation and parole services with a significant percentage of graduate social workers; as well as of detention homes and correctional diagnostic centers and institutions for juveniles and adults where graduate social workers are recruited as members of a professional team. These are, however, but beacon lights. The more typical situation is represented by the fact that so far as is known only about 10 per cent of the juvenile court probation officers for the country as a whole are graduate social workers. Figures are not available for the federal probation and parole service and in social work posts in federal prisons. But rough estimates would put the number of graduate social workers at between 10 per cent and 12 per cent. On the other hand, roughly 60 per cent to 80 per cent of all these personnel are college graduates and would therefore be eligible for admission to a school of social work. Less than one in four of those who occupy social work posts in public training schools are graduate social workers.

There seems to be good evidence for the view that, unless promotion goes by seniority, graduate social workers who go into corrections rise rapidly as supervisors or to key administrative positions in which they influence policy, whether as directors of services or as assistant wardens or wardens in prisons or as superintendents of other correctional institutions, or as chief probation officers, or as members of research teams. In such positions it tends to be forgotten that they are social workers since they are not by definition exercising professional treatment skills, though frequently they must have knowledge of social research methodology and show skill in administration. In these circumstances schools of social work might make a significant contribution by providing for advanced study in the social work administration of correctional agencies.

At the other end of the scale, it is said that some mediocre social work graduates as well as students who have been discontinued at the end of their first year find their way into corrections and are often actively hostile to social work.

There is a tendency for both groups, the best and the least good, to become identified with corrections rather than with the profession of social work. This is particularly prone to happen in certain correctional situations where compromise with professional standards is inevitable; in such circumstances some social workers compromise to the point of losing their professional identity; others leave the field; others arrive at a mutual adjustment or are able to use their social work skill to modify agency practices. Except in comparatively isolated situations, the experienced and skilled professional practitioner is rare, since competence is synonymous with promotion up the administrative ladder as the way to a higher salary and higher status. In any event, with a few notable exceptions, diagnostic and treatment facilities tend to be in institutions. This further skews the development of adequate social work service to the offender in the community—and to his family. The number of qualified social workers in administrative and research positions thus appears to be out of balance with the numbers who are required as field instructors and teachers if social work is to advance in the correctional setting. This total situation must clearly have unfortunate effects on the development of social work methodology in corrections and on the suitability of correctional agencies for students' field instruction. Moreover, many research findings cannot be applied nor adequate diagnostic and treatment facilities be provided without the necessary professional personnel. Some administrators in correctional agencies were aware of this problem and discussing ways of rewarding the good practitioner by increased salary and status. Many social workers are concerned about the difficulty of preserving their professional identity in the correctional field where strong forces operate to pull them into the correctional orbit and, so they complain, they receive too little support from either their professional colleagues elsewhere or from the schools of social work.

Salaries were generally said to compare favorably with those for social workers in other agencies, particularly when good promotion prospects were taken into account. Nonetheless, in one state visited, beginning salaries in corrections were about $1,000 a year lower than in the Veterans' Administration. This, coupled with the lack of training grants, naturally affected recruitment.

It was frequently said that the high caseloads, the distances to be covered and the number of courts to be served often resulted in probation officers spending a large part of their time on social enquiries and miscellaneous court work. In such situations probation and parole was bound to consist mainly of checking up on the client's activities, sometimes by telephone or letter. It was also said that probation and parole officers did not always desire more time for interviews with persons on probation or parole for fear this uncovered problems with which they had neither time nor skill to deal. Sometimes staff supervision was available from graduate social workers but more often than not supervisors had no professional qualifications and were primarily concerned with seeing that legal and administrative requirements were observed. It is clear that many departments of corrections are contending with enormous difficulties of under-staffing and under-qualified staff. This situation, which undoubtedly deters graduate social workers from entering this field, of itself deepens the vicious circle. Nonetheless, no tribute would be too high to pay to those administrators and others in the correctional field who against many odds continue to take pride in their work and struggle to bring about improvements.

While many people stressed the problems referred to above, the general impression seemed to be that career prospects are often very good for men with the right type of "aggressive" personality; that opportunities for social workers interested and competent in research are also good; that certain court, county or state probation and parole services offer satisfactory opportunities to caseworkers; and that some of the most stimulating and challenging opportunities in the whole field of social work exist in multi-discipline professional teams in treatment-oriented correctional institutions. The common statement from the correctional field that they want social workers rather than caseworkers, group workers or community organizers in effect means that social workers in this field will be called upon to use all three methods—and will also need skill in administration and research. This is a job which calls upon the whole of a social worker's actual or potential skill and competence, but it is no field for those who can only function effectively in the sheltered agency, working with the anxiety-motivated rather than the hostile, acting out, involuntary client.

It would be less than realistic not to discuss the disadvantages which are said to exist in greater or less degree in a number of correctional settings. It is not suggested that all these disadvantages are peculiar to corrections. Many, in any event, have far wider implications than their effect on the recruitment or retention of graduate social workers. Some are rigid and pervasive, others subject to swift winds of change, others yet may be modified through better mutual understanding, respect and cooperation between members of the legal and the "treatment" professions and administrators. The following are some of the reasons said to discourage social workers from the correctional field.

A. *Appointment system*—Where appointments and promotions are made by judges, personal bias or political considerations, or ignorance of social work may affect decisions.

Where they are under civil service, personality factors may not always weigh in selection, salaries may be no higher for graduate social workers than for those without a professional qualification, while residence requirements and seniority rules may severely restrict mobility and promotion aspects.

Where appointments are made on a political basis, professional qualifications and personal suitability will not be primary requirements for appointment or promotion; and there may also be uncertainty of tenure.

B. *Uncertainties and rigidities*—This refers mainly to the changes which may happen over-night with change of key person in the power structure or because of political changes. Such changes are sometimes beneficial but they tend not to be seen in this light by professional social workers who have gone to work in a correctional setting with a good reputation and fear negative change.

These uncertainties and work difficulties are centered to some extent on the degree and range of power exercised by judges—the power to appoint, to promote or not promote, to give or withhold salary increases, to dismiss. This same degree of individual power does not exist in a state department under civil service, though staff shortages and heavy workloads may result in rigid practices, with no opportunity for professional advancement or to carry out individualized treatment.

A court may be served by several different judges with different attitudes and methods of working. There may also be rapid change of judges. They may have no knowledge of social work or of how to use social workers. They may see their own function in purely legal terms and be comparatively indifferent to other aspects of the court's functioning, including teamwork and administrative efficiency. Where they think it important to individualize the offender, they may do so by imposing unrealistic controls on the basis of their own hunches, prejudices, and moral values, and with little capacity to communicate with him, thus making the social worker's task more difficult. Where they begin to have some understanding of causation and treatment they may make much better use of social workers but become uncertain about their own role. They may use the court for empire-building, or be anxious to get promotion away from it as quickly as possible, or be motivated by political expediency. But on the other hand they may sometimes be very good indeed, able to give effective leadership and to demonstrate the attitudes of impartiality, fairness and regard for human rights which the law should breed and from which social workers have much to learn. The NCCD Council of Judges is an important means for improving attitudes and practices.

C. *Authority/legal structure conflicts*—Probably all social workers in corrections experience problems and conflicts in trying to hold the balance true between the needs of the individual, parental rights, the protection of the community and the demands of the law, as well as in working in an agency which is not primarily geared to social work or its philosophy. Apart from these inherent problems, a particular correctional agency may have practices which are truly damaging to the offender. Social workers may also be required to perform certain duties which more appropriately belong to law enforcement officers.

D. *Law personnel*—There are often difficulties in working with members of the legal profession and law enforcement officers if their assumptions about the agency's purpose and about human motivation are too inconsistent with social work knowledge or philosophy.

E. *The agency*—Problems arise in working in an agency which is rigid and highly structured in certain directions but often diffuse and unstructured as a setting for the orderly use of social work skill. This is reflected in large caseloads, lack of supervision or consultation services and irregular hours. There is also the heavy strain of continually taking hostility and trying to bring about beneficial attitude changes in involuntary clients caught in a situation in which they fear or are experiencing punishment, social disapproval and damage to their self-image. On the other hand, probation and parole officers sometimes have a good deal more freedom to work in their own way with their clients than in many other social agencies.

ATTITUDES OF CORRECTIONAL AGENCIES TOWARD THE EMPLOYMENT OF PROFESSIONAL SOCIAL WORKERS

It was widely said that social work had been gaining ground in the last few years as an appropriate and desired professional qualification in corrections. As one correctional administrator said: "Even those who don't like social workers would hire them if they could." Against this must be set the view that lip service is being paid to social work because it embodies some of the values and attitudes toward treatment which are accepted though not always implemented in corrections. There is also a good deal of frustration among correctional administrators as a result of their failure to recruit more than a handful of graduate social workers. And also because of what are sometimes interpreted as rigid attitudes or lack of helpfulness on the part of schools of social work. This failure to recruit professional social workers is gravely retarding the application of enlightened diagnostic and treatment policies. Among the conflicting attitudes toward social workers this is one of the factors turning corrections in on itself and away from professional social work.

The following is an attempt to summarize what is said for and against professional social workers in corrections.

In Favor of the Use of Professional Social Workers

Psychologists are needed and used for personality testing, treatment and group therapy; their skill is complementary rather than an alternative to social work skill, but they would not be able to use their clinical skill as probation or parole officers. Sociologists are used in research and for classification and prediction studies in correctional institutions but they have not developed skill in work with individuals or groups. Thus, although psychologists and sociologists are needed to fulfil appropriate roles in the correctional field, the knowledge and skill of social workers are more suited than that of any other profession to bring about the behavior changes which a progressive correctional agency is striving to achieve. This is because they not only have appropriate knowledge about human behavior and motivation about individuals and families and their environment, but also skill in applying this knowledge in social diagnosis and treatment. They know how to interview people "so as to get them really talking." They know something about how to motivate them to change and how to use community resources. This, however, does not necessarily mean that they are exactly what correctional agencies want.

Against the Use of Professional Social Workers

Social workers too often come into correctional agencies knowing nothing about the law or about court procedures, limitations and deadlines; and they are doubtful about the use of the authority inherent in a correctional situation.

They make demands for a type of professional practice and consideration for the client which does not always fit in with the team or with administrative or other practices in the agency. Their point of view may differ too markedly from the legal point of view and judges often do not know how to use them, partly on this account. They may try to influence the judge to take too big risks on behalf of the offender and against the interests of the community. They tend to overlook the high visibility of court decisions in contrast to the low visibility of social work skill, and to be unduly frustrated by the common emphasis in courts and correctional institutions on playing for safety.

They often refuse to work in an agency which does not offer professional supervision ("do they never grow up?"). Their skill and method and their modes of practice may have been acquired with small caseloads of anxiety-motivated voluntary clients in a protected agency setting. If so, they are often almost unable to function professionally with a different type of client and setting. They are often "busy being professional" and do not work sufficiently closely with nor respect the knowledge and experience of lawbreakers which law enforcement officers, house parents and custodial staffs may have acquired.

Sociologists (especially with a criminology major) may be preferred because they know more about the court setting, they are more comfortable with authority and they do not have a professional skill or professional standards which they find hard to reconcile with a correctional setting. Moreover, it is said that they are often better from a personality point of view than some graduate social workers who go into corrections. They may be preferred for these reasons, even though they do not have the skill valued in the social worker.

General

It will be noticed that many of the foregoing points match—though from the reverse angle—the versions given as to why social workers find it hard to function in a correctional setting. Some are the kind of criticisms which many agencies without good orientation programs make about any new professional worker. But they are sufficiently significant to point to the need for further discussion between schools and correctional agencies in order to promote better mutual understanding, to identify possible modifications in agency practice which would result in better service by social workers, as well as additions to the schools' program which would prepare students better for this field and enable them to operate more flexibly in it. In any event, no more than a beginning has been made in identifying the nature of the social work task at various points in correctional agencies, for example, analyzing what probation and parole officers and social workers in correctional institutions actually do and freeing the social work role from certain inappropriate functions now sometimes attached to it.

THE CLERK AND PROBATION*

Clerical services are an important adjunct in the effective operation of a probation office. Frequently, in the selection of clerical assistants, the only concern is with the individual's capacity to type efficiently, and to look reasonably presentable. While the field agent carries the major responsibility for cases, the clerk or receptionist often has the initial contact in the office. For this reason, it is vital that all personnel who come into contact with the probationer have understanding of the types of problems which are a part of correctional work. (Editor's note.)

* * * * * *

From the movies I'd seen and the stories I'd read I expected that when I reported to the parole office on my release from Atlanta I'd be met by a hatchet-faced woman who would start bossing me around right away, but was I surprised! When I opened the door I was greeted by a soft-voiced woman with a pleasant smile who asked my name and a few questions to identify me and then asked me to sit down while she told the officer I was there. Somehow that seemed to start my parole right.

This was written to the warden at Atlanta by one of our parolees shortly after I came to the office. It was then that I fully realized how important first impressions are to men and women reporting from institutions and I have made it a point to be as courteous as possible to everyone coming into this probation office.

New Situations Are Difficult for Most of Us

Anyone going into a new situation is anxious and anxiety, unlike fear or other emotions, is something no one can do anything about. Different people express this anxiety differently; some with an attitude of indifference; some with belligerence; some with shyness or diffidence. A probationer is an anxious person. He probably is somewhat bewildered and is under stress after all he has been through. There is an element of uncertainty which is not pleasant to experience. If the receptionist, who

---

* Reprinted by permission of *Federal Probation*. Jane L. Brewer: The Clerk Also Has An Important Part In Probation, *Federal Probation*, Vol. 19, No. 4, July, 1955, p. 6-9.

usually is the first person to contact him is this new situation, bears this in mind and treats him kindly and with respect, she helps to relieve this anxiety and to put him at ease, making it easier for the officer who is to interview him as well as for the probationer himself. She should never keep him waiting needlessly; prompt service helps to establish confidence. I always make it a point to express regret occasionally if an officer is very busy and the probationer has to wait an unusually long time for an interview. It assures him he has not been forgotten or he is not being overlooked.

I stress this first contact because perhaps we too frequently forget we are dealing with another person who has feelings just as we have. Life is a struggle for the probationer as it is for most of us and the very fact he transgressed the law suggests that life has been more of a struggle for him. He carries an added burden through the stigma of a conviction. There are some people so constituted that their first impression of the probation office will be carried on through the entire relationship and when we bear this in mind we realize how very important is the clerk's part in this first contact. Unlike clerks selling inanimate objects over a counter, we are dealing with persons and to a degree we are selling them self-confidence and self-esteem.

Patience and Understanding Are Important

Few receptionists are called on to meet more different types of people than is the probation clerk. She greets many who are friendly, or cooperative, and at ease; others who are irritable, impatient, or unreasonable in their demands. It is vital that she be courteous, patient, and understanding and never display anger, chagrin, or emotional disturbance even if at times she must leave the office for a few moments to regain her inner composure.

She should remember that one's outward demeanor does not always reflect his true inner feelings. The "cocky, self-assured" individual may, in fact, be covering up a sense of insecurity. A belligerent attitude may actually be a false front for fear, shame, or the unpleasant circumstances in which he finds himself. An apparently buoyant person may be in truth hiding a deep feeling of depression.

Attitudes of defiance, suspicion, bitterness, and depression are symptoms of emotional disturbance. Ofttimes an alert receptionist can bring these signs of emotional upset to the attention of the probation officer before he sees the probationer. They will help him in his counseling. Many times, too, through her friendly, understanding interest in the probationer the receptionist can help him to become more relaxed and at ease and consequently less hostile when the officer is ready to talk with him.

The receptionist must discount her prejudices. They show like a slip below a woman's dress! She meets people of all races and classes. She must treat them as courteously as anyone else who comes to the office and must never show feelings of contempt or indifference.

Others who require the patience and tact of the receptionist are those whose sons, daughters, or other relatives are in prison and a parole plan is being developed. Some of these persons are antagonistic on first coming to the office—"My boy didn't do wrong. They had no business sending him to jail." Others are utterly confused and some are deeply worried for fear they will not be able to work out a plan and the fault will be theirs if the son or daughter fails to make parole. A courteous, understanding receptionist many times can reassure them and put them in a much better frame of mind for the interview with the probation officer. Assuring them of the helpful, sympathetic treatment of the probation officer is one means to this end.

I remember a heart-broken mother who came to this office after hearing that her son was in a federal penitentiary. He had been away from home for some time but she had just learned he had gotten into trouble and had been sent away. I comforted her as well as I could while she was waiting for the probation officer and was rewarded by hearing her say to him, "That nice talking lady in the other room sure made me feel a lot better."

All of this is just applying the "Golden Rule" and treating all who come to the office as we should like to be treated were the situation reversed.

Show an Interest in His Well-Being

Everyone is pleased when interest is shown in his personal achievements and the probationer is no exception. The receptionist can make him feel she is genuinely interested in his welfare without spending an undue amount of time in conversation. A few questions about his family, his health, accomplishments, and general well-being give him the feeling he is really regarded as a person and is understood and appreciated by the probation officer.

If children are brought to the office because the parents cannot arrange for their care, interest shown in them by the receptionist always brings a favorable response. Many parents are apologetic and nervous, fearing that the probation officer will resent the children's presence, and their tenseness is often relieved by a friendly smile and a few pleasant words from the receptionist.

The Receptionist Is Not the Probation Officer

The receptionist, however, must guard against assuming the prerogatives of the probation officer. It is essential that she remember she is the intermediary, so to speak, between the probationer or parolee and the officer but hers is not a counseling or supervising job, and while there are many times when she will have to take messages for the officer she must keep it clear in her own mind and that of the probationer that she is not the officer and it is not her province to advise or instruct the probationer.

That does not mean, however, that she should not be a good listener, especially when she has the time to hear what the probationer is impelled to share with someone, nor that she should not impart what information she is authorized to give that will help him in his relationship with the office.

There are emergency situations in which a clerk perhaps does have to refer the probationer to community resources for immediate assistance when there is no officer available but in so doing she must guard against appearing to be the one to make the decision. I can remember when we were a smaller office I sometimes had to send a probationer out for assistance through a community agency but I tried to do it in such a way that he felt the decision was his and not mine. An appointment would then be made for him to return later to see the officer who would be informed of the referral immediately upon his return to the office. By doing this the foundation is not laid for the probationer to try to see the probation clerk on future visits to the office instead of the officer.

Another danger is the possibility of the clerk's being blamed for things she did not do or say as, for instance, the probationer saying "Miss A gave me permission to do so and so." If the officer knows his clerk does not assume the officer's function in the probationer-probation officer relationship he will know she has not done so this time.

I hardly need state that ordering, forbidding, warning, and threats by the clerk should be avoided absolutely and I am sure that there are few, if any, clerks who would be guilty of such misconduct.

There Is a Way to Ask and Answer Questions

The first question asked by the receptionist is a most significant one. "May I be of help to you?" is one way to assist the probationer in getting started on the right foot. If you know him by name it is even better to say, "May I be of help to you, Mr. Jones?" or, "May I help you, Mr. Jones?"

Incidentally, a good memory for names and faces is invaluable to a probation clerk who has receptionist duties, and is one of the surest means of getting a friendly response and establishing pleasant relationships. Whether he be a government agent, an attorney, a probationer or a parolee, everyone is pleased by being addressed by his right name.

Often the way we ask our questions determines, the kind of answers we get. A friendly, courteous question usually brings the same kind of reply, while short, brusque questions often tend to make the person "clam up" and then it is very difficult to get the needed information.

Questions should be purposeful and not merely to make conversation. The clerk should be sure the probationer understands that the questions she asks are for the purpose of determining to which officer he should be referred and not to satisfy her curiosity. There are those who are reluctant to give any information; tact and patience are required to elicit the needed information. The clerk must never allow herself to show irritation although sometimes she must be firm.

Telephone etiquette is also important in asking and answering questions and imparting information. A well-modulated voice and courteously asked questions get by far the best results in seeking information by telephone and skill in listening long enough to get the necessary facts but termination of the conversation when such facts are obtained is usually attained only through experience and practice.

In answering the telephone, too, "May I take a message for him?" or "Will you leave your number and I'll ask him to call you" is always helpful to the probationer if the officer is not in at the time of his phone call.

Office Demeanor Too Frequently Overlooked

Office relationships should be professional and businesslike at all times. First names should not be used by officers or clerks when there are probationers and parolees in the office even if the atmosphere is informal enough to permit it when only members of the staff are present.

We should never discuss cases with staff members in the presence of probationers and their families, either in the waiting room or the probation officer's office.

A restful, pleasing waiting room with magazines and books available should be provided. It is the receptionist's responsibility to help maintain a dignified, pleasant atmosphere in the waiting room and if she adds little personal touches, such as a bouquet of flowers, a vase of leaves, a plant or two, a colorful bowl, or other appropriate bit of decoration, she can make the waiting room very comfortable, and attractive indeed.

We Must Be Able to Laugh at Ourselves

I have found that a sense of humor is sometimes necessary especially for one who has been in the service for many years. I remember a probationer, reporting in from Seattle on transfer, after a few visits to the office saying to me, "You remind me a lot of the girl in the Seattle office only she is *lots* younger." Another time a conditional releasee, reporting in from a penitentiary after his third time in and out since I have been in the office, said "Gee! Are you still here? I thought you'd be retired long ago."

Many humorous situations occur where probationers and parolees are concerned but here we must be very careful with our mirth. What seems very funny to us may be very serious to them and sometimes humor is very cruel.

We must be able to laugh at ourselves. We all make mistakes and if we can take correction gracefully and with a smile instead of going around the rest of the day pouting and with hurt feelings we will do much toward keeping the office atmosphere serene and happy. A temperamental clerk, no matter how efficient, is a very disturbing element in the office.

Chapter Five

INVESTIGATION AND SELECTION IN PROBATION

THE PRIMARY purpose of a preliminary probation investigation is to aid the court in making an informed disposition of a case. When the court knows the offender's previous behavior, reasons for it, and circumstances surrounding it, then the decision as to the type of treatment needed will be more easily determined. In a sense, probation investigation is analogous to the thorough medical diagnostic examination, in which the etiology of the illness is determined and the disposition and therapy is recommended on the basis of evaluation of diagnostic material.

As a diagnosis is not discarded when treatment of an illness is initiated, so the preliminary probation investigation is used by the probation officer as a guide to supervision, and under other circumstances, by the prison classification and other authorities, and perhaps, ultimately, the parole agent. It stands to reason that neither probation officers, prison correctional staff, nor the parole personnel can be expected to assist intelligently those under their supervision without adequate information as the basis for such advice and guidance.

Though in some jurisdictions the probation officer may make recommendations regarding the disposition of the case, it is the court which is vested with the power to impose probation or other form of treatment; likewise, the power to determine the conditions or requirements to be imposed on probationers. Sometimes conditions are pecuniary, in the form of restitution, the payment of fines or other assessments, or the support of dependents.

Statutory provisions regarding the duration of the probation period vary greatly from state to state. In some jurisdictions, it is assumed that the term of probation should be analogous to a period of incarceration, and as a consequence, the maximum term allowable for a particular offense is generally imposed. In other states, a maximum period, generally not exceeding five years of probation supervision, is assigned. Elsewhere, the probation peri-

106

od is apparently subject to no limit, and the assignment is made entirely at the discretion of the court.

It appears obvious, then, that there is no uniformity in the probation period in the United States. Likewise, it can be assumed that there is an unevenness in the quality and type of investigation which precedes assignment of probation. Certainly, also, selection is based upon a multiplicity of factors, sometimes the least used among which is the offender's capacity to benefit from the period of community supervision. Yet there is no disagreement among those who are well informed in the probation field that the adjustment factor should be the one of prime consideration in the selection of individuals for probation.

PRELIMINARY INVESTIGATION FOR PROBATION*

Although there is no standard form for all preliminary probation investigations, the following outline provides a guide which should be useful to all persons concerned with the preparation of a report of adult investigation. (Editor's note.)

* * * * * *

A. THE LEGAL HISTORY OF THE OFFENDER

1. *Offender's Previous Court and Institutional Record.*
    Brief statements about police contacts and past offenses including mitigating and aggravating circumstances surrounding each offense, if such information is available. If previously imprisoned, how did the offender behave during his incarceration according to institutional reports? If offender has been on probation or parole, state his reaction to such correctional treatment and recorded results as reported by probation and parole authorities.
2. *Statement of the Present Offense*
    State accurately dates, time, place and manner in which the offense was committed. State whether offender has been in detention or on bail, for how many days and what amount. Information under this section will generally be obtained from court records, complainant, witnesses, co-defendants, etc. Record offender's attitude towards and behavior while in detention.

---

* Reprinted by permission of the New York State Division of Probation. From *Manual For Probation Officers* (5th ed., rev.) 1945 p. 128-133.

3. *Statement of the Complainant*

Describe complainant's attitude toward offense, offender and feelings regarding disposition of the case.

4. *Statement of the Offender Concerning the Present Offense*

Statement of the offender concerning the offense. Occasional use of offender's own words, when they typify his attitudes, education or otherwise individualize him, may be advisable.

5. *Mitigating and Aggravating Circumstances of the Offense*

a. General

Was the offender a leader, a follower, or a 'lone wolf" in the commission of crime? Was the offender intoxicated or under the influence of narcotics when crime was committed? Did offender resist arrest? If weapon was used in perpetration of crime, when, where and why was it obtained? Has the offender cooperated with the law enforcing agency and to what extent? (Identification of confederates and assistance in recovering proceeds of the crime) Does injured party fear reprisals because of the arrest?

b. Crimes Against Property

Was there a series of crimes? Amount of property damaged or stolen? How much has been recovered and still remains unrecovered? What became of the stolen property? Was the complainant insured? Was complainant reimbursed by surety company and to what extent?

c. Crimes Against the Person

What is the extent of complainant's injuries? (Working time lost—expenses incurred by complainant—permanent injuries, etc.)

d. Sex Offenses

Age, education, mental condition, religion, reputation and chastity of complainant. Has complainant acquired a social disease or become pregnant? Has there been an offer of marriage and what are the attitudes of the parties involved toward each other and their situation? Other pertinent social data concerning the complainant and complainant's family.

6. *Codefendants*

Record their dispositions by the court. Are codefendants friendly or antagonistic toward defendant?

B. OFFENDER'S SOCIAL HISTORY

1. *Early Life and Education*

Give date and place of birth. Verify ages whenever necessary to determine court jurisdiction and disposition (i.e., eligibility for commitment to institutions with age restrictions). Describe any outstanding events or circumstances in his early life such as separation, desertions, or divorce of parents, an unnatural home environment, placement in an orphanage, boarding home or institution, early training and supervision of offender. Relationships between the offender, his parents, guardian, relatives and companions. Attitudes and behavior of offender during his early life. His reaction to various types of discipline. Information about Children's Court record may be placed in this section rather than under "legal history" on face sheet, if so desired.

Information about offender's school attendance record, school behavior record and school work record should be included in this section. What are the reasons, if any, for his failure to make a school adjustment? What are the opinions of the teachers who came in contact with him?

2. *Employment and Economic History*

Describe work habits, cooperation or lack of same, and types of work done. State and, if necessary, discuss reasons for changes, in employment. What are employers' opinions of the offender? If offender is unemployed, give reasons for, efforts to secure work and attitudes concerning the same. Include information about army, navy, marine and coast guard service.

State all sources of income. State assets of offender both in real and personal property. Generally state obligations of offender. The degree of detail in this section will depend upon the type of case. If restitution or support payments may be expected, more detail will be needed to prove degree of financial ability to pay.

3. *Character, Habits, Associates and Leisure Time Activities*

Record available information about offender's use of alcohol, narcotics, sex practices and gambling. If excesses are noted, which have a direct relationship to the offender's criminal behavior, greater detail will be necessary. With what type of person does the offender associate?

How do offender's associates influence him? How does offender use leisure time? (Hobbies, types of reading and active membership in fraternal organizations.)

4. *Marital History*

   If offender is married, describe circumstances surrounding marriage (childhood romance, short courtship, premarital pregnancy, etc.), date and place, and by whom performed. Describe their compatibility, and for separations, divorces and subsequent marriages, re: the same information as required for the original marriage. Describe the role of each parent in raising the children and children's attitude toward the offender.

5. *Religious Training and Observances*

   Faith, name and address of church and name of priest, minister or rabbi. Describe his frequency of attendance and his attitude toward the effect of religion. Is there a difference of religion in the home and how does it affect the family life?

6. *Mental and Physical Condition*

   Describe diseases which may have materially affected or limited in any way the offender's normal physical and social development or future social adjustment. If offender has been examined by a psychologist or psychiatrist, give summary of report and give direct quotation of any recommendation made by these authorities. State when and by whom mental and/or physical examination was given.

7. *Offender's Family History*

   a. Wife and Children

      Give a brief history of wife and her role in offender's personality and social growth. Significant information about wife and children which has bearing upon the case. In abandonment and out-of-wedlock cases give *verified* birth dates of children.

   b. Parental

      Describe offender's father, giving age (year of birth), occupation, personality, attitude toward the offender and any special characteristics which may have particularly affected the offender and which bear upon his present situation. If convicted of a crime, give pertinent information concerning conviction. If deceased, cause, circumstances and date of death may be important.

  c. Maternal

    Same information.

    If offender raised by persons other than his parents, give above information regarding them.

  d. Brothers and Sisters

    Pertinent information regarding their activities and their attitude toward offender. Behavior which has or may have some relationship to offender's behavior.

8. *Home and Neighborhood Background*

    Describe the type of home and neighborhood, length of residence in this home, its general cleanliness, adequacy and atmosphere (cheerful, drab, etc.), facilities in the neighborhood for social resources and recreational outlets. If present home is an elevation or decline in family standard, state causes and results.

9. *Community Attitude Toward the Offender*

    Describe neighborhood and community attitude toward defendant and the offense, if obtainable.

C. OTHER INFORMATION

1. *Resources Available for Treatment*

    Summarize pertinent findings of resources and agencies which have attempted to aid the offender reported by the Social Service Exchange or Central Index, describe their impressions and prognosis if not included under another topical heading. Also describe any resources which are available as potentially constructive factors (job, interested relative, etc.) .

2. *Summary of the Investigation*

    This section should briefly sum up the situation (describe and analyze in an unbiased manner) . It should contain both assets and liabilities in their relative weight and importance. This section should be a clear and honest picture of the offender and afford the court an opportunity to be aware of the offender as a whole.

3. Recommendation by the probation officer should be based on the findings of the investigation. In his role as an unbiased third party, the probation officer's recommendation should be logical and have basis in the body of the report.

4. Investigation to be signed by the probation officer who made the investigation and to be approved by chief probation officer.

5. *Judgment of the Court*
   If this is included on face sheet, no repetition is necessary.

CONDITIONS OF PROBATION*

Selection for probation is predicated, in part, upon the offender's willingness to abide by the conditions which are imposed upon him. Unquestionably probation conditions should be individualized to the greatest extent possible, but the need for certain conditions to apply to all probationers is not a contradiction to that principle. (Editor's note.)

*   *   *   *   *   *

"The court has placed you on probation, believing that if you sincerely try to obey and live up to the conditions of your probation, your attitude and conduct will improve both to the benefit of the United States and of yourself."

After reading this pronouncement in the concluding paragraph of the federal probation system form entitled "Conditions of Probation," the newly selected probationer is asked to affix his signature to this paper beside that of the probation officer in order to signify a mutual acknowledgment of the terms of sentence. Thus is inaugurated a formal relationship between the court and the probationer. To the legalistic mind this might appear to be a contractual one by virtue of both parties having entered into a fixed agreement; to those entertaining a custodial bent, it may indicate the establishment of an officer-ward relationship; while to others, it represents a supervisor-client relationship as found in social work.

Regardless of which of these contrasting viewpoints one accepts, it is agreed that serious and far-reaching responsibilities have been assumed by both parties. The probationer may be expected to initiate at once changes in his mode of life in order to bring about compliance with the agreement. In using this form of

---

* Reprinted by permission of *Federal Probation*. Richard F. Doyle: Conditions of Probation: Their Imposition and Application, *Federal Probation*, Vol. 17, No. 3, Sept. 1953, p. 19-22. Footnotes are omitted.

treatment the court, in its attempt to correct the probationer's faulty social attitude and forestall his committing further antisocial acts, designates certain conditions of probation. But the court's obligation does not end with the imposition of these conditions, for its probation officers are required by statute to "use all suitable methods, not inconsistent with the conditions, imposed by the court to aid probationers and bring about improvements in their (probationers') conduct and condition."

Practices in Imposing Conditions of Probation

The purpose of this section is to cite practices followed by both federal and state courts in imposing conditions of probation and to offer comments in the hope of stimulating greater thought and care in their selection and application. Before discussing these practices it would seem appropriate to comment briefly on the historical background of this form of sentence. The release of offenders by the court under specified conditions is not new, as it was used as early as the year 1820. At that time the magistrates of Warwickshire, England, adopted the expedient of passing sentence of imprisonment for 1 day upon a youthful offender on condition that he be returned to the care of his parents or master, "to be by him more carefully watched and supervised in the future." This enlightened attitude was not shared by most early courts which in the main were governed by a spirit of revenge and desire to inflict punishment. Gradually, however, and especially in Massachusetts, the birthplace of probation, courts took cognizance of the degradation that existed in the prisons and elected to spare a few selected offenders from this contamination. Usually this consideration was extended only to those individuals who had committed trivial offenses or to those the court wished to reward for service to the state. In more recent times this negative approach has given way to a positive one, whereby the courts now expend untold effort in behalf of offenders through probation departments and diagnostic and guidance clinics, as well as various social agencies. This change of attitude created the need for the greatest of flexibility in imposing sentence, and probation offered the method for its fulfillment.

The response to this opportunity has not been gratifying largely because of the indifferent attitude displayed by numerous courts, particularly the lesser courts by their slipshod, haphazard sentencing practices. Altogether too frequently sentences are passed intuitively without benefit of sufficient facts, and in many instances the offender is not supplied with adequate information as to the terms of his probation sentence. Yet compliance is expected by the court and commitment may result when violations occur. In a comparatively recent case the Michigan Supreme Court ordered the freeing of a prisoner when it was shown that he had not been properly informed as to the terms of his probation by the sentencing court, which had insitutionalized him after finding him guilty as a probation violator. The Federal Probation Act and a number of state statutes require that the probationer be furnished with a written statement of the conditions of his probation.

General Conditions of Probation

Many courts in their approach to the difficult problem of designating terms of probation adopt minimum requirements for all probation cases. These general conditions are more often than not conservative in tenor as illustrated by the list used in the federal probation service. Consequently, little controversy ensues from their usage for, aside from the conditions restricting travel and requiring periodic reports, the probationer is not being asked to fulfill any obligations that are not normally expected of all law-abiding citizens. In a few instances in which the probationer is employed in a capacity such as a salesman, truck driver, or seaman, the restraint imposed upon his traveling might prove to be a handicap, as may the requiring of written reports from an illiterate or poorly educated person. Likewise, the required personal reporting to the probation office by an invalid or by one who lives at a considerable distance might prove burdensome. In such cases these should be waived immediately, for to insist on compliance to unreasonable terms will only result in disrespect for the entire probationary order.

Special Conditions of Probation

It is within the category of special conditions that one encounters the unusual and often undesirable factors. Probation statutes are liberal in character and enable courts to designate practically any term it chooses as long as the probationer's constitutional rights are not jeopardized.

Speaking of constitutional rights recalls to mind an episode that occurred in Detroit a few years ago when one of the local newspapers reported that a federal judge, in placing two young girls on probation, stipulated that they were not to have dates. This statement by the paper was entirely erroneous; but before it could be corrected it had been given nationwide circulation by both the press and radio, resulting in much protesting over the lack of understanding and inhumane treatment by the court. One person wrote directly to the President, proclaiming that the "sentence was unconstitutional in that it interfered with their unalienable right to life, liberty and the pursuit of happiness." To the writer's knowledge this is the only time that the general public was bestirred from its apathy about the context of probationary terms.

Unrealistic conditions.—Strange as it may seem upon first thought, the very liberality of probation statutes sometimes works to the detriment of the probationer by permitting courts to stipulate unrealistic terms. As frequently happens, harm is done in an effort to help; and when this occurs it is invariably due to the court's lacking sufficient facts or to its desire to impose its own code of morals on the probationer. Charles H. Boswell in his article, "If I Were a Judge," points out that courts, particularly juvenile courts, rather frequently impose unreasonable terms:

> Any judge who believes that delinquent children in their middle and late teens should remain home after dark has forgotten his own adolescent years. Requiring youngsters to be home early every evening is only extending an invitation to youngsters to violate probation conditions. It is also unrealistic to expect to separate two boys who live next door to each other or to expect a seventeen year old boy to give up smoking when he has had the habit for two years. The condition of requiring youngsters to attend church is also frowned upon by probation officers. This kind of requirement tends to associate the church with punitive action. Of course, we all want youngsters to have religious experiences but compulsory church attendance is not the way to achieve that goal. In fact it is more likely to turn the

youngster away from the church than it is to get him to seek the aid of church leaders of his volition.

Fine as a condition.—Perhaps the most commonly applied special conditions relate to a fine or restitution to the aggrieved party who has sustained a financial loss arising out of the offense. As a rule these are not objectionable, although there is a tendency on the part of a few courts to make the probationer "feel the sting of paying." If this severely taxes his capacity, hardship may result not only to him but to his family. One minor objection to the designation of these requirements may come from the probation officer who dislikes being cast in the role of a collector, but this is insignificant when viewed in the light of other factors.

Special place of residence.—On occasions it is found desirable to order the probationer to establish residence away from the community in which he is sentenced. In such cases care should be exercised to insure adequate supervision so that harm may not come to the residents of the other locality through the uncontrolled releasing into the community persons infected with venereal and other communicable diseases so as not to endanger the health of others.

If it appears that the defendant is suffering from a mental illness, he may be instructed to seek the help of a psychiatrist or mental clinic. Indication of his willingness to cooperate in such a plan should first be secured; otherwise little success can be expected.

Treatment of alcoholics and narcotic addicts.—Some courts are prone to place excessive drinkers on probation after admonishing them not to drink or visit places were liquor is sold. Strict compliance to this order would prohibit them from entering innumerable restaurants and eating places, particularly in large cities where liquor is more often than not available to patrons. At any rate it is unwise to release an alcoholic into the community unless some treatment plan is inaugurated, for without it he is most apt to violate his probation in a relatively short time.

Under the act establishing the narcotic hospitals, federal courts are empowered to commit narcotic addict offenders as probation patients with the condition that they remain in the hospital until pronounced cured of their addiction. This sentencing practice can best be applied to those whose history indicates relative freedom from prior criminality.

Spending part of probation in jail.—While it is believed advisable to commit probationers to hospitals in certain instances, it does not follow that it is good procedure to commit probationers to county jails or other correctional institutions for the first 60 days of their period of probation as permitted by some state statutes. The imposition of such a sentence tends to defeat the very principles and advantages of probation treatment by subjecting the probationer to the degrading influences found in institutions and by causing dislocation in his employment and family life, not to mention the resultant stigma that is attached to one who "has done time."

Denying privilege to drive a car.—Another condition not infrequently designated is the restriction that the probationer may not drive an automobile, This seems to stem from a punitive desire on the part of the court; and in many cases it results in hardship, especially where a car is needed for transportation to and from work. Cars are no longer a luxury but, on the contrary, are, indeed, a necessity in most localities; therefore, the imposition of this restraint tends to decrease the likelihood of a satisfactory adjustment. Unless the probationer has clearly demonstrated that he is an unsafe driver and a hazard to the public, the privilege of operating a motor vehicle should not be denied him.

Requiring marriage.—Occasionally courts grant probation with the special provision that the probationer enter into marriage. This requirement is generally made in order to provide a paternal name for the unborn child or for one born to the couple out of wedlock. The intent of the court is admirable but it is unlikely that the marriage will prove a harmonious one under those circumstances.

When Conditions of Probation are Violated

As was found in the imposition of conditions at the time of sentence, current practices in respect to the violator vary widely. Some courts insist that the probationer who fails to comply in any manner with his probation terms be brought immediately before the court for a hearing, while others possessing keener perception into human behavior recognize that the task of readjusting an individual's attitude is a slow and often discouraging process. These latter courts prefer that the probation officer handle in his own way the minor infractions and bring to their attention only the more serious breaches of probation conditions. Certainly the judge should be notified when a probationer is convicted of another offense, except possibly minor traffic violations or others of relatively petty nature. It would seem, moreover, that there should be greater comity between the court in the handling of offenders who are subject to sentences in two or more jurisdictions. There is much to be gained by permitting one court to assume the dominant role in disposition so as to avoid entanglements that might later arise in eather probation or institutional programs. In the event that commitment has already been imposed by the other court and is felt to be of sufficient magnitude, then probation should be terminated at once so as not to hamper institutional and release plans of those officials holding him in custody. Conversely, if probation is granted for the new offense, then it becomes incumbent on the respective probation offices to evolve means for the avoidance of duplicating supervisory efforts.

Getting the Facts Before Revoking Probation

The pronouncement of any judgment by court is usually difficult and frequently results in developments of great consequence not foreseeable at the time of its rendition. With this in mind any competent and conscientious jurist strives to lessen this condition by securing as many facts as possible pertinent to the issue before giving his decision. Where a trial is held, facts concerning both the offense and the offender are brought to the court's attention through testimony which does assist the court to some extent, at least in determining sentence. In cases where guilty or *nolo contendere* pleas are offered, the court does not derive even this scanty benefit from the courtroom proceedings, but frequently is the recipient of biased information from both the prosecuting authority as well as from the defendant or his counsel.

Time has proved that the best method of supplying information to a court searching for vital facets in the history and personality of a defendant is the presentence report. Indeed, a presentence investigation should be mandatory in the case of any felony conviction, since it is of immeasurable assistance in shaping sentence, whether it be an institutional commitment or probation. It is appreciated that it is not always practicable to secure these in the lesser courts; but in those instances in which probation is granted and a dearth of information concerning the defendant exists, the court should use utmost caution in imposing any special conditions.

When a presentence report has been supplied the court should review it with the probation officer prior to sentence, for no matter how well a report may be written, the possibility of misinterpretation exists. It further follows that a written statement of the terms of probation should be supplied to the probationer, preferably by the jurist in the courtroom. This would tend to add dignity and importance to the proceedings and at the same time provide an opportunity for the defendant to accept or reject the sentence. It is to be noted that in England probation may not be granted to offenders over the age of 14 without their consent. Usually offenders granted probation are pleased by the court's action and will accept any reasonable terms to avoid institutionalization; however, this is not always the case as reflected by the following account:

MARQUETTE, MICH., March 13.—Mrs. Alice Frazier preferred prison to the terms of freedom which would forbid her from associating with the man she attacked with a knife.

Convicted of a felonious assault on Eugene Belmore, a taxi company operator, she rejected three years' probation for a one to four year sentence in the Detroit House of Correction.

"Do you agree to the terms of the probation?" Circuit Judge Glenn W. Jackson asked Mrs. Fraizier.

"No," she replied in tears.

After she declined a chance to "think it over," Judge Jackson pronounced sentence.

"I hope by the end of your term you will get over your infatuation for this married man, and that you will live a normal life," Jackson told her.

Both Mrs. Frazier and Belmore have families.

Conditions Should Be Realistic and Purposeful

In conclusion it can be stated that the imposition of purposeful and realistic conditions of probation is essential to successful treatment; that they can best be selected after the submission of an adequate presentence report; that these should be presented in written form to the defendant in court for his acceptance or rejection, for unless his wholehearted approval is obtained, rehabilitative efforts will be met with only superficial response without appreciable benefit to the United States or to the probationer.

Chapter Six*

PROBATION SUPERVISION AND TREATMENT

T HERE are two methods, broadly speaking, by which probation endeavors to protect society.

The first is legalistic. It imposes discipline through various restraints and restrictions which are placed upon the conduct of the offender. While a willingness to agree to the conditions is precursor to granting of probation, the ability of an individual to abide by those rules and regulations will determine his success in that status. Thus, as a means of social control, the legalistic method has a value which cannot be ignored.

Restraint and restriction have certain coercive value, but force without counselling services is unlikely to incur a true change in the character of the individual. The second method then, one of re-education and re-direction, is far more subtle. Influencing and changing human behavior is a very delicate and difficult task. In the treatment process, the probation officer attempts to have the offender see himself as he actually is—as a person who has not been playing the game according to the rules of society—and to modify that self-picture through actual change of personality so that the offender can become a law-abiding, contributing member of the community.

Obviously, there is no one way of treatment with the law violator. While there are some generic similarities to be found among all people, and the offender is no exception, each personality is made up of a number of elements which are blended together in proportions and relationships which are unique to the individual. Thus, direction and education must follow a pattern dictated by the needs of an individual.

External changes can be effected through an alteration of his social environment and associates, but internal changes must accompany such social alterations in order to assure that the offender will not recidivate. It is through a fusion of these external

---

* See also, Chapter X on parole supervision and treatment.

(social) and internal (psychological) therapies that the probation officer directs his energies.

The establishment of a relationship (rapport) between the agent and probationer is a first step, but not the only one. Treatment involves a plan which is workable and practical with regard to the offender's background and capacities. Moreover, it demands continuity, for therapy invoked at the whim and fancy of the probation officer, without regard to the needs of the client are apt to do more harm than good.

From time to time, the probation officer is faced with the situation where a community agency is better equipped with specialized personnel to render the services needed by the probationer. Such services should be utilized whenever possible, and the probation officer should make it a part of this duty to know what his community has to offer by way of auxiliary services. This is especially true when the needs of the offender are manifested in some special behavioral disorder.

In dealing with the individual on probation, there is frequently a proneness to treat with him "as if" he were in a vacuum. Behavioral problems have their genesis in a number of sources. The probation officer must be alert to the family situation of his client, particularly where the wife or other family member seems to be the subtle instigator of the offender's anti-social conduct. Where it is not feasible to remove the offender from such an environment, the probation officer might well consider the use of private social agencies to assist in the social readjustment of family members not on probation.

Social adjustment is the goal in probation. The techniques employed in obtaining this end result can be the product of many disciplines. What matters is the end result and not the academic label attached to the method used. The aptitude and skill of the probation officer and his participant associates define the degree of success which shall be obtained.

PROMISCUOUS GIRLS ON PROBATION*

In response to the civilian and military pressure during World War II, numerous social agencies attempted to offer an effective

---

* Reprinted in part by permission of the National Progation and Parole Association. Evelyn C. Hyman: Holding the Promiscuous Girl Accountable for Her Own Behavior, *NPPA Yearbook, Bulwarks Against Crime,* (1948) p. 190-201.

rehabilitation service to the prostitute. Baltimore's answer was the Protective Service for Girls, a service that works with girls who are arrested for prostitution and placed on probation to us by the courts—and girls who come to us of their own accord, seeking help with their promiscuity. Most agencies have approached the prostitute and her problems with a need to examine the causes for the girl's behavior. They have gone into the past to find reasons for the present. The unique focus of the Protective Service for Girls is that it works with the girl and her present problem. This has proved to be a vital dynamic in helping her to change.

We know that the promiscuous girl, like the rest of us, has her weaknesses. We see her greatest weakness in her projection of blame for her plight onto others. But we see no value in making her relive her past. We attempt to help her to live more positively in the present. Our focus is on helping her reorganize her strengths. Maybe you think a prostitute does not have strength. It is only natural to believe that the girl who has always said "yes" is a "weak sister." From our experience we know that many promiscuous girls have real strength but that most of them are using it negatively. Their very coming to us is a sign of strength, for it is very hard to take help from another person. Have you ever lost your way while driving along a strange road? How often have you, instead of asking directions, just fumbled along alone hoping you'll come out all right? Just as such independence is a common trait among all of us, so it is typical of the prostitute, but additionally, when she seeks help, she must fight her embarrassment and feelings of guilt. And so if she gets to the point where she can come to us for help, she is already one step on the way toward being different. As we relate to this inherent strength, we make it possible for the girl to begin affirming herself as a person.

The Protective Service for Girls has carved out an authoritative casework method in which we hold the girl responsible for some demonstration of an attempt to change. Just her saying she wants to do differently is not enough. Whether the girl comes to us voluntarily or on probation, we hold her to our requirements. One of the most important of these requirements is keeping regular appointment with her worker. This is a big order for the prostitute—a girl who has been sleeping all day and living at night must rearrange her entire mode of living to get to our office during business hours. More than this, she will find it hard sharing with another adult the problems she has created for herself as a result of her own promiscuous behavior.

Another requirement is that the girl live in a neighborhood where she feels she can stay out of trouble. Invariably this means moving to an entirely new neighborhood and living differently. But we cannot merely require her to move without helping her to get located. If she has no place to go and no funds we will pay her room and board at the Salvation Army Women's and Children's Residence until she can take over for herself. If having her own room or apartment seems right, we will refer her to accredited room registries or discuss neighborhoods with her.

In addition, we require that all girls have an examination at the health department. This can be a very fearful experience as it involves the possibility of having to face the fact that they may have contracted a venereal disease. Very often it is in discussion of this requirement with her worker that for the first time the girl begins to trust as she shares her former behavior and present apprehension.

Finally the girl must secure dignified employment. And that means she cannot go back being a waitress or barmaid in cheap restaurants or taverns where advances of the men customers are part of the job. This is, for many girls, the most difficult of requirements. Before this, she has not applied through an employment service but picked up jobs with the same casualness as she has picked up men. She has little to give her confidence in making application for a totally different kind of job. But at the state employment office she will be met as a person claiming a right, and respected as a person capable of making the best choice for herself. All of this is new and fearful, of course, but another important experience for her.

These requirements provide a structure against which she can test her strength and against which we both may evaluate her desire and efforts toward change. We believe they give her the opportunity to know that she can live within authority and not be destroyed by it.

A Trusting Relationship

At the start, in order that she will feel supported in her smallest efforts, she will have frequent appointments with her caseworker. This is one of the most important factors in helping her change, for it gives her an opportunity to have a meaningful relationship. While her caseworker is always expecting of her and holding her to some evidence of change, she is at the same time always there for the girl, showing that she cares. We believe that only through such an experience in relationship can the girl begin to trust and be capable of trusting relationships outside.

During these interviews with the girl, we will not take over the making of any decisions for her but will help her with the process of making considered choices. For instance, many times, girls will ask during their first interviews, "But I can't go to a bar, can I?" or "Don't I have to be home by ten o'clock?" To these we answer, "Can you go to a bar and keep out of trouble?" and "*You* feel you'll get into trouble if you're on the streets at night." And so in our discussion we put more and more responsibility for decisions back on her. It is up to her to ignore the wolfish whistles of the boys. She must use her own strength to refuse the first drink, and each time she demonstrates to herself that she can do these things and not be destroyed by the decision or the doing, her sense of pride and respect for herself increases. As she takes on this stature she expects more and more of herself, and requires less holding up by the caseworker. It is certain that she has begun to think of herself not only as a person with obligations but also as one who has rights, when she can begin to make some demands of her own. Very often the meek little wife will tell her alcoholic husband that his drinking must stop. The heretofore patient woman will serve notice on her non-supporting male that he must be a more responsible father. In putting out such expectations for a better life for herself, she is demonstrating that she has begun to internalize the authority needed to live more affirmatively.

Just as we make use of expectation and requirement in working with the promiscuous woman, so we make dynamic use of time. Since she had no purpose, and had felt no achievement, living has seemed endless. We know this to be unrealistic, for all experience is limited—broadly by birth and death, and more partially by the completion of each endeavor. In order to help the promiscuous girl get hold of some wish to achieve she must feel some awareness of time. To this end we consciously put time limits on all our expectations of her. For instance, the girl who is on probation for a year may feel that this is forever, and therefore much too long for her to remain out of trouble. She can feel beaten before she starts. We therefore discuss with her how she can manage today, whether between a Friday and Monday appointment she can keep out of trouble, and then since she was able to do so for a week, is there not reason to think she can continue for another week? We know that movement is slow and growth never straight ahead. The girl must be free to fail and know this will mean rejection. With the same consideration of its dynamic value, we set a time limit in which we will expect the girl to secure employment, report to the health department, and come to a decision about her living arrangements. And so the girl begins to succeed in different phases of her living. She is then made aware of her growth by being given fewer appointments and more responsibility.

This process of engaging the prostitute in being accountable for what she does begins in the very first interview. This interview is most often in places to which her antisocial behavior has brought her—the prison, the jail, the health department, the police station or the court. Here her characteristic of projecting blame is most outstanding. We hold her to deciding whether she wants to remain in such a static state or whether she desires to move ahead.

It is often very difficult to hold the promiscuous girl accountable for her behavior in these first interviews. That it can be done is illustrated in the following piece of case material:

Interview in a Lockup

Miss Henson is a tall, slim, fair and rather attractive young woman of twenty-three, who was extremely negative, frightened and quite tightly put together. She quite obviously trusted no one and yet was somehow pleading for someone to care about her.

I began the interview by telling her my name and that the

judge had sent for me because she was found guilty of prostitution. Although her lower lip trembled and in a few seconds she cried, she at once retorted with great belligerence. "I know it, but I am not guilty of anything. I didn't do it. I didn't do nothing to be arrested for." I thought that if she felt she was being held and sentenced unfairly, she had better say so to the judge. With the same bitterness she jeered at this idea. She knew and she thought I too should know that "those vice squad men" who had arrested her, and the judge all stick together. I said I didn't know that, but if she felt that way even though she had done nothing, I supposed she would have to serve her time in prison. Miss Henson said she didn't want to go to prison! There was no reason why she should. All she had done, she said, was to go to get something to eat with this fellow who stopped and talked with her as she came out from the midnight movie. Then as they were in the restaurant, he had given her some money. She didn't take it "to have intercourse with him as they said in court." All she had done was take the money. Did I see anything wrong in that? I wondered why she thought a friend of such a few moments would be giving her money. She said she didn't know—and I said I didn't believe that. She asked me if someone wanted to give me some money, wouldn't I take it? I said we were talking about her. She had taken the money and was in real trouble because of it. I believed that she had been around enough to know what she was doing and to know it was against the law. But Miss Henson said she absolutely did not go with this man and didn't intend to. I held that she knew what she was doing, and why she had acepted the money, and had had previous experiences of this kind. I couldn't believe she too didn't consider it strange to accept money from strangers. Showing her first yielding, Miss Henson said that was right, she knew it was wrong and against the law to do what she was doing, but she said, "I'm so confused I don't know what I'm doing."

I said it could feel like confusion—I thought she was afraid and worried about herself. She had been pretty much on the loose for a few weeks now, on her own, away from her family. I supposed she and her family were having trouble and she didn't seem to be caring what she did. Miss Henson very rapidly and defensively told how she had first gone away to Pennsylvania for a short time. Although since her return to Baltimore a few weeks ago she had not gone home to live, she stoutly attempted to impress me with the fact that she is a girl who had a "good mother and stepfather." They would be disgraced if she went to prison. I wondered if they knew of the trouble she was in. Miss Henson said her mother did, but she was not in court today. Miss Henson then began anew to fight for herself. She said even though she had accepted this money, which was wrong, she had never gotten into trouble before. I asked if it were not true that a few years ago she had to go to the health department. Miss Henson quietly but quickly agreed. I said it sounded then as if she had been running around for quite a while. She started again to cry, saying she didn't want to go to prison and didn't feel she should. I said maybe that was the only thing for her. I had come over with the intention of taking up the possibility of her being on probation, but I realized now she wasn't really ready for that. Real angry, Miss Henson said she could be on probation. She didn't *want* to go to prison, but that wasn't reason enough for me to be willing to tell the judge we would give her a try on probation. We then had quite a struggle. Miss Henson said, "The trouble with you all is you never want to give anybody a chance. All you want to do, when a girl gets in trouble, is to send her away to prison." I let her know this was how she looked at it. For my part I believed in giving everyone who seemed able to use it, not only a chance to do differently, but help in doing that also. Miss Henson said she wanted a chance. She didn't want to go to prison. She knew some girls who had been to prison, and when they came out they did lots worse things than when they had gone in. "They swore a lot and did a lot of things." I said she seemed to like being a part of this group. And I didn't think swearing was new to her. I did not think she could behave differently because she was so tied up with this group; hence considering probation seemed futile. Miss Henson, with real determination and at the same time a desperate tone, said she could drop her friends. They hung around and she did, too, at the Bijoux and the Overland Bus Station. She didn't think much of it now, it seemed, and wanted quickly to separate herself. I could agree this could have a lot to do with her getting into trouble, but I doubted she could make a break, and there would be just no point in being on probation if she weren't going to be able to do differently. She said she knew and she could. After all, "I have a mother and father—and parents help a girl, don't they?" I thought it was good she felt hers would—that was real important—but it would be she who would be on probation, not they. Miss Henson said that was all right. She could still do it. She could be different. I said I wasn't sure—she hadn't said much to convince me yet that she thought she was doing anything that needed to be changed. Miss Henson put the blame on everybody else. She said, "I know I have to change. But I'm not all bad like"—and as she stopped, I said, "people think you are"—and she agreed. She then said, "I know I have some good in me—everybody does —and I could be different." I agreed everyone did have some good, but it seemed to me as if she really didn't care. Miss Henson said, "I do care. I don't know why I've been doing all these things. I'm all confused." She said, with a lot of feeling, that being in the jail for these few days had been enough. It was the first time and "awful."

I wondered what she saw that could be different—why did she think she had been prostituting? Miss Henson said very frankly, "Because I don't have enough responsibility." She explained that she had gone out just about every night. She said that she had to give up her job because of this situation. Then, added, she also takes care of a sailor's baby. She denied this was her child, but that she and the sailor want to be married as soon as he can obtain a divorce. While I could understand her feeling of boredom with this situation, I had no idea how these things could be changed so she could feel more "responsible." Miss Henson said, "I do—I could get a job." She felt that different plans would have to be made for her mother who was ill. Anyway, she said, she is better now, and more able to care for herself. I felt she was too quickly trying to make everything plausible and easy. I knew it would be harder than that, and I doubted she could get hold of herself so simply.

Miss Henson said she knew she could. She said, "If I ever get out of this, I know I could be on probation. I'd go to Pennsylvania where I don't go with this kind of a crowd. After all, you know a girl's environment is what makes her get into trouble. I know I could be different some place else." I said I did think environment was mighty important, but I knew it wasn't everything. What a person really wants for herself has a lot to do with it, and if she were on probation the hard part would be that she would have to remain right here in Baltimore—and still change —stop prostituting. Miss Henson was startled that she would have to remain in Baltimore, but quickly recovering, said if she had to stay she could and still be different. She sounded so sure—how could she? Miss Henson said, "Because I have a will. And if I say a thing and make up my mind to do it, I can. I know I can. You can't know unless you give me a chance to show you." I thought she had something there. However, I said neither the judge nor we were anxious to try someone on probation if she wasn't going to be able to make use of it. And she should be the least anxious, for if she did violate, it would mean serving her time anyway. Miss Henson realized this, but said she knew she could do it. She knew she'd try as hard as possible and "that's the most a girl can do, isn't it?" I thought it was. Miss Henson was much quieter now. As I stood up I said I'd be talking with the judge now. I felt her attitude was somewhat different from what it was when we started. She was seeing that she had a part in getting herself into this trouble—and while I still had my doubts, maybe she could do something to get herself out of it. I would tell this to the judge and then it would be up to him to decide if he wanted to send her over to our office where we could talk more specifically about probation and decide if she still wanted it and could use it. Miss Henson sat with her head lowered, and said nothing as I left.

In this one brief contact, her first with the agency, Miss Henson met someone as strong as she who was not judgmental but who continually held her to a recognition of her part in her arrest. When she could begin to accept this, she was then held to deciding whether she could and wanted to do anything differently. The fact that she felt she could was the basis for my recommendation to the judge that she be given an opportunity on probation. From then on she began taking over responsibility for herself. She came from the courthouse to our office alone, she has kept all appointments, and recently, after evading all attempts on the part of the health department for over a year to get her to report for treatment, she has gone to the Rapid Treatment Center and been cured of syphilis. While Miss Henson, who is still on probation, is experiencing many difficulties in meeting our requirements and saying "no" to the boys, she is able to continue because she knows we believe in her ability to change. By relating to the girls' strengths and showing them that we care and have respect for them, we are able to help most of them through to successful endings. And it is because of this firm warm belief in them at the beginning that many of them come back to say, as one recently did: "What means most to me are those first hard times I had with you."

This is a broad picture of how we hold the promiscuous girl accountable for her own behavior. It is a strong, direct, authoritative method of helping people come to something for themselves. It is carried by our conviction that people who are not in harmony with society cannot be in harmony with themselves. And its real authority is in our belief in people, their right and capacity to live with that most precious gift of all, human dignity. Not only for the sex delinquent but for all of us this dignity comes, in part at least, from being accountable for and able to live with our own behavior.

THE PROBATION OFFICER AND SPECIAL PROBLEM CASES*

A great heart specialist, addressing a body of general practitioners, told them that they, the general practitioners, were the real heart specialists for they saw the early development of heart disease, they saw the beginnings of the trouble, the could take measures to heal and to cure, to prevent and to advise, long before the patient came to the so-called specialist who saw too much of the end product of a series of events when it was too late to be of much service.

In the correctional field the probation officers are the real specialists.

Final answers to many of our most perplexing problems of human behavior await the result of their observations, their wisdom, and their knowledge to tell us how a normal baby with all potentialities for good grows into an individual whose lax moral standards, thoughtless hedonism, callous conscience, and rebelli-

---

* Reprinted by permission of *Federal Probation*. Manly B. Root, M.D.: What the Probation Officer Can Do For Special Types of Offenders, *Federal Probation*, Vol. 13, No. 4, Dec. 1949, p. 36-46.

ous aggressiveness make of his character and personality a person who has to be locked up by society for its own protection.

Alcoholics

Drinking in general is certainly to be discouraged in your clients. The reasons for this are many. It is at best an expensive luxury which any man struggling to make his way in the world can ill afford. How often do you and I listen to the woes of a client who tells of the hard financial struggle he has had, but has to admit that he has found money for drinks. Alcohol, a most remarkable drug, has as one of its many effects the lessening of inhibition—that control which, like the governor of an engine, keeps the mind from following up rush and impetuous desires, keeping the human spirit from running away with itself. With the loss of this governor, moral standards evaporate till "anything goes." Alert intelligence, the ability to tap the reservoir of past experience and judgment is relaxed. Of all men, our clients need acute judgment and self-watching perhaps the most, and yet they so often tempt fate by taking into their bodies that drug which is specific in its ability to put the censor to sleep.

Social Drinking

Again, drinking usually takes place, at least for most of our clients, in what we call bad company and in a mentally and morally unhealthy environment, where ideals are low, moral standards are lower, where profanity and vulgarity are the rule, where it is smart to flout ethical ideals, where criminal exploits are often planned, and where a man can put away his timidities and reserve and become great by being especially daring in the company of those who are ready to exploit him. Such a man becomes a ready tool; and we all know that a great number of violators would not have resorted to folly except for their drinking.

The time of drinking is also important. Most "moderate drinkers" do their drinking in the evening, the time passes quickly, and soon it is morning. The client, with an overpowering need for prompt appearance at work in the morning, has a hard time getting there if he has been drinking up to a few hours before he is due at work. To avoid this, many resort to Saturday night drinking, a pretty well-established custom among us. This is better than weekday drinking, but it is hard to hold to this; and even so, it does not encourage church attendance where a man may at least hear a weekly lecture, concentrate for a brief hour on good ideals, and live in an atmosphere of high aspiration—at most find a philosophy and a faith in a way of life led by the Greatest of Counselors.

As in all categories, let us not be dogmatic. Let us not forget that a great many of us drink, that the drinking of millions of persons does not get them into trouble. If a client's drinking is done wisely and socially, it is best to point out the dangers, to advise abstinence for reasons discussed above, and then not to worry to much about it. We have no right to expect our clients to maintain standards higher than the average; we are foolish and insincere if we expect them to maintain standards higher than our own.

Drinking by Neurotics

Drinking by neurotics takes place when they turn to the sure but dangerous and only temporary relief from the tensions and conflicts which torture them. Clients whom you know or believe to be neurotic should be helped to understand this. Get all the psychiatric help and advice you can, but *much,* sometimes *most* of the assistance the neurotic needs has to come from you, from the parole advisor, and from friends, and the family. What seems a blessing to a neurotic individual in his ever increasing search for peace of mind—namely, alcoholic escape from the harsh cruelties of reality— becomes, because of its effects, only another cause for tension. So the neurotic must learn from you if he has not already learned it from us, that the alcoholic "treatment" only adds other symptoms to be treated. In other words, the neurotic can never safely drink. In this connection, an allied group of patients—the psychotic (insane) —often drink heavily as a manifestation of early symptoms of mental disease. Drinking then becomes part, not a cause, of the mental disorder. We must be on the lookout for this especially in persons who have not been heavy drinkers previously. Much time can be lost and much harm done by the failure to recognize this type of symptom-drinking.

The Alcoholic Defined

The true or "real" alcoholic belongs in a different category. He is not primarily neurotic nor psychotic, though he may become so as indeed any person with one disorder of personality, character, or mind may develop another disorder.

For our purposes and for our discussions and explanations with our alcoholic clients, an alcoholic may be defined as an individual who is unusually sensitive to alcohol, in whom alcohol produces character and personality changes, so that he does things he would never do while sober, often with amnesia of incomplete memory for the acts. It is realized that this definition of an alcoholic stresses only one factor; namely, alcoholic sensitivity. Complicated physical and emotional factors, together with social and cultural diatheses, unite to produce an individual driven by forces he does not understand and cannot control to seek happiness in the very cup which makes such a fool of him and jeopardizes his chances for happiness and success. Unconscious conflicts, particularly in the field of psychosexual pathology, inferiority broodings, and aggression-submission battles within the personality are frequently at work. The various combinations of these factors produce acute and chronic states of mind characterized by emotional tensions which certain individuals cannot stand. These tensions can be dissolved in alcohol which seems almost specific in its ability to lessen the tyranny of the superego, which is the psychoanalytic name for conscience—a sort of emotional governor which provides the civilized restraint necessary to keep us from yielding freely to our emotions and instinctive drives. Alcoholics, as well as neurotic and psychotic individuals, cannot handle all this conflict and retreat into their varied forms of escape and phantasy. An alcoholic, then, is a person who has developed the particular alcoholic method of achieving peace of mind; effective for the time being, but disastrous for his integrity, his character, and his future success. However, in initial talks with alcoholics all this cannot be discussed. They eagerly grasp at the sensitivity idea which relieves them for the time being of moral guilt feelings, and at the same time makes very clear the important point that they cannot ever safely drink. Later, less superficial analysis of deeper mechanisms is necessary.

A "pure" alcoholic is quite normal and socialized when not drinking; shows varying degrees of irresponsibility and character faults when drinking. Less liquor is usually necessary to make him intoxicated than is the case with the average man. The Alcoholics Anonymous organization teaches its members that they have "an allergy of the body and an obsession of the mind."

For the initial contact I have found it effective to talk to the alcoholic somewhat as follows: "You are sensitive to alcohol in much the same way as other persons are sensitive to ragweed or strawberries. When we have allergies, it means that we react to certain substances differently from the average man. These reactions may be physical as shown by hay fever or the hives; they may be mental as in insomnia after coffee; they may be in the field of character as shown by your behavior after a few drinks. So the stuff (alcohol) is pure poison to you. Others are able to drink without doing themselves any harm. They would probably be better off if they did not drink; they would certainly save money, but they can get by with it—at least for a time. You are different, it is not your fault; but because you are different it is literally a matter of life and death to you, a matter of success and happiness or failure and disgrace. This is not due to any moral weakness or character fault; it is a matter of this allergy of yours. You can never 'handle' liquor but it can and has put you in jail."

Contrary to common opinion, the alcoholic does not have a "craving" for drink between his bouts. His backsliding occurs, or his return to drinking after leaving prison takes place, not because of any craving. In the great majority of cases it happens under one of two circumstances. First, the man takes his first drink after a time of abstinence in company with other drinkers, just to be sociable, or because of trouble or sorrow or happiness, despair or celebration. Second, the man drinks in the mistaken impression that he is not really an alcoholic, that he merely drank too much before, that he can be a "normal" or "social" drinker. Once an alcoholic does take a drink, there is truly craving of a malignant sort, and all the king's horses and all the king's men cannot stop him drinking until his bout has run its course. We must use all our persuasiveness and all our ingenuity and all our influence to convince the alcoholic that he cannot ever become a social drinker. He must never take a single glass of beer or liquor; his only hope of safety and success and happiness lies in understanding that *once an alcoholic, always an alcoholic.* He may get away with it at times, but he cannot afford to take a chance.

Alcoholics Anonymous

Alcoholics Anonymous appears to be one of the most successful organizations ever developed by victims of any disorder for their own improvement. One of the strongest reasons for its success is probably the fact that it *is* a victim-sponsored and managed organization. It is easier to be helped by persons like yourself, by people who have gone through the same struggles you have and have won out, than to be treated or preached at by others who have no way of knowing how you really feel about things. "A.A.," as the members call it, has helped drinkers to stop their drinking where parents, wives, clergymen, doctors, and psychiatrists have failed. It has rescued men from the skids by thousands. There have been backsliders, of course, but there are many, many successful men whom it has rescued from the alcoholic's seemingly inevitable end. If an alcoholic can be induced by you to meet with and join an A.A. unit, you have performed one of the most helpful of services to your client. In my opinion you should have A.A. literature in your offices and give or loan it to your alcoholics to read and study.

Not all alcoholics can be interested in A.A. No one joins until he is convinced that he cannot refrain from drinking by his own efforts; he must seek some help from without his own personality. By confession and discussion of his alcoholic troubles before other alcoholics, by helping others to stop drinking, by open-meeting consideration of the whole problem, by association with fellow victims the A.A. member becomes fired with the enthusiasm and faith and confidence which keeps him dry from day to day and from year to year.

The members practically date their life from the day they took their last drink, realizing the life and death nature of the problem.

By all means, get the help of A.A. for your alcoholics if at all possible.

Drug Addicts

In most cases users of narcotics are criminals only incidentally in their need to supply their habits. To them all other needs are subordinate.

An addict who is getting all the drugs his system requires is apparently quite a normal individual. This is in striking contrast to the alcoholic problem, for the alcoholic is quite normal when not drinking. The stories of "drug crazed" criminals are fantasy. The drug addict is "crazed" when he craves the drug and turns to criminal activity to get it. All drug addicts must, if they are not wealthy, turn to some kind of criminal activity because they cannot earn enough to buy their drugs; and as many have told me, "I don't have time to work."

It is practically impossible to control, except under close supervision, under guard, an addict who has an active habit. He must get his daily dosage or suffer severe pains, terrible anxiety, and mental agony. Such a man is in need, of course, of hospitalization or imprisonment under medical supervision.

A former addict, just released from hospital or prison, presents serious problems for his supervisor. Some drug users, deprived of drugs while in prison or hospital, wish to live without drugs; others look forward to getting drugs at the earliest possible moment. Certainly some of them do go for days, weeks, and months without drugs; some who have used drugs stop their use. If he wants to get along without drugs there is at least some hope for him. Remember that he is a sort of lost soul, longing for the drug which alone can make him feel normal. If he is trying to do the right thing he leans heavily for support and encouragement on you, on friends, and his family. The best advise you can give him is that he stay away from people and places which have been associated with his habit in the past. Many an addict has gone for a long time without drugs, courageously carrying on the good fight, only to backslide after meeting an old addicted friend or visiting a place which has fostered his habit in the past.

Many addicts in their honest search for respectability try to choose a lesser evil. They must find some surcease from the agonizing tension of their drug-longings. They want to stay free from narcotics so they try drinking as a substitute. This shows their dependence; it brings new troubles of its own, it does not help at all, and it usually leads back to drugs.

There is a difference of opinion as to whether everyone can become addicted. In studies of addicts certain types of personalities are found, but I believe with many others that anyone who uses drugs for a long time will eventually be "hooked." The man of character and good sense will not try drugs initially for the thrill which unstable personalities seek, but I believe that certain addicts correctly trace their addiction to long-continued use of drugs during painful illnesses. This is a danger which all physicians realize and try to avoid.

As a final word regarding addiction, let me urge you to try to understand the terrible hold it has on the human personality. You may be unable to see an addict without disgust and revulsion, but remember that his need of drugs is partly physiological. The longing for drugs in an addict, deprived temporarily of his accustomed dosage, is probably comparable only to the longing a man lost in the desert feels for water. I have tried to understand, in talking to addicts, how strong their craving is. I have told many of them that one of the strongest longings of a human being is for sexual satisfaction and have asked them to compare that with the desire for drugs. Without exception they have told me that there is no comparison—that the craving for narcotics is far greater. We can talk to the addict about will power, but the will power necessary to combat narcotic craving is a hundredfold stronger than any we nonusers have ever been called upon to face.

Marihuana

The general belief at present is that the dangers in the use of marihuana have been greatly exaggerated. We read formerly of its terrible effects, and some of these seem to have been fairy tales. Its use is to be discouraged, but it is non-addicting, it probably causes little or no trouble, and it certainly is not an important contributor to criminal activity. When a prisoner tells me he committed a crime when intoxicated or because of his need for narcotic drugs, I frequently believe him; when he says he was under the influence of marihuana, I do not believe him. Marihuana seems to alter the sense of time, to exhilarate the individual; but that it influences him to perform acts outside his usual moral code is probably not true. It is against the law to have it or sell it, and this law is probably a good thing.

Psychopathic Personality

It is an old idea that certain people, not insane, feebleminded, epileptic, or neurotic showed such variation from the usual standards of their cultural level that a special name must be given to their kind. They have been called moral imbeciles and psychopaths and many names between these designations, and still we do not know how or why they are as they are. The conception is a very useful one—and yet a very dangerous one—for we are likely to fall back on it when we do not understand a man. By calling him a psychopath we are somehow unconsciously relieved of the necessity of trying to understand and help him. And if we fail to supervise him successfully, how delightful to tell ourselves that he was a psychopath whom no one could have helped.

Psychopathic Personality Defined

Fifty psychiatrists will give you as many definitions; and notice how they squirm as they give them! There is none of the assurance which we have when we tell you about dementia praecox or general paresis. The definition is usually one of exclusion. If a person does not conduct his affairs with ordinary judgment, he acts impulsively, if he does not profit by experience and mistakes, lacks the capacity to plan wisely, goes through life sinning, blundering, stumbling as though trying to get himself into as much trouble as possible and trying to get himself hated or killed —and if we cannot prove that he is feeble-minded or insane—then we say he is a *psychopath* if he is not neurotic. Most of us are sure that there is such a person, but the danger lies in making a diagnosis by recounting all the troubles into which the man has plunged, and then calling him a psychopath because of this history. You probation officers in the field must help us understand these people. It may be that here is a special type of personality, it may be that they represent a type of real mental disease as Dr. Hervey Cleckley and Dr. Ben Karpman believe. It may be that they are "rebels without a cause" in the words of the title of Robert Lindner's book. Or it may be that they do as they do because of mental conflicts, or as a result of experiences in early life which would have made anyone a psychopath. We simply do not know.

The great medicolegal dilemma presented by these psychopaths is this: are they sane or insane; responsible or not responsible. Legal procedure at present considers them sane and responsible; and unless and until we are more sure of the belief of some of us that they are irresponsible, the present legal attitude would seem to be the most practical. For we must remember that they often are persistent evil-doers and if we ever excuse them from punishment as we do the insane and feebleminded, we must have an appropriate disposition, for they cannot be allowed to mess up themselves and the world without restraint. The only possible disposition would be similar to that of the insane; namely, commitment to some sort of a hospital, not for a definite term but for an indefinite period—till cured. The psychopaths and their lawyers would hardly appreciate this. The present common cycle of court to mental hospital and back to freedom and on to delinquency and court again would be many times extended. The probation and parole officer has little to do with this dilemma. At present he must consider the man sane and try to guide and influence him as best he can.

Characteristics of the Psychopath

Outstanding among the tragic characteristics of the psychopath is his inability or at any rate his failure to develop loyalties. The probation officer, in his management of ordinary clients, relies, to a large extent, on this loyalty which he tries to develop toward himself, his friends, and his family. The psychopath must not be expected to develop this loyalty, so we who deal with him lack a very useful tool. We must steel ourselves against being shocked when these strange people talk so penitent and ashamed and friendly and loyal and loving, and then within days or even minutes act in a way which shows that these emotions have no meaning whatever for them.

It is easy to recount the peculiarities and sins and weaknesses of the psychopath. It is harder to give advice as to how to help him. My advice will not be very helpful as I am one of those who regard the problem of the psychopath as well nigh hopeless, as far as our influencing his thought, idealism, and behavior. I repeat my theme song—"do your best." The only hopes I know of lie in three main categories.

Many psychopaths become more normal as time goes on. I can attribute this only to a gradual maturity. So much of the behavior of a psychopath seems explainable on a basis of delayed or stunted emotional maturity, particularly in the field of appreciation of the rights of others and in the concept of their personalities, characteristics, and desires in relation to the same desires of others and of the state. The professional criminal has, we believe, normal appreciation of these things but chooses to ignore them. The psychopath does not seem to have it. Many psychopaths mellow and seem to develop this socialization, and in this maturity lies our greatest hope. I have asked many of them who seem to have matured—at least to the extent of finally learning to restrain themselves enough to build up a good record in prison—what in their opinion could have been done earlier to have helped them to adjust at home, at school, in correctional schools, in prisons. Their answer invariably is to the effect that nothing could have been done—"I just had to learn my lesson the hard way."

By trying to rid yourself of the hoplessness of giving up trying to help a psychopath you can always say to yourself, "maybe this kid is not a psychopath after all." You will experience many heartaches and cruel disappointments, but you may also rid yourself and your client of the feeling of utter frustration, and may find ways to help him to a better way of life. So try it, and if you fail, don't feel too bad; if you succeed, yell for joy!

I don't believe it to be irreverent or far-fetched to say that it is a miracle of a sort when one of these irresponsible, blundering persons suddenly or gradually settles down and begins to act like a normal human being. This happens in prison and happens to your clients. Then is the time to try, as we do, to find out what caused the change; and then to try similar techniques on similar clients when they come along.

Extra supervision and guidance obviously are needed, far more than are required for other types of offenders. The psychopath of course resents the very supervision of which he is in such crying need. In a way he will hate it, and yet I am sure that they know they need it. They like to talk about their troubles. They like to exaggerate their good points and accomplishments, they like to tell of the sins and unwise behavior of others. They love to ask for favors, and they do want your good opinion. While they are offering their excuses, and offering fancied or rationalized evidence in mitigation of their misdeeds, there is a chance for us in prison and you in the field to discuss, advise, and offer guidance and leadership. Some of the words of wisdom you offer for their benefit may not be wasted. And remember that for some strange reason most of the psychopaths who become criminalistic are of average intelligence or better. Others in close contact with the man—employer, friends, family—should be taught to encourage conversation, to praise when possible, to warn wisely, to help form a solid rock of stability which these people need as a refuge. It is, of course, an art to advise and counsel without being too "preachy." Our counseling efforts must be highly developed to be at all effective in helping these people. Concentration as much as possible in conversation on "neutral" subjects, matters of interest to the client which carry no emotional charge and which have nothing to do with right and wrong are advisable here. In "passing the time of day" with our clients much can be done in building up friendship or at least friendly feeling which is the most important factor in establishing rapport which is so necessary if we are to influence successfully another person, psychopathic or not.

It is better to have psychopaths live with others and work with others, than to have them lead more solitary lives. There are exceptions, but the constant break of other people's needs and rights and emotional drives must be on hand to be used by the psychopath, if his maturity begins to develop. This is in line with their need for special supervision and guidance. Employers, friends, and family need not know that the client is considered by you and by us to be a psychopath. Probably they usually should not know this. But they should be told that the client is unusual, that he is "nervous," that he needs extra help, that he frequently needs to be left alone, that he can be talked to sometimes, and not at other times, that he is often disappointing and disloyal but that you are trying to help bring out the best in him. Get them interested in the fascinating, though difficult, problem of helping and influencing for the better a peculiar individual who "needs just the help that you can give him. That is why I am asking you to take a special interest in him."

Sexual Deviates

The attempts to understand sexual deviation are hampered by our lack of knowledge of what constitutes a normal or average sexual life. Kinsey's recent book and the multiple of reports and publications concerning it have confused rather than enlightened us. Honest attempts at understanding this important part of life are to be encouraged, of course, The complicated physical and emotional factors involved are far beyond the scope of this paper. Here we must be a little dogmatic and call sexual life "normal" when the individual turns for sexual expression to those of the opposite sex, and manages his sexual life with discretion and self-control to the extent of receiving and giving happiness from the relationship and avoiding the flouting of laws and customs of society. The highest ideal, of course, is that all this will lead to a happy marriage and the formation of family life.

Most Common Sexual Deviations

The most common sexual deviations which concern us in this paper are the following:

Uncontrolled heterosexuality.—Persons who offend in this manner belong in general in one of two groups:

(1) Individuals whose sexual aim is union with one of the opposite sex, but whose relationships never develop to the point of real enduring satisfaction. Such are the so-called "Don Juan" type among men and the so-called "nymphomania" type among women. A neurosis of a severe type is usually the basis for these conditions.

(2) Psychopaths whose sexual life follows the same pattern of

irresponsibility as the rest of their life activities. They seduce and rape in their restless hedonistic search for the satisfaction which they never really find except for the passing moment.

Active homosexuality.—These persons have as their sexual object a person of the same sex; as their sexual aim, sexual union with the other person. They desire the masculine role, acting toward their homosexual lover as a normal person would toward a lover of the opposite sex.

Passive homosexuality.—These persons have as their sexual object a person of the same sex; as their sexual aim, sexual union with the other person. They desire the feminine role, acting toward their lovers as normal persons would toward lovers of the opposite sex.

Remember these distinctions: the active homosexual (when a man) treats a male lover as though he were a female. The passive homosexual (when a man) treats the male lover as though the lover were a male, and he (the passive homosexual) a female. All three of these types may be aggressive or not; that is, they may seek the lover or may respond to the lover's seeking. All three may be constantly true to their abnormal type, or may be what we call facultative; that is, sometimes "normal" and sometimes "abnormal." In the field of personality distortions hardly anyone is the same sort of person all of the time.

Polymorphous perverse sexual state.—There are individuals who seem never to crystallize their sexual aims or desires. They are essentially children or at most adolescents in their psychosexual behavior and attitudes; are ready to try any kind of sexual expression, particularly if it seems smart to them or if they have never tried it before. Some of these are probably psychopaths, others are probably definite victims of neuroses.

I realize that the foregoing is such a brief discussion that it may only have led to confusion in your minds. There is no way of really making the matters simple. These conditions all lie in the field of sexual pathology. Those of you who are really interested in this complicated and involved field of study may read psychoanalytic works. They, again, may only further confuse you. The very best introduction to a serious attempt to understand the sex deviate is to read Freud's *Three Contributions to the Theory of Sex.* As an antidote to all this, and to restore your sense of humor, and to keep you from worrying too much about it, I suggest that you read Thurber and White's *Is Sex Necessary?* Best of all, in most cases, study the individual you are trying to understand, to help, and to guide, and get all the psychiatric advice you can. And to revert to my theme song, do the best you can.

One more word about helping your client with his sex problems: Advise and discuss, but do not be "preachy." Almost everyone has some peculiarities and worries and guilt feelings and conflicts about his or her sex life. Common sense discussion is of tremendous help if you can become genuinely interested and avoid being, or at least acting, shocked. The sexual difficulties of most people, serious as they are, tend to fade away as they mature. It may or may not be "normal" but think of the many people you know as good people and yet who have transgressed our sexual code.

How Tensions May Be Relieved

Remember that you cannot control another person's sex life. You can only give guidance and leadership.

Many clients will appreciate talking over their sex life and problems with you; others will not. Clients of this sort are worried and ill at ease, no matter how much they may deny their anxiety. If they will talk these important matters over with you, the mere talking may do much good, especially if you can keep your own emotions under control and do not show them even if your clients shock you. Much of the good done by doctors, by friends, and by priests at the confessional, comes from what psychoanalysts call catharsis—letting off steam and relieving tension by talking to a sympathetic listener. Another point to remember is that the tension caused by a person tortured by psychosexual pathology can be relieved in only four ways, as follows:

(1) Frank acceptance of the abnormal sexual desires and frank yielding to them. This results in the individual becoming an overt participant in his particular kind of sexual pathological activity. He is then no longer ashamed of his longings and activities, enjoys them, and considers the people we call normal as narrow-minded. Tension leaves him for he has avoided conflict about the matter.

(2) Frank acceptance of the abnormal sexual desires but refusal

to yield to them. This results in some tension because of the constant restraint, but the acceptance of the abnormal desires does away with the more serious conflict which always occurs when an individual refuses to admit his personality or character peculiarities, sexual or otherwise. His mental state is then to be compared on a heterosexual level to the normally sexed man or woman who for some reason remains unmarried and continent. He is consciously exercising self-control, not fighting an inward conflict.

(3) Relief of tension by sublimation. This word, which is taken from physics, refers to the purification of an impulse or tendency or desire into a socially acceptable form of activity. This is not done consciously like the solution discussed under (2), but is an unconsciously developed mechanism. Its explanation lies in the field of psychoanalytic theory, not at all universally accepted. It is pretty generally believed, however, that many people find happiness by satisfying their antisocial tendencies in a way which does good instead of harm. To give specific examples of this sublimation in a paper prepared for nonmedical readers might cause embarrassment. Suffice it to say here that any overpowering interest or vocation or avocation which your clients show may lead the way to a possible sublimation of antisocial or abnormal sexual tendencies.

(4) Repression of the sexual conflict. Another and always tragic solution of an individual's conflict about his sexual peculiarities involves its repression. According to psychoanalytic theory, at least, such a person is actually able to repress his conflict. Thus a homosexual, for instance, comes to believe that he is not a homosexual at all. If this were all, it would be a happy solution. Unfortunately for such a patient—for such persons then become psychotic—the repressed desires remain active and seek repression in some way. These ways take place through delusions and hallucinations in which homosexual threats seem to come from other persons. Depending upon the subject's personality makeup, varied symptoms may develop and the individual becomes the victim, as he sees it, of a hostile world which is trying to force him into homosexuality, and of hallucinations and voices which accuse him of the very perversions he has repressed. Thus a person cannot safely repress his desires without becoming psychotic or exhibit some sex deviation.

The only safe way of keeping his mental health are the first three alternatives. It is probable that we can do little to help the probationer as to the way in which he solves the conflict, but we should try to lead and advise him to accept the second or third alternative rather than the first or last.

In talking over these sexual peculiarities and conflicts with a probationer, the strongest talking point is somewhat as follows: "You are for some reason unusual in your psychosexual life. You cannot help this, but you can and must accept it if you are to remain mentally healthy. The desires which you have and which society calls abnormal cannot be allowed free sway. You must exercise self-control and it may be no more difficult than the control which you use in other fields of personality."

I tell a homosexual man that he cannot help being what he is, but that he can control it, just as a more normal man controls his heterosexual impulses. This conscious control is a far different matter from repression, for the latter involves splitting of the personality—pretending that he is what he really is not. He is never as effective an individual as is the man who accepts his peculiarities and succeeds in controlling them.

Aggressive Sexual Psychopath

Another type of sexual abnormality, the victims of which are really in danger, are the so-called aggressive sexual psychopaths. These persons are of different personality patterns but are similar in their aggressiveness. The case history and medical and psychiatric opinions usually have spotted most of them. Share your knowledge and opinions with your professional co-workers and get what help you can from doctors and clinics. Many states have put into effect laws which provide for indefinite commitment of sexual psychopaths. Become familiar with these laws if your state has one. If you suspect or believe or know that a client, or anyone for that matter, has or is likely to attack others, particularly children, you must not take the responsibility of keeping it to yourself. State authorities or city police should have the benefit of your knowledge in order that they may get medical advice and act as seems best. Remember that these unfortunate but dangerous individuals cannot or have not developed the normal or controlled adult status of heterosexual love as a force to be sublimated or refined toward marriage and family ideals. They long for sex expression and, not being able to make love in the usual way, turn in desperation to rape or sex intimacies with young children. The fear of being caught and the intense feeling of guilt may then lead to the killing of the victim. Try to inspire them with higher ideals, help them with common sense sex discussion. But do not keep it to yourself; otherwise you may have plenty of reason for guilt feeling yourself if your client is involved in one of the sex crimes.

Neurotics

It is beyond the scope of this paper to go into the classification and description of the sorts of nervous disorders to which the human mind is susceptible; the same applies to psychotic (insane) people, discussed below. You are not expected to be a psychiatrist, but you do have to deal with neurotic (nervous) clients. Get all the help you can from psychiatrists and other doctors; learn some of the danger signs which may point to the presence of a neurosis; learn common sense methods of advice and management. Try to learn how far you may safely go before the client *must* seek medical help. And remember that the doctor will probably need and request help from you, friends, and the family.

Neurotic persons frequently are nondelinquent for the probable reason that neurotics are persons who succumb to their conflicts submissively, while delinquents, on the other hand, aggressively try to fight their way out of their dilemma. But we do have nervous clients. Many of these "nervous" clients, however, may be frustrated psychopaths and we need a great skill to distinguish them from the true neurotics. Again, much "nervousness" is an early expression of physical disease which makes early medical examination and diagnosis necessary.

Common Danger Signs

Anxiety, brooding, undue worrying, insomnia are all possible symptoms of neurosis. Moodiness, inability to think clearly or to concentrate, inattention to family and employment responsibilities—these may all be evidence of neurosis rather than merely character faults. Frequent physical complaints and the so-called "hypochondria" may become as serious and crippling as actual heart or stomach disorders. A whole new field of medicine, as most of you know, is concerned with what we call psychosomatic disorders; i.e., mental conflicts converted into physical complaints and illnesses in a rather mysterious way, probably through the complicated connections between emotions, ductless glands, and the sympathetic nervous system. We must learn that much actual physical pathology begins in emotional conflict, and that after a time the process may become irreversible. When this happens the physical disorder is the important thing. Certain disorders are believed to always begin in mental conflict; as for instance toxic goiter, gastric ulcer, and migraine. You may be out of your depth when you try to do the best you can for these patients, but most of their treatment and management will fall upon you.

How the Neurotic Can Be Helped

Naturally you will have to fall back on the help of doctors wherever you can, but the necessity of doing much of the actual advising yourself makes it imperative that you become as informed as possible about these symptoms. The things you can do are mainly as follows:

Common sense advice may or may not help. Try it. Not all neuroses are so very serious and a good, interested friend is sometimes all that is needed. Very important as a measure of your ability to hely a nervous client is your ability to enter into his feelings, to understand the things he is worrying about, to be able to put yourself in his place and find out what you would do. You will really be a partner of your client in his struggle and you will attain a chastening sense of humility in your probable realization that he is grappling with problems which would have stumped and thwarted and de-energized you as much or more than they have tortured him.

Time spent in letting all clients, and particularly nervous clients, talk it out is usually well-spent time. There is a limit to your time, of course, and you have to use common sense in budgeting it. But the turning point in the improvement of many a neurotic patient has been the privilege of talking himself out to a sympathetic listener.

A few words of advice concerning the tone of our remarks when talking to neurotic people may be helpful. We must remember that neurotic symptoms, though not based on physical pathology, are very real to the patient. A general air of encouragement is in order, but the breezy "cheer up" usually does more harm than good. It is not in order to belittle the patient's symptoms. Many neurotic patients are driven to despair by our constant inability to understand their condition as they see it. Above all, do not refer to the complaints and symptoms as imaginary, for indeed they are not. They frequently are beyond our understanding, and they lie outside the realm of ordinary physical disease. Nevertheless, a neurotic suffers from exceedingly crippling and embarrassing disorders. A true neurotic is not a malingerer, but usually is considered one. He probably should be regarded as an "unconscious malingerer," no more responsible for his mental tensions, worries, and phobias than is a diabetic responsible for his faulty pancreas.

Neurotic symptoms and neurotic patients are susceptible to two kinds of treatment. The underlying cause, usually unsolved emotional conflict, can be helped by analytic psychotherapy; this lies within the province of the psychiatrist, should not be attempted by others. Replacement and suggestive therapy, however, is given by doctors and lay alike, often better by the latter. Sympathetic understanding, cheerful attitudes toward getting well, and suggestions and advice regarding everyday living can be attempted by all. It is probably in the field of helping the patient to develop healthy vocational, avocational, and recreational interests that you and the patient's family and friends can be of most help. A neurotic person does not have time to worry and fret if he becomes busy and interested in outside interests; often, but by no means always, this is true. The danger in this kind of treatment lies in the fact that even if the patient feels and acts normal, his unsolved emotional problems still remain. They sometimes evaporate, but often they do not; and if they do not they are likely to break out anew at any time.

Psychotics

Many of the points discussed in regard to neurotics also apply to the psychotic (insane person). Psychoses, however, are much more serious, much more dangerous, far less likely to be affected by anything you can do. Out of any group of persons, certain ones are going to be psychotic.

Danger Signals

You must be familar with certain danger signals which may point to a possible mental disease. Among these are the following:

(1) Any change in character or personality. Any indication that the person seems to be a different person from his usual self.

(2) Unwonted withdrawal from the society of others and from activity formerly enjoyed.

(3) Undue exhilaration or depression.

(4) Fear of going insane. Neurotics frequently say this, and need to be encouraged that they are not. It is all right to similarly encourage psychotics, or potential psychotics as well, but reassure the patient, not yourself. Don't try to diagnose mental disease, or a neurosis either.

(5) Fear of being controlled, of having the mind read, of not being one's self, all common early symptoms.

(6) Presence of paranoid ideas (ideas of persecution). In our work where our clients so often are already antisocial and interpret prosecution as persecution, it is frequently difficult to differentiate between truly paranoid ideas and surly hatred of the world which is, indeed, often "against them." The psychotic paranoid ideas tend to be fantastic and impossible, but are not always so. All ideas of this sort place the client under suspicion.

(7) Fantastic delusions (false ideas) are characteristic of psychoses, but here again it is often hard to tell.

(8) Hallucinations (false sensory impressions) are certainly evidence of mental disorder.

A doctor, preferably a psychiatrist, must be called to examine a man you suspect of mental disease. Unfortunately we are not always sure at first, so you may have to worry your way through early symptoms.

How the Psychotic Can Be Helped

States have different laws regarding emergency, observation, and regular commitments to state psychiatric hospitals. You must be familiar with these. A doctor and also courts are needed to obtain commitments. Emergency commitment often may save the patient's life; accordingly, you should know the quickest way to obtain a commitment in your community.

Common sense advice is needed here, of course, but such advice is usually for the family rather than for the patient when there is actual mental disease. Do not depend upon your knowledge of mental disease, good though it may be. The responsibility for the commitment and care and treatment of mentally diseased patients rests with the state, its courts, and its doctors.

It is well to remember a few points about psychotic persons.

Paranoid patients frequently believe they are in danger and have to defend themselves. They are thus potentially dangerous. Anyone who knows of the possibility of a paranoid condition must share that knowledge and get the best advice possible, or bear a good share of the responsibility if disaster occurs.

Depressed patients are always potentially suicidal, and must be guarded every *second* till proved not suicidal.

As is the case with any disease or abnormal condition, the earlier diagnosis and treatment can be secured, the earlier may improvement result. It frequently may become one of your responsibilities to counsel with families of clients when commitment to a mental hospital has been advised. The strongest talking point is: The danger of stigmatizing the patient by residence in a state hospital is far less than the danger of putting off treatment and commitment till it is too late for the most effective treatment.

Any nervous or mental disease in a person who has had syphilis should be considered possibly due to syphilis of the brain and spinal cord unless examination of the spinal fluid shows that this is not so.

Our old friends of several pages back cause us a lot of trouble in our consideration of possible psychoses. I refer to the psychopaths, those who are sort of "half crazy" all the time, and who develop both real psychoses at times and strange behavior which may not be actually psychotic at other times. In this connection, your judgment probably will be as good as the doctor's, possibly better; and you both often will be unsure of your ground. Use the best combined judgment you and the doctors can summon, and even then prepare to be often outwitted by the psychopath.

Casework and Professional Assistance

The problems we have discussed in this paper are difficult, will tax your casework techniques to the limit. But we all have to fall back on the "common sense" and "do your best" techniques I so frequently have cited. But your special skills will also be called into play. And in most of your communities you can summon doctors for their diagnosis and treatment, clinics with their medical-psychological-social work services, and community agencies with their casework and recreation facilities. Churches, clubs, settlement houses, employment services, private citizens—one or more of these often can help us turn the tide when our own strength is not enough.

And remember two things: (1) Any agency or person who is successful in helping you will be as proud of the result as you are; and (2) Don't be afraid to give generous credit when you have been helped. The fields of social work intermingle. A concerted attack often may solve problems which a single individual or agency cannot. You are professional men. I hope that this paper may have thrown a little light on some of the most difficult professional problems you have to face.

THE PROBATION WORKER AND THE COMMUNITY*

A vital part of the social worker's equipment is a knowledge of and an ability to use skillfully the resources of his community in helping the client to reach the most satisfactory solution of his difficulty. No matter how dedicated the individual caseworker, no matter how well he relates to his client or uses the professional skills at his command, he is of necessity limited not only by the boundaries of his capacities, but also, by the policies, function, and material resources of his agency.

This generic statement is nowhere more applicable than to the function of the probation and parole worker. For example, during the course of a pre-sentence investigation, the probation worker may become aware of a number of contacts that the individual awaiting sentence has had with a variety of community agencies.

---

* Printed with consent of the author, Howard W. Borsuk, from an original, unpublished manuscript. Florida State University, 1957.

The probation worker will then need to communicate with these agencies in order to obtain a rounded picture of the individual under investigation which in turn will provide part of the basis of his description and interpretation of the offenders' situation to the judge. The judge will then be able to arrive, within the limitations of the law, at a decision which, hopefully, will be of simultaneous benefit to society and the offender. This will pre-suppose not only a knowledge of the existence of these agencies, but the scope of their services and how they work. In the pursuit of helping the offender abide by the conditions set by the court under probation and helping him deal with the constellation of problems that influenced the commission of the offense, the probation worker may become aware of certain contributing situations, the effective handling of which are beyond his personal resources and the scope of the agency he represents. Similarly, the parole worker, in helping the paroled offender adjust to his social environment in a way that is both satisfactory to himself and society, notes the existence of situations barring the attainment of this goal. In both instances the worker will need at his fingertips a knowledge of those agencies in his community which will be of help not only in supplementing his efforts but sometimes in dealing with a crucial life problem of the client.

The process of referral is far from perfunctory and calls for the mobilization of skills and understanding which are not in the least obvious. The offender must be physically available to his probation or parole worker, perhaps at stated intervals according to conditions set down. Certain aspects of his life are open to investigation on the part of the worker. His relationship with the worker must then, of necessity, carry elements of authority. In this he has no choice. He does, however, have a very significant choice, whether or not to use the worker as a source of help in regard to his situation. The same element of authority is not present in his relationship with voluntary community agencies. He is free to choose whether he wants to contact the agency to which he is referred or not. The voluntary agency may pose any number of emotional threats to him. The nature of the connection between the voluntary agency and the court may be unknown to him and constitute an additional threat. To deal with these problems the worker must bring to bear all the skill available to him.

Unfortunately, a detailed analysis of this process is not possible within the limitations of this article. The reader, of necessity, needs to be referred to the pertinent literature, as Walter A. Friedlander's *Introduction to Social Welfare* (1955) ; Arthur E. Fink, Everett E. Wilson and Merrill B. Conover, *The Field of Social Work*, (1955) ; and Herbert Stroup's *Social Work: An Introduction to the Field* (1948), for a more complete consideration.

Another word of caution. This study presents an array of agencies which are commonly available to residents of large metropolitan areas. Smaller aggregates may have only a portion of these agencies existent in the community or may have a smaller number of agencies which combine several functions. Rural and semirural communities are, of course, generally the most poorly serviced of all, and the worker in this case may sorely tax his frustration threshold in finding appropriate resources for his client.

The Family Agency

The Family Agency in many ways represents the core agency of private social work. It has been in the past entrusted with providing financial assistance for the "worthy poor" and is still identified by a large section of the public as essentially in the business of offering tangible assistance to the indigent. Although family agencies are continually engaged in defining their functions, certain trends may be discerned. The advent of the great depression overwhelmed these agencies in an avalanche of financial need. It became increasingly clear that the alleviation of financial distress because of its magnitude and its permeation of the entire economic system was a public responsibility, to be discharged through publicly controlled agencies, in most instances, local Departments of Welfare. While most family agencies still make provisions for financial assistance, it is given generally on an emergency basis only, when, for instance, the local Department of Welfare must impose some kind of a waiting period before actual monetary help can be given or when for some reason the client in actual need is not eligible for the Department of Welfare's services. The emphasis is at all times on the constructive use of this assistance and maintenance. Financial aid is not given except in the above last circumstance. The function of the family agency can be currently defined as involving the preservation and restoration of harmonious family relationships and the prevention of those conditions which would lead to a disruption of this kind of relationship. In the pursuit of this objective emphasis is placed on healthy personality development as well as the satisfactory social functioning of individual members of the family. The various services of the family agency are utilized toward this end. They may involve solely a counseling service in respect to a marital difficulty, difficulties in the parent-child relationship, problems involving the adjustment of the aged to current living, or pre-marital difficulties centering on relationships with the opposite sex. In addition, problems concerning severe mental illness are dealt with in which the objective is not direct treatment of the individual who is mentally ill, but rather with the many problems that accompany this condition, such as referral to psychiatric resource, the effects on the family, necessitating, perhaps, a reorganization of attitudes, feelings and living arrangements. In short, the family agency deals with the entire gamut of social and psychological problems that the family may become heir to in our complex civilization. Although this definition of function reflects the shift from the administration of tangible services to a more intangible stress, various other services within the agency, if available, may be called upon as part of the process of help. One such service might be *homemaking service* to temporarily relieve a situation in a family whereby the physical presence of a substitute mother is called for, for instance, in the absence or incapacitation of the wife or mother because of illness, psychiatric or other consultation. Another growing development which may be mentioned, is *fee charging,* commensurate with the client's ability to pay, still another reflection of the shift from dealing only with indigent clients to servicing every segment of the community. Help is given within the structure of the client-worker relationship involving office interviews, customarily on a weekly basis. The primary method is that of social casework, and the fundamental service is administered through the person of the caseworker as representative of the agency. It is obvious that the probation or parole worker in his contact with the offender will come upon difficulties of this nature in his client. He may want to consider referral to a family agency which would have at its call greater resources for dealing with the difficulty and provide a focus that would be different, and as such more helpful than his own. Sometimes the family agency in smaller communities may combine its function in one administrative setting with that of a child care agency.

Child Care or Welfare Agencies

Under this heading would come those agencies which deal with the placement of children, either on a permanent or temporary basis. This may involve placement for temporary care in foster homes or institutions or placement with a selected family interested in adopting the child. In some communities these agencies combine both functions in one administrative setting, in others these functions are administered by two distinct agencies, the foster care agency and the adoption agency. The services of all child care agencies have at their base, the philosophy that for healthy physical and emotional development, children need to have the experience of family living. The best possible setting for this to take place is within the natural family. When circumstances do not permit this, e.g., severe neglect on the part of natural parents which defies efforts at alleviation, or other for the moment insoluble physical and emotional problems, foster family placement is indicated. Although institutions are generally felt to be poor substitutes, they may be considered as more helpful to the child when his emotional damage is such that a successful adjustment to family living is not for the time being possible for him or when placement is for so temporary a period as to make the stress and strain of adjusting to foster parents not worthwhile. In the case of temporary care the effort is on helping the natural parents reassume their parental responsibilities in a way most helpful to their child and themselves. In the case of children placed for adoption, the stress is on finding adoptive parents who feel the lack of children keenly in the completion of their otherwise successful family life, and who will be able to give the adopted child all the love, warmth, and acceptance that will make for his emergence as a socially and emotionally competent adult. One of the essential elements in this process, except in the eventuality of a court order, is the exploration with the natural parents of alternative solutions to placement and if placement seems the only feasible alternative, that it be arrived at through mutual agreement and acceptance.

In relation to the utilization of these agencies, it may be that the offender's children manifest some type of problem behavior, the resolution of which would assist the probationer's adjustment.

Again, the primary method is that of social casework. In small communities private agencies with these functions may not be available. In this case, the Child Welfare unit of the local Department of Welfare may assume some or all of these services. The typical large urban private child care agency will have psychiatric consultation, testing facilities, perhaps medical services and shelter facilities as well.

The Child Guidance Clinic

A more specialized child care service is that of the child guidance clinic, whose principal function is to offer help in relation to severe emotional disturbance in the child. Here the primary service is a psychiatric one focused on the child's disturbance. This does not mean that the inter-relatedness of the family as providing the setting for the problem is ignored. The family's involvement is seen as a vital part of the helping process. Perhaps the delineation of the clinical team characteristic of the child guidance agency will provide a clearer concept as to its function.

We have mentioned that the fundamental service is a psychiatric one. Operationally this implies that the psychiatrist has both the responsibility for direct treatment of the child and general supervision of the team which cooperatively deals with the total problem. The psychiatric social worker typically deals with the parents, the focus of help being directed to the parent's part in the problem, planning for both a shifting of attitudes and restructuring of the family's relations with the child.

The psychologist has the responsibility for the administration and interpretation of any number of psychological tests which will be used as an aid to complete the diagnostic picture.

Of late, both social workers and psychologists in many child guidance clinics have been entrusted with direct responsibility for the treatment of the child, usually under psychiatric supervision. Thus, there has been some blurring of the lines of demarcation between the various disciplines. However, the function remains the same, therapy for children with emotional disturbance.

Characteristically, the child guidance clinic is a private agency, usually confined to large urban aggregates. It may exist, however, as a division of service in the larger mental hygiene clinic or within a university setting, the principal goal of the last being the provision of training for future practitioners. Some of the smaller child guidance agencies may be staffed solely by psychiatric social workers and psychologists, principally because of the unavailability of psychiatrists. However, there is usually provision for psychiatric consultation. Fees may or may not be charged, depending on the setting.

The Mental Hygiene or Mental Health Clinic

Here, too, the principal service is usually a psychiatric one. In structure the Mental Hygiene Clinic duplicates that of the Child Guidance Clinic, treatment being provided for the adult with severe emotional problems who is still able to function outside of a mental hospital. Family members may be seen by the psychiatric social worker, depending on the situation, for purposes of making a social study which will be integrated into a coherent diagnostic framework, and which will aid in the evolvement of the treatment plan. Again, family members may also be seen by the psychiatric social worker in order to deal with their part in influencing the disturbance and to effect subsequent changes in the family atmosphere. The social worker will commonly have the additional responsibility of utilizing various community resources that will aid in the patient's social adjustment. Again, as in the case of the Child Guidance Clinics, treatment responsibility has been increasingly assumed by social workers and psychologists, and some of these agencies in small communities will be staffed solely by members of these disciplines.

The Mental Hygiene Clinic may operate as an outpatient clinic of the psychiatric divisions of large metropolitan hospitals or as self-contained clinics without a hospital affiliation. In some communities they may be private agencies supported by fees and voluntary contributions, in others, they may be public, tax-supported institutions, and in still others, a mixture of both.

Vocational Guidance Agencies

Specialized agencies providing vocational guidance are usually confined to large urban centers. The best of them provide testing services, to determine vocational aptitudes and interests, help focused on problems, emotional and otherwise, blocking a successful vocational adjustment. They may or may not include a placement service. Many of these agencies charge fees, sometimes based on ability to pay. The services are administered by trained vocational counselors who will also make use of other community resources, when indicated.

Social Group Work Agencies

Under this category, we might list any number of agencies, such as Settlement Houses, Neighborhood Centers, and YM or YWCA's. Their primary purpose is to provide a constructive group experience for their clients. These group experiences may take the form of activity in special interest groups, such as arts and crafts, little theater, social clubs, etc., or in guiding activity for various segments of the community such as the aged, etc. Although the emphasis has been traditionally on youth, an increasing interest is displayed in the problems of the older groups of the population. Although, again, these agencies typically exist in large urban centers, group work activities may be found in small communities under the aegis of the "Y" or Salvation Army. Some of these agencies will have professionally trained group workers, in supervisory capacities.

We might also mention in considering group work resources, camping facilities which often operate as a service of various group work agencies. Although the use of adult camps is not as yet wide spread there is an increasing trend in this direction.

There are many more specialized categories of agencies in the arsenal of social welfare. However, the probation and parole worker will, in his work with the offender, rarely have to call on the services of agencies other than those mentioned. Throughout the above there has been an emphasis of private agencies. It might be worthwhile to note that public agencies often combined with their material assistance function, offer highly skilled counseling help. As was pointed out in the foregoing, the publicly supported Department of Welfare has the responsibility for administering maintenance financial assistance. However, local practices not only as to amounts, budgets, but in respect to policies concerning eligibility for emergency assistance vary greatly.

UNDERLYING PRINCIPLES IN PROBATION COUNSELING*

Effective counseling implies a relationship between two people in which the counselor attempts to create conditions which will facilitate increased understanding on the part of the counselee of his life situation, and promote the necessary freedom to act in accordance with the understanding. Many criminal acts result from internal compulsions or external pressures of which the individual is only vaguely, if at all, aware. Increased understanding would bring into sharp focus the motives underlying his behavior. If he is to be a responsible citizen his freedom must be maintained —freedom with all of its social implications. Unless he is to be kept under continuous surveillance he must be free to decide whether he will continue his own present way of life or, if he is to change it, to do so in his own good time and for his own good or bad reasons. There is no half-way station in this conception of freedom. While a person is on probation he is not free—he is conditionally released. He must understand this. He must understand that his achievement of actual freedom depends not so much upon conformity with the rules imposed by the terms of his probation, important and necessary as those rules are, as it does upon the liberating effect of insight into himself and the social and psychological forces impinging upon him in the intimate social grouping (the community) of which he is a part. With this kind of knowledge and understanding he may begin his ascent toward freedom. The probation officer's task is to create the kind of at-

---

* Reprinted in part by permission of *Federal Probation*, and the author. Robert H. Dalton, Ph.D.: Value and Use of Counseling Techniques in the Work of Probation Officers, *Federal Probation*, Vol. 16, No. 4, Dec. 1952, p. 17-22.

mosphere or climate in his counseling relationship with his client that such increased understanding may be facilitated. Here we shall discuss some of the attitudes and practices which have been found to be effective in promoting optimal counseling conditions.

1. *Respect for and faith in the other person.*—The counselor tries to understand how the other has come to feel, think, and act as he does. He does not belittle the struggle the other has made and is making to solve his problem. At the same time the counselor must believe that his client has the potential capacity to solve his problem, given proper understanding and conditions.

2. *A realistic attitude toward oneself.*—Before we can properly understand another person we must know ourselves. We must know our own emotional involvements and tender spots—our own unsolved problems. We must know the areas in which we are inclined to look upon others in light of our weaknesses and strengths. Until we possess such knowledge we may unconsciously encourage a client along the very lines which we would consciously seek to have him avoid. Self-knowledge leads to greater objectivity and fairness in dealing with another. It also enables us to concentrate on the solution of his problem and prevents attempting to solve our own problems at his expense through the relationship.

3. *An attitude of complete honesty at all times.*—The foundation of all effective counseling is confidence. The client will test you in a thousand different ways, and dishonesty is the surest way to undermine his confidence. One example will suffice. Where the probation officer is attempting to prevent recurrence of criminal behavior his attitude toward the cultural sanctions should be made clear to the client from the beginning; otherwise misunderstanding is likely to develop in the relationship. In other words, the client should know whether the probation officer is going to side with the law-enforcing officials or with the client himself in the fact of any breach of the terms of his probation.

4. *The establishment of good rapport in the counseling relationship is essential to effective treatment.*—Good rapport is primarily a function of the individual attitudes and dispositions of the counselor. It also is based upon the natural likeableness of the

two partners and the way in which the situation is structured. Where there is an explicit common goal and the limits of acceptable behavior are clearly understood there is the best chance for success. This calls for the probation officer to decide upon the role he shall take. Shall he be judge, shall he be friend? He cannot realistically take either of these roles. Shall he be a friendly counselor? If so, what does this imply, and how shall it be clarified for the probationer?

5. *The practice of patience, the ability to listen and withhold judgment or too ready advice or interpretation, help to facilitate a good counseling situation.*—It is not the counselor's job to demonstrate how quick he is in understanding or solving problems; rather he should seek to help the other to gain in self-confidence and the ability to solve his own problem. He may never be able to do it; and this we must recognize and be willing to face. We may not be able to help some people—we must be able to fail. When we have achieved sufficient security to be able to fail without too great threat to ourselves, we will then be enabled to relax and provide a constant, sustaining support for our clients. This is one of the paradoxes of counseling: as we achieve the ability to accept failure in working with a client our chances of success with him increase.

6. *Study of the person's life history.*—How one has met typical life situations at home, at school, with his gang, in the community institutions, in his work situations, and in his marriage indicate his patterns of adjustment and adaptability. From this appraisal of the trends in his past behavior and for the way in which he handles himself in current crisis one can gauge the integrative capacity of his ego. One can better judge what to expect of the client and under what conditions to expect it. One may come to know when encouragement, support, and reassurance are indicated, and when suggestion, advice, and other forms of pressure are necessary. One may even discover that under the peculiar concatenation of unfortunate and tragic circumstances in the life of a client crime may be the only solution to his difficulties—the only solution, that is, which will keep his personality from complete disintegration.

Crime Arises from a Complex Background of Conditions

I should like to suggest that individual counseling is not the only method and frequently may not be the best method of treating criminal offenders who are on probation. Difficulties arising out of group situations may be more readily solved in groups than in individual consultation. Let us briefly inquire into the relevance of this statement.

Everyone is born a potential criminal. He becomes an actual criminal by virtue of the learnings which he acquires in the course of his development in social groups. This being so it becomes exceedingly significant to know the kinds of learning situations to which he has been exposed. With such knowledge we may not only help him to understand how he acquired certain traits and dispositions, but we may also be able to modify the current situation so that repeated reinforcement of old behavior patterns will not occur.

Two of the most prominent background learning situations in youth which influence the development of criminal tendencies are the home and the gang. According to dynamic psychology, the individual may have a basically sound personality structure but act out against society as a result of group identification. On the other hand he may have a personality warped by contagion through long and intimate association with sick and depraved parents. In either case his behavior is to a large degree a product of an interplay of dynamic forces over which he has little, if any, control. This interplay of forces has to be understood and modified before the individual's behavior can be changed. Or he has to be removed from the situation into a more healthy one, in addition to receiving individualized help.

This calls for a larger undertaking than the probation officer alone can possibly shoulder. Crime thus conceived makes probation become a community responsibility, and the job of the probation officer that of seeking, harnessing, and co-ordinating the human resources within communities which may be brought to bear upon the general social improvement and specific corrective measures where they are needed.

PROBATION TREATMENT IN DELINQUENCY*

Regardless of the nature of the delinquency, the major contribution in direct treatment by a probation officer will consist of forming a strong, friendly bond to the delinquent—a relationship that will let the delinquent know the probation officer is on his side, and that the probation officer believes the child is behaving in the only way he knows how. The probation officer must really believe this deeply, or the delinquent will have little use for him for, at best, it is difficult to get the aggressive delinquent to accept an adult as an ally. He has thought of the adult for too many years as an enemy who cannot be trusted. Many have been disillusioned repeatedly by adults and, though the individual delinquent senses the probation officer as his friend, he prefers to withhold significant information for a long time. If, as is occasionally the case, the probation officer is so conditioned by his own early experiences and training that he has a condemning attitude toward the delinquent's behavior, and to him, this will soon be sensed. He will not depend on what the probation officer says any more than the probation officer will rely on his remarks. As a delinquent he has had to learn to spot his friends quickly, and he will detect by a frown or sudden quietness or tenseness that the probation officer cannot accept him deeply. A sensitive probation officer may have difficulty in retaining a feeling of warmth for a boy who struck his mother who has just returned from the hospital; for an adolescent girl who got in after midnight after repeated promises and assurances this would never happen again; for an aggressive boy who tells in a convincing manner that his school work is satisfactory though the probation officer knows he has not been to school since the last interview. In this connection, the probation officer probably never will reach the stage when one of these clever delinquents will not be able to really convince him of his sincerity while he is telling a succession of lies.

---

* Reprinted by permission of *Federal Probation*. Hyman S. Lippman, M.D.: The Role of the Probation Officer in the Treatment of Delinquency in Children, *Federal Probation*, Vol. 12, No. 2, June, 1948, p. 36-39.

To complicate matters, there are delinquents who will have no respect for the probation officer if they can outwit him. To some extent this may be due to a need to be punished and to have their aggression checked. More often, however, it is an expression of their narcissism; they form their relationships on a narcissistic basis and can only develop a tie to someone who can outsmart them. Fortunately, this group is in the minority, because underlying this behavior mechanism is considerable emotional conflict that is resistive to treatment in the hands of the most experienced therapist.

The probation officer may be discouraged if his success seems to end with having formed this bond of friendship with the delinquent. He is aware, through talks with the foster parents, school, and others, that a given delinquent suffered greatly as a young child; was subjected to scenes of cruelty by an alcoholic mother, and knows he was illegitimate, and yet he tells the probation officer nothing of these facts. He becomes defensive when his family is referred to and prefers to stay on a superficial level. At the same time, he looks forward to coming in, and he has been more pleasant in the home and school—there has been a lessening of the delinquent behavior. The probation officer, acquainted with psychiatric literature, knows the part played by early emotional experiences in the development of delinquent behavior, is anxious to do something of "real value," and wants to discuss the early life experiences with the delinquent. The delinquent will give the kind of material the probation officer wants only when he is ready to do so (and he never may be ready)—when he is sure of him—when he is convinced the probation officer won't be critical of him or think less well of him, or can be relied upon not to repeat to the foster parents or the judge what he tells the probation officer. It is routine to assure him early in the treatment that what he tells the probation officer is in confidence, but it may be months before he is sure of this.

In some instances the delinquent talks freely from the outset. Usually, however, if this is the case, he will tell the probation officer what he has told others, and the telling will add little to the treatment. In some instances there will be a great deal of talking, much of which is intended to leave the probation officer with the feeling of trust in him, but which actually is a defense against revealing significant material.

There will be many delinquents who never will disclose traumatic experiences even after long periods of casework with them. They may continue with their delinquency, and admit this to the probation officer, but want to maintain contact with him, and so the probation officer is not justified in concluding he has not helped a delinquent because his delinquency persists. He may have checked a career in crime by his casework, but may never know this.

The interview is the chief tool of the probation officer in his treatment work. The capacity to be relaxed and get the delinquent to relax develops only after experience. It will not develop quickly if the probation officer is working under the pressure of a big case load, or is on a staff that demands quick results. One cannot speed up casework on order without affecting the result. The delinquent, it must be recalled, has been sent to the agency; he has not come for help. He would have preferred to go on in his own way of delinquency, to have his pleasures without meeting reality. He has little interest in our taking this only adjustment he knows away from him. He has enjoyed the behavior that has furnished him an outlet for his hostility to a society that has rejected him and that he in turn has rejected. He must be wooed for a long time, in many instances, to keep the resentment down, if he is to continue trying to behave acceptably. There will be more temptations that will pull him back to delinquency than will keep him working with a social agency. Any pressure may start him off on a delinquent career if it stirs up the resentment that made him delinquent in the first place. The task of keeping the delinquent close to the probation officer is easier if he can find something tangible in the treatment that allows the delinquent to feel the probation officer is doing something for him. In the larger cities membership in a Y.M.C.A., a part time job, tutoring help, and removal from sources of unhappiness are useful.

Effecting Changes After Confidence Has Been Established

After the probation officer has gained the confidence of the delinquent, he will be in a position to make those changes in the delinquent's surroundings which he believes are important. The statement is made in this manner purposely because of our interest in the individual delinquent at this point in the discussion. One can make many changes in the environment that will not touch the delinquent, unless he is interested in seeing these changes made. The probation officer will be much further ahead in getting him to see the value of living in a foster home, before moving him. Many of our failures in foster-home placement of the older child result from the fact that everyone wants him in a foster home except the boy himself. He wants to be with his own neighborhood group, prefers his companions in school and the home that he may be able to dominate. To give him a choice early between a delinquency institution and a foster home does not help matters much, because then the foster home represents to him a method of punishment. It is a different matter if he is told later in the treatment when the probation officer's counsel means something to him, that he will be smart to get away from a neighborhood that is largely responsible for his delinquency and give foster-home placement a trial, especially if he is told that the probation officer's interest in him will continue and the probation officer expects to see him often while he is trying to make the new adjustment.

Probation Officer Must Expect Failures Too

It may be well, also, to realize before beginning to deal with delinquents that probation officers will fail with at least half of them through no fault of their own. We often make the mistake of wanting to cure all or most of the delinquents we see. If half of them are helped we still will have done a great service to society. The reaction to the delinquent will be different if we keep this fact in mind. We will be gratified then by the number who improve rather than disillusioned by the number who fail.

In the group of those delinquents who are most likely not to respond to treatment are the mentally retarded, those with organic disease of the central nervous system, and those who are deeply conflicted emotionally. An adolescent who belongs in these groups needs special care that the probation officer alone cannot provide. This does not mean, however, that advantages of casework should not be supplied the delinquent just because the possibility of curing him is remote. Actually, intensive casework may provide the best means of diagnosis—of obtaining the information that will help decide on the need for institutionalization.

This leads to the subject of the neurotic delinquent who has been one of the chief interests of the psychiatrists dealing in problems of social psychiatry. I purposely shall avoid discussing the treatment of the underlying emotional conflicts of the neurotic delinquent, because there is little in the intensive treatment of such an individual that will be a part of casework, without the help of a psychiatrist. Such conflicts are of an unconscious nature, are deeply imbedded, and can only be brought to light by the psychiatrist trained in psychoanalytic techniques.

There are certain phases of the treatment of the neurotic delinquent, however, that can be carried on by the caseworker. First, and foremost, is again the development of a relationship that will lessen the need to vent his hostility on others and to attack himself. Psychoanalytic observations have demonstrated the presence of an excessive amount of cruelty in the neurotic delinquent who reacts to these deep drives with a feeling of guilt and a need for punishment. Most agencies have had experience with adolescents, bright enough to know better, who have managed their delinquencies—without being aware of it—in such a way that they were apprehended easily and punished. What happens in the everyday life of the delinquent is that small frustrations in the home, and in the school, stir up the more serious underlying frustration that has always been with him. To be denied the lesser things means again that they are not loved, that they are rejected, and that their efforts to change the status quo will never get them any place. The probation officer must keep in mind the fact that the neurotic delinquent almost invariably comes from a family where other members, particularly the parents, are neurotic, and that there are, therefore, numberless opportunities for stirring up the feeling of hopelessness and revolt. The probation officer may be an all important person in breaking up this vicious circle. A positive tie may make it possible for the delinquent to find the kind, accepting parent in the probation officer unless the delinquent is too overwhelmed with guilt. To the delinquent it may mean that all adults are not cruel and rejecting, but it will not mean this during the first few weeks. He will have to be convinced of the probation officer's being well-meaning, and consistent, over and over again. If, and when, he can give up his need to change his own parent and accept the probation officer as a substitute, in some instances the delinquency will stop—there will be no more need for its existence.

At the same time it may be possible for the probation officer to work with the neurotic parents, at least to see that something is done for them. Sometimes it is inadvisable for the same probation officer to work with the delinquent and the parent, because of jealousies that arise and the possible needs of each to interfere with the satisfaction of the other. There are many things that can be said about the casework treatment with the family of the delinquent, but I am omitting them at this time. It is sufficient to say that unless this casework is done, the work with the individual delinquent in most instances will suffer.

To get back to the problem of direct treatment with the delinquent—the probation officer must keep in mind the fact that in most instances the delinquent is suffering from feelings of inferiority. These grow out of his school failure and his rejection in the home and community. The school failure has resulted from a lack of motivation and the development of poor work habits, since school work is hard work and the child does not work unless he is making somebody happy through his work. This feeling of loyalty is usually lacking in these delinquents. Sometimes the feeling of inferiority comes from a feeling of guilt related to masturbation and other sexual practices. The delinquent may be sensitive about an alcoholic father, or psychotic parent.

Anything that will strengthen the ego of the delinquent will lessen his feeling of inferiority and in turn make him feel more secure. The biggest ego boost will come from the realization that he is good enough, and worthy enough to be accepted by the probation officer. If the probation officer can get the delinquent's permission to go to his school, talk to his principal and teachers, the probation officer may be able to arrange the delinquent's schedule in a way that will make it possible for him to enjoy school. Perhaps he can change his school or be allowed to drop one of his subjects. The probation officer may even motivate him to study for the first time in his life. He may be able to get the school to help him in his attempts to change the delinquent's attitude toward school and life.

Checking Emotional Disturbances One of the Main Functions of the Probation Officer

To sum up, one of the probation officer's main functions will be to check anything that emotionally disturbs the delinquent. He will have to search carefully among the various situations to which the delinquent is exposed and reduce friction wherever possible. In the home, he may locate favoritism for another child, an overly critical father, a nagging, rejecting aunt. These influences will have to be controlled or the irritation will continue daily—hourly—and keep the boy in a state of turmoil with a need to fight back either to punish or in an attempt to reduce the tension. In the school, he may be trying to do 7th grade work though only able to do 5th grade work; or he may be able to do 7th grade work well, but be totally deficient in reading. The failures to compete successfully with his fellow students can cause more or less continuous unrest. Or he may be picked on by several older boys, or under the influence of an older sexual pervert whom he fears, and feel guilty and ashamed of this behavior. These and many more precipitating factors may keep him in a state of conflict or rebellion which invites the many forms of behavior that neurotic delinquency assumes. This does not mean that there is a lesser need than always to get at the underlying unconscious factors also, but this is not the function of the probation officer.

Perhaps the probation officer will be fortunate enough to get him to discuss spontaneously his preoccupation with sexual problems an anxiety about what will happen because of his masturbation. The probation officer's assurance that masturbation does not cause insanity, and his continued acceptance of him in spite of his behavior, may go a long way towards relieving the delinquent of tension and worry. The prevailing attitude in all his contacts with him must be one of optimism, and this must persist when the probation officer fails and the boy is sent to an institution. The probation officer's interest in his welfare must continue so that his relationship can be re-established when he leaves the institution.

Demands for quick decisions present themselves more often in dealing with young delinquents than with other child welfare problems. Pressure is applied to get immediate action because the community wants to be rid of the delinquent's hostility and aggression. It would be unfortunate if the probation officer yielded to this pressure and formulated a plan before he knew all the important contributing factors. One learns by experience that there are few real emergent situations that cannot wait long enough to permit thorough study—without which needless errors are made. To deal intelligently with each child, so that a diagnosis of the child, and of the total situation in which the child finds himself, can be established, requires a limitation of cases assigned to the individual worker. There are few probation officers who can handle successfully a case load of more than thirty or forty young delinquents, and when one hears that a probation officer is dealing with 100 to 150 juvenile delinquents, the conclusion must be reached that most of the cases are inactive, or the work is of a superficial nature.

I purposely have emphasized what a probation officer can do with young delinquents, independent of the help he can receive from a child guidance clinic or an out-patient psychiatric department in a hospital, because so many probation officers are not in a position to take advantage of these services.

A THERAPEUTIC APPROACH TO PROBATION AND PAROLE*

There are two major approaches to the treatment of criminal behavior. One approach assumes that criminal behavior is learned in the same way as any other kind of behavior. According to this approach, the presence of criminal behavior does not indicate the

---

* Printed by permission of the author Albert E. Quade, Ph.D. from an original unpublished manuscript. Florida State University, 1957.

presence of neurotic, maladjusted, or antisocial personality traits. The other approach sees criminal behavior as a manifestation of such neurotic tendencies as inferiority feelings, irrational hostility, self-hatred, etc. This paper is directed toward those cases of criminal behavior where there are observable manifestations of personality maladjustment and where some form of psychotherapy is indicated. Although what follows is related to the probation officer, the same approach is also applicable to the work of parole officers in particular and counselors in general.

An individual placed in the role of a counselor, has, generally speaking, three major problems confronting him. First of all, there is the problem of how to relate to his client. If he errs in relating himself properly he finds that his own behavior is more inclined to reinforce the defenses of his client, thereby reinforcing his general maladjustment. To avoid the danger of making the client worse, the counselor is usually advised to be respectful of the patient's individuality, to accept him as a person, to treat him honestly and fairly at all times, to be consistent in his approach. The beginner, generally, has no difficulty in finding sufficient books and articles to advise him as to how to approach his client.

The next problem is that of diagnosis. The counselor must develop his ability to take the content materials presented to him by the client and organize them into some kind of a consistent structure. Those trained in the traditional schools are most likely to organize the material according to the theories presented by such pioneers as Freud, Jung and Adler. An academic psychologist is more likely to organize the material along the lines of learning theory. The sociologist will organize the same material according to development of the self-concept within a group structure. *So far as effective counseling is concerned, the question is not which of these theoretical orientations is most important, realistic, or popular, but rather that the counselor be firmly rooted in one or another of them.* Generally speaking, skilled counselors in one discipline have about as much success as skilled counselors from other disciplines. A strong theoretical background is of great importance in assisting the counselor in defining the nature of the problem, and assessing its most probable causes.

The third major problem is that of therapy. There are many aspiring counselors who can orient themselves well to the treatment of the client, and can develop excellent rapport with their clients. They move onto the stage of diagnosis and do a very creditable job, but they are often surprised to see that after extensive hours of diagnosis there are no apparent changes in either the client's attitudes or his behavior. It is unfortunate that from the therapeutic viewpoint an excellent diagnosis sometimes functions only to increase the client's negative conception of himself. The mother, for example, who has been taken into custody for abandoning her children, may plead that she is fearful that her children might die. This might be properly diagnosed as a rationalization of an unconscious death wish. Unfortunately, for the client, this only serves to destroy her defense mechanisms and leave her more vulnerable to her own negative attitudes toward herself as a person.

We are concerned here with both the problem of diagnosis and the problem of therapy, giving special attention to those techniques which are therapeutically effective.

The primary consideration in any form of therapy is the extent to which the client manifests self-acceptance. Various schools of psychological thought have assigned different terminology to this concept, but basically, they all treat it similarly. The analytic schools refer to self-acceptance as ego strength. The sociological and psycho-sociological refer to this as *self concept*. This concept easily distinguishes between the well adjusted individual who adjusts the satisfaction of his needs to the culture in which he lives, and the maladjusted individual who is unable to adjust himself to society. There is usually a definite and predictable relationship between how an individual sees himself and how he adjusts that self to his cultural milieu. The individual who is basically satisfied with himself as a person assumes, unconsciously, that other people, once they come to know him, will find him as likeable as he finds himself. His general behavior pattern, therefore, in the presence of other persons is to express himself so that others come to see him as he is and develop a basis for liking him.

A person with a negative self concept, or low ego strength, dislikes himself with varying degrees of intensity, for possessing feelings, attitudes, that run counter to his moral and ethical standards. Not liking himself, he is never able to find concrete reasons why other persons would find him likeable. Horney believes that there are three general adjustments the individual makes to negative self concept. First of all, the individual is strongly inclined to reject his own convictions as a guide for life, and to use instead the approval of others. Counselors of sexual delinquents are often surprised to find that the actions of the sexual delinquent run counter to her own moral convictions. Seeing herself as an unlikeable individual, the sexual delinquent is left only with sex to use as an attraction to the male. Since, in this case, the need for approval is an over compensation for the feelings of self-disapproval, such individuals will be found engaging in behavior which violently contradicts their own moral codes, but which they feel will bring them some measure of approval from others. The same principle is at work in delinquent gangs. There are many adolescents who are not proud of the behavior patterns in which they engage, nonetheless, they continue these patterns seeking the approval of their peers.

A second adjustment to self-rejection is hostility. The hostile client, like the compliant individual discussed above, is almost completely organized personality-wise to believe that the rewards of life are attainable only by submission to the whims, desires and caprices of others. Whereas the compliant individual sees no alternative and prefers to maintain the existing pattern, the hostile person rebels at the belief that he will not be accepted as an individual. The over-expression of hostility does not really differentiate the hostile client from the compliant individual. There is about as much hostility in the compliant individual, but since expression of hostility would run counter to attempts to win approval, the compliant person inevitably represses the hostility. The primary motive in both personality types is over compensation for feelings of self rejection.

A third adjustment to a negative self concept is withdrawal. This individual can see no reasons why other individuals will accept him as a person. Whereas the hostile client becomes angry with others because they refuse to accept him, the withdrawn person sees no reason for acceptance. His only alternative is to retire from people. If he enters into crime he is likely to be a "lone wolf" operator. One should not assume that his client will fall clearly into one or another of these categories. Some clients will at times be compliant, and alternate this with periods of withdrawal. Some clients may vacillate between stages of withdrawal and hostility. A number of combinations are possible. This need not be confusing to the counselor, however, since he may safely assume that in each case, or in any combination of cases, the basic problem remains that of a negative self concept.

The primary function of diagnosis is to probe behind this superficial veneer of compliancy, hostility or withdrawal, and show the client that his basic motive is an attempt to win affection from others, even though he sees nothing about himself that merits approval, acceptance or affection.

The primary objective of therapy, then, is to increase the client's self-acceptance to the point where his behavior is no longer governed by the approval or disapproval of those about him. It should be apparent to the reader that a brilliant diagnosis may leave the client with only a more painful feeling of how unlikeable a person he is, and may give him no clues as to what factors produced such negative feelings, and what behaviors might assist the client in overcoming them.

Another objective of therapy is to get the individual to a point where his behavior is self-determining, is consistent with his own moral and ethical codes, and his convictions about life in general. These two objectives are not at all inconsistent, since the individual, once he realizes the nature of the factors which made him dislike himself and comes to see himself as a likeable person, builds self respect by sticking to his convictions and defending them even though this might bring disapproval or hostility from those about him. This does not mean that we attempt to assist the client in reaching a position where he is no longer interested in the approval of others. What he should come to realize is that approval is wholesome, but that it is unhealthy for him to go to the point where he violates his own convictions to win that approval. The better adjusted person is very aware of approval from others but he will not yield his individuality to violate his convictions in order to win more approval. The very fact that he defends his convictions and often thereby wins greater approval, gives him the feeling of pride and self respect that he did not have previously. Attempts to compensate for self-rejection by winning the approval of others appears to be disturbingly common. Unfortunately, the practice is almost always self-defeating. The individual usually starts out submitting to others in order to gain certain goals. As the process continues, however, the goals become sacrificed to win approval. In the end the client is left without a feeling of identity or individuality. It is erroneous to assume that there are no goals, objectives, or convictions in these clients. What is more likely is that these have been repressed in favor of approval. An understanding of the following behavior patterns will assist the counselor in making a more correct diagnosis of his client, and will orient him more directly toward the therapeutic process.

(a) Probation officers are too often deceived by the semantic meaning of the term "compliancy." They expect to see an individual groveling, apologetic, and retiring. On the contrary, an extremely compliant individual might superficially appear to be quite friendly, outgoing and talkative. The clue, therefore, is not so much in the overt behavior of the individual as much as it is in the content of his conversation. If the probation officer listens closely he will begin to realize that although client may speak fluently, feelings are never manifested. The client may go into great detail describing experiences which he has had, but he at no time reveals to the probation officer the nature of his emotional reactions in those experiences. He has a good reason for not doing so. He is afraid that not liking these feelings in himself he will provoke similar negative reactions in his counselor. For example, he may describe a situation in which the average person would become angry. At no time in his discussion does the client indicate he was angry, nor does he indicate any angry feelings as he recounts the situation. He fears that this anger will be punished by the counselor. If the tendency in the client to conceal feelings is especially strong, the counselor will note a "flatness" in the client's tone of voice. Other clients, somewhat more sophisticated, will attempt to conceal their feelings, attitudes and opinions, behind a veneer of popular cliches. The absence of feeling should always be reflected back to the client, so that he becomes aware of the fact that in his social interactions with others he represses those feelings which constitute the essence of his being. A well adjusted person is quite free in expressing his feelings on all matter of subjects. Such a person is easy to relate to because others know where he stands. In the maladjusted person, there are usually feelings of inadequacy or fear of failure so far as human inter-relationships are concerned.

(b) The second important characteristic which may also appear in disguised form, is the feeling of worthlessness. The only mani-festation of this in the initial counseling situation may be an apology for wasting the counselor's time. Most clients in a mar-riage counseling situation are baffled by the question, "Do you feel that you are a loveable person?" The juvenile delinquent and the adult criminal is also equally baffled by the question, "Do you feel that you are a likeable person?" Often such individuals will respond glibly that they are. When the counselor follows up with a question such as, "What is it about you that is likeable?" the client is again baffled and usually incapable of offering a single trait of his personality that he sees as likeable. At this point the untutored counselor almost inevitably hastens to reassure the client that he is indeed likeable, and almost inevitably client interprets the reassurance as a selfishly motivated attempt on the part of the counselor to appear kind, polite, and interested. Ex-perienced counselors realize that assurance rarely accomplishes more than a temporary good feeling in the client. There is a high correlation between the ability to accept one's self as one is and the ability to accept others as they are. The well adjusted coun-selor, therefore, who basically accepts himself, will also be in-clined to accept his client. It may surprise him that this appar-ently likeable person suffers with such intense feelings of self hatred.

(c) Another clue to self-rejection is over-emphasis by the client of the importance of achievement. Finding nothing in himself likeable to other persons, the client often takes the second alter-native of achieving goals which will bring acceptance and respect. Such individuals are characterized by compulsive achievement drives. In some cases they actually do achieve high levels of attainment. Unfortunately, this does not solve their basic problem, since they feel that the acceptance that they have now gained is still not on the basis of themselves as an individual, but rather on the basis of achievement. Such individuals are inclined to be dissatisfied with their own achievements, and continually strive toward more acceptable and socially approved achievements. Our culture places great emphasis upon personal improvement and achievement. If he is not wary, the counselor may be deluded into accepting this aspect of his client's behavior as a normal trait in this culture. Consequently, he may overlook the fact that an attempt to better one's self is based psychologically on the premise that one is not good to begin with. Juvenile delinquents are often inclined to define delinquent acts as forms of achievement. The "stoolie" is often an useful adjunct to law enforcement because some criminals are so inclined to boast about their criminal achievements. In law violations, were this not an essential part of the dynamics of self-rejection, many criminals would go unapprehended. The law violator is often averse to going straight because the achievements of a more mundane life are not sufficient to compensate for his feelings of worthlessness. He abhors the more quiet and inconspicuous life of the law abider. The drive toward achievement does not always motivate the individual toward criminal behavior. In fact, an identical drive may lead the individual to achieve eminence in a profession. It is noteworthy that even though professional achievement may command respect many such individuals are incompetent to carry on wholesome relationships with their family, friends, and colleagues. The criminal achiever often finds himself in the same predicament.

The notion that achievement can be a matter for therapeutic concern may be obscured by the fact that we live in a culture which puts great emphasis upon individual achievement. There are two factors which the probation officer should be cognizant of at all times. First, he should remember that the individual may be using achievement to mask feelings of personal unworthiness; and secondly, that the avenues toward achievement may take anti-social tendencies and appear as criminal actions. Because of the feelings of unworthiness and inferiority are so great, the normal daily rewards and achievements of the law abiding citizen may be insufficient compensations for the maladjusted individual. Achievement is meaningless to him unless it supersedes the achievements of the average person. Furthermore, the achievements of the maladjusted individual serve only temporarily to over-compensate for the feelings of inferiority. Consequently, achievements must come frequently, and must be outstanding.

The feelings of inferiority which usually underlie strong achievement motives may, on occasion, be temporarily masked by the fact that a recent achievement sufficiently over-compensates for the feelings of inferiority. Considering the gang, his peers, and the criminal group as his frame of reference, both arrest and sentence may serve only to reinforce in his own mind the achievement factor. The probation officer attempting to reorient the probationer to an acceptable socially conforming type of life, may often overlook the fact that the rewards of this type of life are insufficient to over-compensate for the feelings of rejection. He may struggle with persuasion, cajoling, reassurance, and many other tricks of the trade, and still find that he meets with defeat. His real problem is that he is not properly oriented to the basic emotional impulses arising from within the client.

So far as therapy is concerned, it is important that the individual be brought to realize that the basic motive force behind his tendency to engage in criminal behavior is his strong sense of self-rejection. The first attempts on the part of the probation officer to relate this information to his client may result in a considerable amount of defensiveness on the part of the probationer. Accusing the probationer of being defensive or resisting, usually serves only to increase the intensity of the defensiveness. There is another important vital element which underlies the major problem. In order to preserve some measure of self respect, the individual is strongly inclined to rationalize his perception of life, and to project this rationalization into his understanding of the world of people in which he lives. Each individual develops his self concept out of the reflections he receives from the treatment accorded him by others. If the treatment he receives is essentially negative in the nature, the materials he has to use to build his self concepts are essentially negative. In his developmental period most of these negative reflections were from those close to him, parent figures, relatives, peers, etc. The individual "generalizes" from his own particular experiences and expects similar treatment from all those with whom he comes in contact. He is able to build a quite logically consistent conception of the world of people in which he lives, which is highly consistent with his own developmental experiences but which might be quite contradictory to the attitudes and outlooks of the probation officer, whose background was probably more favorable and more accepting of him as an individual. When the probation officer attempts to persuade his charge to accept the idea that he is a likeable person and that he would be even more likeable if he conformed to social norms, his comments sound essentially strange and unrealistic. The first resistance of the probationer, therefore, should not be immediately interpreted as an unwillingness to accept what the probation officer offers. The counselor should understand that although his own comments are true, they do not strike his client as being either true or logical. The client might wish with all his heart that what the probation worker says is true. His own experiences assure him that, although this would be a desirable state of affairs, it is not a realistic approach to life. The probation worker and the parole worker are often accused by their clients of having a ridiculously unrealistic attitude toward real world in which life must be carried on.

Secondly, the attempts on the part of the probation officer to inform the client of his feelings of inferiority might meet with defensive measures; because, although true, these interpretations conflict with the image the client has of the kind of a person he wants to be. A male struggling to manifest at all times, red-blooded, masculine behavior, might be inclined to be strongly resistive to interpretations which reveal him to himself as being less than what he wishes to be. A straightforward presentation of this type of diagnosis often leads to resistance. The probation officer must take another approach to the problem. He should remember that this individual strongly wants approval from others, in fact, this is his *raison d'être* for living. Because he is so desperate for the approval of others he often, as indicated above, attempts to do what will please others. If the counselor approaches this as a self-sacrificing attitude, the individual is much more likely to respond favorably to it, since there is implicit a sense of injustice to the client. Instead of seeing the probation officer as an antagonist, he comes to see him as someone who is sympathetic with his position. Unfortunately a probation agent is often deceived by the antagonistic and hostile attitude he receives. It does not seem to him logical that there lies behind surface behavior strong self-sacrificing feelings. If he can accept the assumption that self-rejection lies behind compliancy, hostility and withdrawal, he will not be so inclined to be thrown off the track by the more aggressive responses.

Once the compliant or self-sacrificing aspect has been accepted by the client, the next task of the probation agent is to reinforce the conception. Although the client may have been aware of feelings of inferiority, he either has not gained insight into their influence on his interactions with others, or they seem so right that it has never occurred to him to question them. One approach to this type of reinforcement is to encourage a client to pay close attention to the manner in which he responds to those with whom he must interact. He should be encouraged to note how many times he feels free to assert himself, and how many times, comparatively, he tries to go along with those with whom he interacts. The client will often return to the probation officer overwhelmed by the degree of submissiveness in his own behavior. On the other hand, it is surprising how often the client is able to persuade the probation officer that these interpretations are basically incorrect. The client often attempts to prove his own self-assertion by citing incidents in which he spoke sharply to those with whom he interacted. If the probation officer will look closely he will notice that those to whom the probationer speaks sharply, are people who "don't count." They are underlings whose approval is not particularly important. The picture immediately changes when persons whose approval is important is discussed. It is important at this point to realize that no effective therapy can be expected until the client has accepted his diagnosis of his behavior and its motive.

If the client accepts this diagnosis, and if the diagnosis is reinforced by measuring the diagnosis against actual behavior, the next step is to encourage the client to test the hypothesis of self-assertion. First attempts at self-assertion on the part of the individual will be essentially reflections of the maladjusted personality with which he is already troubled, and the assertions are likely to be both unrealistic and anti-social. The first impulse of the probation officer is usually to react against these attempts of self-assertion, since they are both unrealistic and anti-social. This impulse on the part of the probation officer usually counteracts the first healthy tendencies. Unfortunately, the role of the probation officer is often so defined that he is given no freedom whatsoever to respond to these first maladjusted self-assertions in an accepting fashion.

Suffice it to say in this paper, that a considerable amount of analysis and reorganization of the probation officer's role is necessary if he is to become an effective therapist attempting to reorganize the attitude, impulses and feelings of the client toward a more conforming attitude toward society's expectations. Although the probation agent accepts these negative assertions on the part of his charge, this does not mean that he agrees with these self-assertions. The assertions may be essentially emotional in nature, and may be attitudes of resentment or hostility toward the probation officer. The fact that the probation officer, an individual of some importance in the client's life, is willing to accept these feelings manifested toward him, is sometimes the first experience the client has had in asserting himself to an individual in authority, and having assertion accepted. The acceptance by the counselor often forces the client to reconsider the intent of his hostile gesture.

As the individual learns to assert himself as an individual, a number of his outstanding symptoms begin to diminish. Second, as he asserts his opinions and feelings, he finds that they are at least respected by others. His own esteem in his ability to affect people is enhanced. As he moves into the stage of asserting himself, he often becomes confused. He is attempting to reach toward a better adjusted orientation toward the world in which he lives, but he is required to do so with a maladjusted personality. The confusion arises over the fact that some of his self-assertion involves hostility developed by his maladjusted attitude.

He sometimes finds severe defeat in attempts at self-assertion, because instead of being defensive of his rights and expressions of himself as a person, these self-assertions are often expressions of his negative attitudes. This point should be clarified with the client. If the attempts at self-assertion are successful, the client begins to experience a sense of freedom he has never known before. He feels better since he is defending his convictions; he feels better that individuals outside himself respect those convictions, and he sees a world of freedom to himself opening before him.

Again, he is somewhat inclined to be defeated by the maladjusted personality with which he is operating. Very often, although he senses and realizes the great implications of freedom, he has not yet given up his conception that other individuals are domineering, exploitative, selfish, greedy, etc. He now begins to build defenses to protect the measure of freedom he has attained.

Usually, his first defense is that of complete emotional and economic independence from others. He may begin to manifest to his probation officer an apparently healthy interest in preparing himself for some occupation. The counselor should look closely at the motives of the client at this point. Very often the client believes that although his freedom is a wonderful experience, it will be taken away from him. He continues to believe, at this point, that others still expect him to comply before they will give him personal and social rewards. The individual now believes that this is not possible, and begins to build a world of total independence. His inclination in this direction should be again brought to his attention. When he reaches a state of sound personal and social adjustment, he will have come to realize that his early attempts to generalize and assume negative response from everyone is erroneous. On the contrary, he should not be persuaded to believe the opposite is true, i.e., that all individuals are kind and generous and faithful. Instead, he should arrive at a point where he is able to differentiate between those who are accepting and trustworthy, and those who are not.

This transitional stage between the client's old maladjusted conception and the development of newer more realistic conceptions, will be a stage of confusion, disorientation and sometimes crisis. The old conception, although erroneous, was a conception which gave him a feeling of security. As he moves into the newer conception he feels insecure in the transitional stage. He has no definite convictions one way or another to orient himself. He is caught between seeing the error of earlier conceptions, and yet not being sufficiently persuaded to accept the realities of the newer conceptions. To terminate the counseling at this time presents dangers to the client, because he has less to orient himself to than he had before the diagnostic and therapeutic periods began.

During the entire period of time in which the probation worker has been attempting to show the client the nature of adjustment to life, there should be attempts to show the probationer how his feelings of self-rejection developed in his early developmental era. From the causative analysis of those factors in early developmental years which created his self rejecting attitudes, the client often infers that given other circumstances he would have developed differently. The counselor should watch closely to see whether the client draws this inference. If he does not, the counselor should make it his responsibility to specify this implication clearly.

Implied in this corrective approach is the educational function of the counselor. Too often the client is beset with the idea that his behavior is inherited. So long as he believes that his tendencies toward crime are congenital he cannot believe that anything can be done about them. The counselor's attempts to emphasize the causative relationship between background factors and personality development show the client that there were alternative modes of development.

The counselor's effectiveness is often counteracted by the age of the client. This approach will be much less effective with a client fifty years of age than one closer to twenty. The older client will have fifty years of reinforcement of his erroneous concept toward life. The probability that this can be altered in the amount of time available to the counselor is minimal. On the other hand, this approach will be highly effective with the youthful offender who has not as many years of experience which serve to reinforce his negative and anti-social conceptions of life. Another important factor which affects this approach to correction, is the degree to which the client believes he can trust his probation agent. The very fact that he is on probation may incline the client to conceal from the probation agent those very experiences which necessitate thorough analysis. The probation worker is therefore beset by handicaps which do not ordinarily confront the counselor whose clients come to him on a voluntary basis. In ordinary circumstances, the material related to a counselor by the client will be held in the strictest of confidence at all times. For the probation officer this is not usually the case. He is required, often times by law, to place in the probation's file an accurate record of what transpired as his knowledge of the client increases. Those agencies whose organizational structure prevents the probation officer from holding in confidence material presented to him by the client can expect to have a higher rate of recidivism.

If the client responds to this form of treatment with a greater acceptance of himself as a person, he inevitably develops a greater acceptance of, and respect for, those about him. He discards his old notions of compliancy, or hostile resistance against compliancy, and develops pride in his own new found ability to accept and respect others for what they are. It should be noted that an implicit assumption underlying this approach, is the faith in the client to develop a more socially conforming attitude given the freedom to do so. The counselor who does have the faith in the clients who come to him will find the approach discussed here entirely unsuitable to his own personality.

MEASURING THE EFFECTIVENESS OF PROBATION*

Probation today is well establshed as one of the most common methods of handling criminal offenders. In the California superior courts, the proportion of persons placed on probation ranges from 20 to 65 per cent of those convicted, depending on the county. The general state average is 44 per cent. At least 95 per cent of delinquent youths declared wards of the juvenile court are placed on probation. There is an ever-increasing use of probation in the case of misdemeanant offenders convicted in the inferior courts.

---

* Reprinted by permission of California Youth Authority. Ronald H. Beattie: *Measuring the Effectiveness of Probation,* California Youth Authority Quarterly, Vol. 10, No. 2, Summer 1957, p. 33-36.

The probation departments of the State report a higher case count for such cases than for those received from the superior courts. In fact, if every suspended sentence were to be considered a grant of probation, then the inferior court probation placements would exceed more than 200,000 cases a year. With probation playing such a dominant part in the handling of criminal offenders, it becomes a matter of importance to seek for methods of selection and supervision that seem to produce the most satisfactory results.

Probation should be more than merely a method of assigning convicted offenders to the administrative control of a probation department. Probation supervision implies not only keeping track of the probationer, but also the positive responsibility of rendering aid and counsel to the probationer and assisting him to adjust to his life situation without resort to criminal behavior. In fact, probation responsibility is becoming recognized more and more as involving professional casework methods and treatment of these offenders.

How is the general effectiveness of probation to be determined? Today, the major emphasis on the methods of handling convicted offenders has shifted from objectives of retribution and deterrence to the more positive aim of rehabilitation. By this is meant primarily that the offender will refrain from engaging in further criminal conduct. While the matter of working with human individuals to change or modify their general course of behavior is a most complex operation, the final objective can still be stated in reasonably simple terms; to reduce the repeated criminal conduct of the offender, or to prevent it entirely. Thus, one of the basic measurements as to the effectiveness of the process is to be found in the behavior after they have been placed on probation.

In the first place, it must be pointed out that measures of rates of recidivism are of necessity stated in negative terms. Many practitioners argue that the success of correctional treatment should be measured in positive terms rather than in negative violation rates. However, as the only commonly accepted objective of these treatment procedures is to minimize repetition of crime, these procedures can be measured only in terms of the amount of repetition that exists. This type of measurement compares with the standards that are used to determine the general health of the community which is to be measured in terms of morbidity and death rates. In the same way, the general health and effectiveness of correctional treatment is to be measured in the criminal behavior (i.e., violation) rates, and presumably the lower the rate, the more effective the treatment.

Measurements of the effectiveness of probation in these terms will not be the same for the different areas of probation. A somewhat different yardstick will have to be used for each of the three probation operations, adult felony, adult misdemeanor, and juvenile.

Felony Probation

In the case of felony probation, the amount of serious criminal behavior that occurs on the part of probationers during their probation period becomes a measure of the effectiveness of the probation operation. Much more attention and care must be given to recording the facts of criminal behavior on the part of persons on probation in order to insure the validity of recidivism rates and to demonstrate the level of criminal conduct. Possibly, credit can be taken for progress even if the probationer continues in criminal behavior if it can be shown that such behavior is of a diminishing seriousness in degree.

Inasmuch as felony probation is used in about half of the cases convicted, the matter of selection of offenders for probation as contrasted to either prison or jail sentence is a factor of considerable importance in the ultimate effectiveness of the probation operation. There are bound to be differences in the violation rates for different kinds of offenders who are placed on probation. To determine in what cases violation rates may be high and in what cases low, and the general circumstances and conditions of supervision that are associated with these differentials, will aid materially in evaluating when probation can be used most effectively, under what conditions of supervision, and how long such probation should be in effect.

Misdemeanor Probation

Probation at the inferior court level offers an even more difficult problem in determining what criteria might be developed for measuring the effectiveness of probation. Persons placed on probation by these courts are involved in problems of behavior that are not criminal offenses in the same sense as crimes against persons and property. These include many offenders charged with drunkenness and disorderly conduct, prostitution, or vagrancy. Even the offenses of simple assault and petty theft do not arouse the level of concern for persons and property that the felony offenses of these types do. Public opinion as a whole is not too concerned about the punishment of misdemeanor offenders in terms of retribution and deterrence; and, until very recent times when probation services became more widespread, there was little concern about rehabilitation. By and large, this is a class of offenders that is considered more a nuisance than a danger to society, and there is even some disagreement as to the degree of surveillance to be given such offenders. Even a repetition of minor offenses is not considered as too aggravating. In fact, it is generally expected and anticipated. How under these circumstances can any criteria be designed to measure the effectiveness of probation for such misdemeanor offenders? Presumably the general objective would be the same as in felony cases to reduce or eliminate the possibility of misdemeanor offenders repeating their offenses. The knowledge of further misdemeanor behavior must come from identification and conviction records that in instances of misdemeanor offenses are often most incomplete. Before measurements of this kind can be developed, there will have to be first a real concentrated effort made to record in accessible form and in uniform terms information on all misdemeanor convictions.

Juvenile Probation

Practically every juvenile who has been declared a ward of the court for delinquency is placed on probation, and very little incarceration is used in these cases. Seldom is a juvenile committed to the Youth Authority or a county camp until he has already been supervised and treated for some time under probation. In the juvenile area, therefore, there is not a great problem of differentiating between those who will be placed on probation and those who will not be placed on probation. How is the effectiveness of treatment to be measured in these cases? If the criteria of success is that there should be no further conflict with the law, there is a particularly difficult problem of actually defining juvenile conduct that is in "conflict with the law." The span of officially recognized juvenile misbehavior is so broad that it does not coincide with the scope of criminal offenses. The natural exuberance, and irresponsibility of youth often lead them into activity customarily described by some unevaluative form such as "wayward" or "incorrigible." There is a certain inherent rebellion and conflict with the processes of parental and social control throughout adolescence, and the fact that a youth on probation continues to show some conflict with authority is not necessarily to be used as a measurement of failure. In the juvenile field there have never been developed consistent records of behavior on the part of probationers which could be uniformly used to indicate from time to time and place to place the amount or degree of violation.

Possibly the most logical approach to developing criteria for juvenile probation would be to record as violations only those traits or behavior activities which are of a serious nature, and yet it is very difficult to distinguish from the information available in juvenile records those acts which reflect serious offenses from those that may reflect much less serious conduct. It seems unlikely, however, that much progress can be made in the juvenile probation field until there are more specific definitions of the types of behavior that occur on the part of the probationers, until some agreement is reached on what constitutes sufficiently serious misbehavior to be gauged in an evaluation of the effectiveness of probation, and until a systemic procedure for recording such information for summary and analysis is evolved.

This discussion has basically indicated that to measure the effectiveness of probation in terms of the purposes of probation recognized by the community, the criminal behavior of probationers will have to be identified and recorded in such a way as to produce a yardstick for this measurement. One method of describing criminal behavior would be to set forth the actions of the probationer in terms of the number of recorded violations or revocations of probation. The great weakness in this procedure is that such information is not readily or consistently available, and extended efforts must be made to record the necessary data.

Complete information should be in the record not only for the purposes of determining violation rates, but also as a part of the case history of each probationer. Actually criminal behavior is not always synonymous with official revocations or violations. To get at the real problem of the general effectiveness of probation, it is the actual criminal behavior that must be determined, classified, and compared.

There are many other areas of measurement which will have to be evolved as the processes of probation supervision become better developed and applications are made in line with scientific controls. It may be possible to determine degrees of adjustment or movement on the part of persons under probation treatment who do not violate the laws so that it can be better determined what the real positive values are of certain types of treatment in certain types of cases as against mere absence of negative values. But such developments can hardly precede determination of basic differences of violation rates among different classes of probationers. In any event, the objective is to develop a standard measurement. We have to have a mean or established norm on which to judge whether or not changes take place under different conditions or circumstances. It is not too important whether the norm be considered high or low as long as it is uniform and consistent, for the real evaluation of probation effectiveness comes from determining how much variation there is from the norm, and not from any inherent meaning as to how high the norm is set.

The development of criteria and plans for measuring the effectiveness of probation must come about through the thinking and constructive criticism that is engendered on the part of the practitioners in the field. Those who are responsible for the statistical collection, analysis, and evaluation can only carry out their part of the service when the information available and the classifications that are used are uniformly accepted by both the practitioner and the research technician as representing real measurements of what goes on in probation.

Chapter Seven

PAROLE: ADMINISTRATIVE ASPECTS

IN AN EARLIER chapter, we considered the historical development of parole. Now, we are proceeding to examine in detail the administrative components of parole practice.

Those charged with the administration of parole policy can be said to have four prinicipal functions. The first of these is to select and place prisoners on parole. The second is to aid, supervise, and provide continuing control of parolees in the community, according to conditions previously established. When the parolee has reached a point in his parole experience that supervision is no longer required, the parole board, as its third function authorizes the discharge of the individual from that status. On the other hand, if the parolee violates the terms of his parole, either through a technical violation or the commission of a new crime, then it is the function of the board to determine whether revocation and return to the institution are necessary.

If the selection of candidates for parole is skillful, there is a favorable possibility that the individual will react satisfactorily to community custody and treatment. Where, at the other extreme, paroles are granted indiscriminately to relieve congestion in prisons, then the abuse will be manifested in a poor success rate and a negative public opinion toward parole.

The parole board is generally the policy-making group with regard to parole. Since parole has the dual goal of *protecting society* and *rehabilitating* the offender, there is always the danger that one or the other direction may be over-emphasized by board policy.

Where the board is solely interested in community protection, (and to some extent it is desirable that the board have such an orientation) the parole agent will be directed to stress rigid surveillance, and allow no flexibility with regard to conformity to conditions. At the opposite extreme, when rehabilitation becomes the sole consideration, the parole officer may permit the community to be endangered by excesses of misconduct of the parolee, using revocation of parole as an undesirable "last resort" method.

Obviously a balance is desirable. When an individual is unable to withstand the pressures of the community and conform to prescribed community mores, and where he is unable to utilize the counseling which his parole officer is ready to provide in the freedom of the community, then it is the function of the parole board to return the parolee to the closed environment of the institution.

On the other hand, as with probation supervision, restraint and restriction, without counseling and other indirect services, are unlikely to effect any true change in character of the individual.

Variations exist, of course, between the different jurisdictions insofar as the nature of restrictions placed upon the parolee are concerned. Uniformity of parole conditions are both desirable and necessary. The National Council on Crime and Delinquency, the American Correctional Association, and the Council on State Government have strongly recommended the adoption of standardized rules of parole practice. The National Conference on Parole (1956) recognized the need for uniform practices and attempted through its nation-wide representation to develop standards which the States may follow in the revision of their own parole policies and procedures.

There now exists, between the States, an Interstate Compact on Parole, which permits the parolee to seek residence and employment in jurisdictions other than the one which incarcerated him, enlarging the opportunities available which may result from a change of employment. A continuing problem, of course, is that of what to do with the individual who has detainers filed pending his release from prison. Should such individuals be granted parole? Can a uniform practice be developed in the United States.

Only as the parole board functions as an integral part of the whole correctional system can it be expected to serve its maximum usefulness.

STRUCTURE AND FUNCTION OF A PAROLE BOARD*

A Right or a Privilege?

From time to time parole boards are confronted with the contention that parole is a matter of right, even though the courts have held quite definitely that it is not right but rather a privilege. If parole were assumed to be a right, it could be exercised by the inmate only when he attains a certain status. (It does approximate a right in the Federal Youth Corrections Act, which guarantees at least a try on parole for two years in certain instances.) The factors which could still restrict parole, assuming it to be a right, are inaccurate or poorly thought out methods of computing time, ineligibility for the prescribed status for certain period, and the loss of status due to forfeited good time. If we called parole a right it is conceivable that the following factors would serve to safeguard the right: statutory requirements for periodic reconsideration, a formal request for reconsideration, and a petition for resentence.

Regardless of our speculation as to whether parole is a right and the insistence of some of those known in prison parlance as "jailhouse lawyers" that parole *is* a right, the cases uniformly hold that parole is not a vested right. From a purely legal point of view and according to parole statutes, parole is a matter of grace and not of right. The federal parole statute of 1913 provided that prisoners serving definite terms were eligible for parole on the service of one-third of their sentence. This limitation still prevails, except for life sentences or sentences of forty-five years or more, in which instances the inmate must serve at least fifteen years before he becomes eligible for parole.

Parole is a privilege accorded at the discretion of the paroling authority. The intent of the framers of the parole law is to provide a latitude which will permit the parole board to develop techniques to change basic attitudes. The board's discretion is not unbridled; it is restricted by the ineligibility of certain offenders for parole, the time which must expire before eligibility is established

---

* Reprinted in part by permission of the National Probation and Parole Association. Scovel Richardson: Parole and the Law, *NPPA Journal*, Vol. 2, No. 1, Jan. 1956, p. 23-30.

under statute, and the waver by an inmate of his privilege to file an application for parole consideration.

Qualifications of Board Members

The exercise of discretion is further ensured by carefully drawn provisions for the appointment of parole board members. According to the job description, members of the United States Board of Parole must have had special training and experience, and must have attained recognition in law, medicine, criminology, penology, psychology, or sociology. On the federal board we have a psychologist, a sociologist, a former warden, a former state parole director, two former probation officers whose formal training was in law, and two lawyers. We feel that this cross section of backgrounds and experiences gives us a quasi-judicial administrative agency of delicate balance. The points of view and disciplines represented—psychological, penological, sociological, and legal—are rarely found in any one person. The systematic exchange of views and ideas in individual cases by such a board and a consensus of a majority of three out of five in decisions to grant, deny, or revoke parole give substantial validity to board actions. Also, the fact that the board hears and passes upon applications for parole in thirty-one institutions located in various parts of the United States and yet has the opportunity to sit *en banc*, to discuss similar and contrasting factual situations in a central office before deciding a case, enables us to avoid great disparity and unbalanced justice in our decisions. Such a *modus operandi* makes it possible for us to achieve a high degree of uniformity without the rigidity of conformity.

Appointment of members of the federal parole board by the President of the United States and confirmation by the Senate after a thorough investigation by Federal Bureau of Investigation insure a careful screening as to fitness and integrity. Definiteness of tenure (six years) makes the positions more attractive than if they were retained only at the pleasure of the appointing officer.

Parole Board Functions

The functions of a parole board should be clearly and fully defined by law, in order that there may be no "gray lines" of authority, obfuscation of authority or unassigned areas of responsibility. The law can be an effective support of parole if its definition of functions is succinct.

The board of parole should be given the responsibility for the exercise of all quasi-judicial functions with respect to the grant, denial, and revocation of parole; re-parole and conditional re-release; establishment of rules and regulations for parole and parole supervision; imposition or modification of the conditions of parole or conditional release; issuance of warrants and orders of revocation; and establishment of general parole policies. This authority should be clearly legislated.

Eventually most prisoners will be released from confinement. The question is, which is the better time for release, for both society and the prisoner: (1) at the point during his sentence when there is a strong probability that, with supervision and helpful guidance, he can spend the remainder of his sentence in the community without violating the law; or (2) at the end of his sentence, when he will be returned to the community without the benefit of a competent and understanding counselor during the most critical period of his transition from a controlled situation to a free society? Parole stresses the importance of continuing outside the prison walls the process, begun inside the walls, of modifying conduct patterns by fundamentally changing the individual offender. Thus it is an important procedural and administrative phase of criminal law.

A CRITIQUE OF PAROLE BOARDS*

Some states actually parole prisoners almost indiscriminately, simply to relieve the congestion of their institutions. Such a policy can hardly be condemned enough since obviously, if there was reason to incarcerate the inmate in the first place, no good to the community can come of releasing him merely because of lack of space. Various other practices, brought about by faulty laws or ignorance of administrative officials or lack of proper appropriations for the work, are equally ridiculous and equally far from the

* Reprinted in part by permission of the *Yale Review*, Copyright Yale University Press, Joseph F. Fishman and Vee Perlman: In the Name of Parole, *Yale Review*, Vol. 28, No. 1, 1939, p. 146-150.

true spirit and purpose of parole. While perhaps there is not one state in the Union which provides really adequate funds for a thorough going parole system, it is such States as condone the practices just mentioned which are also apt to provide little and, in a number of instances, no supervision at all for the parolee. Yet they call it parole.

The laws of each state are the beginning of wisdom—or otherwise—regarding the effectiveness of its so-called parole system. They are concerned usually with such broad matters as the institutions to which parole is to apply; how much of the sentence must be served before prisoners can become eligible for parole; in whom the parole power is to vested; and the very important matter of funds to be expended on the work.

So far the legislature of each state has followed its own more or less quaint notions as to what constitutes the establishment of a parole system. Almost needless to say, provisions are varied as the climates from pole to pole.

Out of the legislative source flows a main stream, and from this main stream certain tributaries, which all together determine whether the parole land they vein shall be properly irrigated and as a result beneficently fertile or not. This main stream consists of the body in which the parole power is vested. Sometimes it is the governor of the state, who acts on the advice of a special board or one made up of the officers of a particular institution; or the power is vested entirely in a parole board appointed for that purpose. An outstanding drawback of most of these boards is the fact that their members frequently possess as their sole qualification for such work political reliability and responsiveness to the power which appointed them. While some of these persons may be not only honest and well-disposed but sometimes, through accident, competent in this field, most of the time they are thoroughly naïve as to the factors which should entitle a prisoner to parole.

Leaving out for the moment the paroles which are granted because some powerful person brings sufficient pressure to bear on many of these naturally malleable boards, practically all parole administrators make the mistake of judging a man's fitness for parole by his record of conduct in prison. There could scarcely be a more misleading index to the prisoner's future behavior. One of the long-standing maxims of the "prison-wise" is revelatory: "The quickest way out is through the front door." This means that, contrary to popular belief, life and other long-term prisoners—are frequently the best-behaved in prison. At once they set about purposely to earn as much time off their sentence by good behavior as possible, and, knowing the ignorance of the usual parole board concerning this front, thus to win a parole also. Any number of felons, callous enough not to stop at any crime however atrocious, never violate a prison rule from one year's end to the next. They are, indeed, "model prisoners"—but decidedly poor parole material.

How can the politicians, the business and professional men —specialists in totally different fields—who make up the membership of most parole boards know this? They simply can't. And neither can the legislatures, which actually in some states make parole for the prisoners who have a record of good behavior in confinement *mandatory*. Should a criminal in such places intend on release to kidnap a child and be indiscreet enough to say so, the authorities would still have no choice but to parole him.

The fact remains that the administrative boards themselves are almost universally taken in by such records. They are also customarily led astray by the fact that the candidate is a "first offender." Under the law a first offender is a person who has been caught *and convicted* only once. He may have committed a hundred crimes over a period of years without being caught. Or he may have been caught fifteen or twenty times when there was excellent reason to believe him guilty, but not sufficient legal proof. In other words, he may be an habitual criminal and have pursued successfully a criminal career for a long time. Nevertheless, in the eyes of the law, he remains a first offender. Obviously, the first-offender class may comprise the most capable, the most alert in avoiding detection and therefore, from the standpoint of the public's protection, the most dangerous criminals.

On the other hand, the public is always bitter in its denunciation of parole whenever it discovers that this privilege has been given to a known second or third offender. It may be quite right in doing so. Yet actually, the criterion of the first offender is equally useless as far as a qualification for parole is concerned. The worst of it is that parole boards are as much deluded by this fallacious belief as the uninformed public.

The boards are also in many instances taken in merely by the reassuring appearance and demeanor of the prisoner at his parole hearing. In addition, such an apparently praiseworthy effort on the part of the prisoner as having voluntarily taken educational courses while incarcerated frequently serves to influence parole boards unduly in his favor. Increase in the prisoner's stock of information, however, does not necessarily mean increase in his virtue, and, in some notable instances at least, those close to the criminal have found him studying subjects which will aid him in his crooked pursuits once he is free again. For example, one such convict's devotion in prison to articles on metals and chemicals in the encyclopedia bore fruit on his release in a new ability to make counterfeit money.

Besides these, there are various other items in an inmates' prison record which make an instant appeal to lay boards as grounds for parole. They include such things as the prisoner's "tipping off" the officials concerning an impending escape or outbreak; helping a prison officer when he is attacked by another inmate; or being such a good worker that his skill saves a considerable amount of money for the state. When a prisoner tips off an official, the board often assumes that he behaved as he did because he was "on the side of law and order" when, as a matter of fact, the aid he gave the authorities may have been motivated solely by revenge, by bitterness at the thought of someone else's possible success in getting out, or by the anticipation of some reward for his betrayal. Likewise, his "heroic" act in aiding a guard may have meant merely taking advantage of a long-sought opportunity to bamboozle the parole board, and may have had nothing at all to do with any attempt to "go straight" outside of prison. In other instances too, the prisoner's helpful acts or his seeming desire for self-improvement do not necessarily mean that he has become for good a law-abiding citizen. On the contrary, they may be proof of a cleverness that makes him a greater menace to the public than his fellows.

Only long experience with criminals and close study of their lives can confer on anyone necessary knowledge concerning their mental and emotional slants. This knowledge the haphazard and usually politically constituted lay boards of parole do not have.

PAROLE RULES AND REGULATIONS*

One of the origins of parole is the eighteenth century "ticket of leave," which played an important part in the British administration of Australia as a penal settlement for transported criminals. The "ticket of leave" was a declaration by the governor of Australia which exempted a convict from further servitude and permitted him to seek private employment within a specified district.

The English Penal Servitude Act of 1853, which gave legal status to the "ticket of leave" system, substituted imprisonment for transportation and specified the length of time that prisoners had to serve before becoming eligible for conditional release on a "license to be at large." The license was granted with the following conditions:

"1. The power of revoking or altering the license of a convict will most certainly be exercised in the case of misconduct.

"2. If, therefore, he wishes to retain the privilege which by his good behavior under penal discipline he has obtained, he must prove by his subsequent conduct that he is really worthy of Her Majesty's clemency.

"3. To produce a forfeiture of the license, it is by *no* means necessary that the holder should be convicted of any new offense. If he associates with notoriously bad characters, leads an idle or dissolute life, or has no visible means of obtaining an honest livelihood, etc., it will be assumed that he is about to relapse into crime, and he will be at once apprehended and recommitted to prison under his original sentence."

One Hundred Years Ago

Prisoners released under the act were not supervised, and it did not take long before everyone realized that the only effects of the act were confusion and disorder. A system of regular supervision

---

* Reprinted by permission of the National Probation and Parole Association. Nat R. Arluke: A Summary of Parole Rules, *NPPA Journal*, Vol. 2, No. 1, Jan. 1956. p. 6-14. Footnotes omitted.

and uniform procedure was urged, with prescribed rules and regulations. This was developed in the 1850's in Ireland, where the "license to be at large" was granted to a convict "from the day of his liberation under this order" for the remaining time of his sentence, except that it could be "immediately forfeited by law" if he were to be "convicted of some indictable offense within the United Kingdom" before the expiration of his sentence, or if it should "please Her Majesty sooner to revoke or alter" the license. It was noted also that "This license is given subject to the conditions endorsed upon the same, upon the breach of any of which it will be liable to be revoked, whether such breach is followed by conviction or not."

The conditions referred to were the following:

"1. The holder shall preserve this license and produce it when called upon to do so by a magistrate or police officer.

"2. He shall abstain from any violations of the law.

"3. He shall not habitually associate with notoriously bad characters, such as reported thieves and prostitutes.

"4. He shall not lead an idle and dissolute life, without means of obtaining an honest livelihood.

"5. If the license is forfeited or revoked in consequence of a conviction of any felony, he will be liable to undergo a term of penal servitude equal to that portion of his term which remained unexpired when his license was granted.

"6. Each convict coming to reside in Dublin City or in the County of Dublin will, within three days after his arrival, report himself at the Police Office, . . . where he will receive instructions as to his further reporting himself.

"7. Each convict residing in the provinces will report himself to the constabulary station of his locality within three days after his arrival and subsequently on the first of each month.

"8. A convict must not change his locality without notifying the change to the locality to which he is about to proceed.

"9. Any infringement of these rules by the convict will cause to be assumed that he is leading an idle, irregular life and thereby entail a revocation of his license."

Conditionally released prisoners were expected to inform their employers of their criminal record; if they failed to do so, the head of the police was responsible for transmitting the information.

That was one hundred years ago. Consider, for a moment advances in the welfare of other groups which, like the parolee group, are made up of the scorned, the rejected, the handicapped —say, the mentally ill, or religious and racial minorities, or the economically backward. Compare changes in attitude toward these with any changes, if any, toward the parolee. Compare parole regulations of one hundred years ago with today's.

Fundamental Questions

By and large, parole rules have continued pretty much as they were a century ago. Does this mean that they are satisfactorily meeting their purpose and therefore should not be changed? Does it suggest that there may have been changes in emphasis and interpretation, less obvious but perhaps more important than the fact that the letter of parole rules has changed very little?

Some other questions arise from an examination of parole rules: How are parole rules used? As guides? As coercive devices? As casework treatment tools? Do parole rules help in the community adjustment of the parolee or do they plague him as continuous reminders of his "second-class citizen" status? Are they pitched so high that parole adjustment is unattainable in many cases? Can we establish parole rules which give evidence of awareness of the communities' pressures on the released offender—rules and conditions tailored, as close as possible, to the needs of the parolee and his community?

If it is conceded that parole rules and conditions do not have to be immutable, how can they be modified or amended in specific cases? Should individual modifications be made by the parole officer, or by the supervisor, or by the central office, or by the parole board?.

You may have read, in *Confidential* magazine for January, 1955, an article entitled "Parole—Freedom on a String." The subheading was, "What good is a system that censors your job, bars you from women, and puts you back under arrest without cause?

Parole can be a engine of torture that succeeds in redoubling hatred of law, cops, and penal 'experts.' " A large part of the public still accepts that kind of statement as gospel truth, and we continually see its imprint when we interview prospective parolees, especially those who have had no prior experience with parole. Doesn't this suggest the need for an analysis of our public relations programs so that we may erase or at least begin to minimize these erroneous impressions?

Frequency of Parole Rules

The chart on pages 204 and 205 summarizes the policy of each of the 48 states in regard to parolee behavior. The 24 regulations listed include all that refer explicity to restrictions on behavior. (However, two of them—17 and 19—really indicate parole board action in the event that the parolee violates his parole.)

The number of regulations indicated for a state on the chart does not necessarily coincide with the actual number in the state's official document handed to the parolee upon release from prison. In some states the references to both liquor and narcotics usage, for example, are combined as a single regulation; and in many states the document may include statements that interpret parole board administrative policy as distinct from those that describe what is and what is not allowed in parolee behavior.

It must be borne in mind, too, that a blank in the chart means only that the regulation is not printed in the state's set of rules; it does not mean that the conduct referred to is ignored in practice. This gap is comprehensively covered in many states by the parolee's signifying his agreement to "abide by such special conditions of parole as may be imposed" on him by his parole officer.

In a few states the number of stipulations about parolee behavior and parole board administrative policy exceeds 20. How many of these the parolee can reasonably be expected to remember is a question. Because of this, one of these states includes a regulation requiring the parolee to read the regulations periodically during the entire parole period!

Not a single one of the twenty-four parole regulations appears in every one of the forty-eight states documents.

	Alabama	Arizona	Arkansas	California	Colorado	Connecticut	Delaware	Florida	Georgia	Idaho	Illinois	Indiana	Iowa	Kansas	Kentucky	Louisiana	Maine
1. Liquor usage	2	2	2	2	2	2	2	4	2	4	2	2	2	2	2	2	2
2. Association or correspondence with "undesirables"	2	2	2	2	1	2	2	2	2	2	2	2		2	2	2	2
3. Change of employment or residence			1		1	1	1	1	1	1	1	1	1	1	1	1	1
4. Filing report blanks		3	3	3		3		3	3	3	3	3	3	3	3	3	3
5. Out-of-state travel	1		1		1		1	1		1	1	2		1	1		1
6. Contracting a new marriage	1		1	1	1	1		1		1	1	1	1	1	1		1
7. First arrival report	3		3	3	3	3		3	3	3	3	3	3		3	3	3
8. Operation and ownership of motor vehicles			1	1	1	1		1		1	1	1	1		1		1
9. Narcotic usage	2		2	2	2		2	2	2	2	2			2	2	2	2
10. Support dependents	3		3					3	3	3					3	3	3
11. Possession, sale, or use of weapons; obtaining hunting license			2	2	1	2		1	2	2	2	2	2	1	1		1
12. Travel out of county or community			1	1	1			1	1	1	1	1	1				
13. Agree to waive extradition	3			3				3	3	3					3		3
14. Indebtedness			1							1							
15. Curfew						6					10:30						11:00
16. Civil rights	1			2	2						2						2
17. "Street time" credit if returned as P.V.																	5
18. Gambling		2						2						2			
19. No "street time" credit if convicted of felony					5												
20. Airplane license			1														1
21. Report if arrested					3												3
22. Treatment for venereal disease								3									
23. Church attendance																3	
24. Enlistment in armed forces																	

Key—1. Allowed, but permission must first be obtained. 2. Prohibited. 3. Compulsory.

Maryland	Massachusetts	Michigan	Minnesota	Mississippi	Missouri	Montana	Nebraska	Nevada	New Hampshire	New Jersey	New Mexico	New York	North Carolina	North Dakota	Ohio	Oklahoma	Oregon	Pennsylvania	Rhode Island	South Carolina	South Dakota	Tennessee	Texas	Utah	Vermont	Virginia	Washington	West Virginia	Wisconsin	Wyoming
2	2	4	2	2		2	2	2	2	4	2	2	2	2	2	2	2	2	2	2	2	2	2	2	2		2		2	2
2	2	1	1	2	2		2	2	2/1	2		2	2	2	2	2	2	2	2	2	2	2	2	2	2		2		2	
1	1	1	1	1	1		1	1	1	1		1	1	1	1		1	1	1	1	1	1	1	1			1	1		1
	3	3	3	3	3	3	3	3	3		3		3	3	3	3	3	3	3	3	3	3	3			3	3	3	3	3
1	1	1	1	1	1	2	1		1	1		1	1		1	1	1	1	1	1	1				1		1	1	1	1
1	1	1	1		1		1	1	1	1		1			1	1	1	1	1	1	1	1			1		1		1	
3		3	3	3	3		3		3	3	3	3		3	3	3	3	3	3		3			3	3	3	3		3	
1	1		1						1	1		1					2	2	1	1					2	1	2			1
		1	1		1					1	1	1	1	1		1	1	1			1		1			1	1			1
		3		3		3				3				3	3		3	3	3							3	3			
		1	1			1	1	1	1			1			1														1	
	6							6	6				6	6																
													2		2															
5									5								5								5		5			
						2																				2				
									5	5			5																	
																		1												
						3																								
																		3												
														1																

4. Allowed but not to excess. 5. May be received. 6. "Reasonable hour."

The regulations listed below as in the chart, are in order of frequency.

1. *Use of liquor.*—Completely prohibited in forty-one states; permitted, but not to excess, in four states—Florida, Idaho, Michigan, and New Jersey. No restrictions in Missouri, Virginia, and West Virginia.

2. *Association or correspondence with persons of poor reputation.*—"Persons of poor reputation" are specified generally as other parolees, ex-convicts, inmates of any penal institution, persons having a criminal or police record, etc. New Hampshire policy draws a fine line between association with such persons and correspondence with them, prohibiting the former but allowing the latter when permission has first been granted by the parole officer. In thirty-eight states, both forms of conduct are prohibited; in three other states—Colorado, Michigan, and Minnesota—both are allowed after permission is granted. In six states—Iowa, Montana, New Mexico, Virginia, West Virginia, and Wyoming—the regulations ignore the matter entirely.

3. *Change of employment or residence.* —In thirty-nine states, permission to make such a change must first be obtained through the parole officer. It need not be obtained in nine states—Alabama, Arizona, California, Montana, New Mexico, Oklahoma, Vermont, West Virginia, and Wyoming.

4. *Monthly reports.*—In thirty-eight states the parolee must fill out a monthly report blank and send it to a central agency. He is not required to do so in ten states—Alabama, Colorado, Delaware, Maryland, New Jersey, New York, North Carolina, Rhode Island, Utah, and West Virginia.

5. *Out-of-state travel.*—Allowed, after permission is granted, in thirty-four states; prohibited by Iowa and Montana. No restrictions in twelve states.

6. *Permission to marry.*—In thirty-three states a parolee desiring to marry must first obtain the consent of the parole officer. No such requirement is specified in fifteen states.

7. *First arrival report.*—In thirty-three states the parolee is required to report to his parole officer immediately upon arriving at his destination after release from prison; in fifteen states he is not required to do so.

8. *Operation and ownership of motor vehicles.*—Denied, in thirty states, unless approval of parole representative is obtained; no restriction in eighteen states.

9. *Use of narcotics.*—Prohibited in twenty-eight states; permitted in one state—Tennessee—when approved by a physician. No restriction mentioned in nineteen states.

10. *Support dependents.*—In twenty-seven states the parolee must promise to support his family. No regulation of this sort is specified in the printed rules in twenty-one states.

11. *Possession, sale, or use of weapons; obtaining a hunting license.*—Prohibited in twelve states; allowed, after permission is granted by parole officer, in fifteen states. No restriction in twenty-one states.

12. *Travel out of the county or community.*—Allowed in twenty-five states upon permission of parole officer; no restriction mentioned in twenty-three states.

13. *Agreement to waive extradition.*—This is a condition of parole in nineteen states. No mention of it is made in twenty-nine states.

14. *Indebtedness.*—In eleven states the parolee is allowed to incur a debt only if he has the permission of the parole officer. There is no such restriction in thirty-seven states.

15. *Curfew.*—In six states the parolee is required to be at home for the night at a "reasonable hour." Curfew for parolees is specified as 10:30 in Illinois and 11:00 in Maine. There is no curfew regulation of any sort in forty states.

16. *Civil rights.*—Civil rights, including suffrage and the right to hold office, are lost to the parolee in six states; in one state—Alabama—they may be restored upon application and approval of the request. In forty-one states no explicit mention is made of the civil right status of the parolee.

17. *"Street time" credit for parole violator.*—In six states the parolee who is returned to prison for violation of parole receives credit for all or part of the time he has been on parole. Such credit is not allowed or is not mentioned in the provisions of forty-two states.

18. *Gambling.*—Prohibited to the parolee in five states; no restriction mentioned in forty-three states.

19. *Conviction for felony while on parole.*—In four states the parolee is warned that if he is returned to prison because of a felony he commits while on parole, he will be deprived of all "street time" credit. No mention of this is made in the regulations of forty-four states.

20. *Airplane license.*—In three states—California, Maine, and Pennsylvania—the parolee must obtain his parole officer's permission to apply for a license that would allow him to operate an airplane. Not mentioned in forty-five states.

21. *Report if arrested.*—In three states—Colorado, Maine, and New Jersey—the parolee is required, if he is arrested, to report the arrest to his parole officer. Not mentioned in forty-five states.

22. *Treatment for venereal disease.*—In two states—Florida and Pennsylvania—a parolee who has a venereal disease is compelled to take treatment for it as a condition of remaining on parole. Not mentioned in forty-six states.

23. *Church attendance.*—In two states—Kansas and Nebraska— the parolee must attend church regularly as a condition of remaining on parole. Not mentioned in forty-six states.

24. *Enlistment in armed forces.*—In one state—Ohio—the parolee is required by regulation to obtain permission of the parole officer before applying for enlistment in the armed forces. Not mentioned in the regulations of forty-seven states.

Some Conclusions

A. Excessive Number of Regulations in Some States

As suggested above many of the documents listing "General Conditions of Parole" contain so large a number of regulations that the value of the parolee's signature on the parole agreement is questionable.

They are further weakened when they include, as many do, quasi-legal interpretations of parole board policy. The distinction between *law* and parole board *rule* should be clearly drawn in parole rule documents.

It hardly seems necessary to impose a regulation on conduct already governed by the criminal code. For example, if a state already has a law imposing penalties for the illegal sale or use of narcotics (and most states do have such a law), why make it, superfluously, a parole regulation?

B. General Impracticality of Regulations

Many of the regulations are not realistic and do not lend themselves to practical enforcement. The complete prohibition of the use of liquor by parolees in forty-one states forces us into an unrealistic position that breeds violations and contempt for the value of parole supervision. It seems to me that a "Ten Commandments" form of agreement would provide the framework for more intelligent and functional supervision of parolees.

C. Lack of Uniformity

The lack of uniformity is, of course the most obvious defect of parole regulations. Consider, for example, the regulation which requires the prospective parolee to agree to waive his right to an extradition hearing in the event of his arrest in another state. There is real question about the legality of this regulation. Furthermore, if the regulation were used either universally or not at all, there would not be the confusion and expense that are now the result of the use of Form A-3, "Agreement of Prisoner When Permitted to Go to Another State," issued by the Interstate Commission on Crime in the twenty-nine states where the extradition waiver is not included in the list of parole rules.

Some uniformity of regulations should exist among *all* states, if for no other reason than that the number of parolees living in states other than the one in which they were sentenced is increasing all the time.

Parole regulations in the fifty states should be carefully reexamined—not separately in each state, but in a coordinated fashion. Lack of uniformity, impracticality, and mutiplicity of regulations are not the only defects. Others are redundancy, complexity, legal jargon, inconsistency, and irrelevancy. All of them should be eliminated in the interest of better people.

THE INTERSTATE PAROLE AND PROBATION COMPACT*

Since 1934, when Congress first authorized agreements or compacts among the states "for cooperative effort and mutual assist-

---

* Reprinted in part by permission of *Federal Probation*. B. E. Crihfield: The Interstate Parole and Probation Compact, *Federal Probation*, Vol. 17, No. 2, June, 1954, Footnotes are omitted.

ance in the prevention of crime," each one of our fifty states
has become a full-fledged partner in crime control through the
adoption of the Interstate Compact for the Supervision of Parolees and Probationers. Not even the United States Constitution—
an agreement among all the states, ratified by all the states—can
claim more signatories to a formal compactual agreement calling
for coordinated effort and cooperative practices.

Prior to the formulation of the compact, so-called "sundown
paroles" were the order of the day in many sections of the country
and theoretic parolees literally roved the land with no supervision,
formal or informal. Today, these men by the thousands are under
full, legally binding supervision for the protection of our citizens.
Cases constantly arise where, due to family relationships in
another state, better opportunities for work and a more conducive
atmosphere for rehabilitation will be found if the prospective probationer or parolee can be permitted to transfer to another jurisdiction. But the rehabilitative value of such a move would often
be lost unless there is adequate supervision, advice, and assistance
to accompany the released person when he crosses the state line.
The function, then, of the compact is twofold: (1) It serves as protection to the community through providing effective supervision
and by ensuring a means of retaking offenders who have violated
the terms of their conditional freedom, and (2) It encourages the
rehabilitation of parolees and probationers by permitting their
transfer to a receptive environment where their chances of success
may be greatest.

Statistics gathered by the Council of State Governments indicate that there are in the neighborhood of 12,000 cases handled in
the course of a year under the compact, with some five or six
times as many parolees being reported under supervision as there
are probationers. These figures are admittedly incomplete, especially with respect to probation, and additional unknown numbers
of cases do not enter into the available statistics. Turnover by virtue of new cases and terminations, which roughly balance one
another, amounts to approximately 25 per cent per year.

How the Compact Works

Procedure under the Interstate Compact for the Supervision of
Parolees and Probationers involves the following steps:

(a)   Any state may permit a parolee or probationer to go to any other state (the so-called receiving state) if "such person is in fact a resident of or has his family residing within the receiving state and can obtain employment there" *or* if "the receiving state consents to such person being sent there" even though the residence qualification cannot be met.

(b)   The state to which an interstate parolee or probationer is transferred agrees under the compact to exercise the same care and treatment of such a person as its own state standards require for supervising its own probationers and parolees.

(c)   If a state desires to retake a probationer or parolee who has left its jurisdiction under the terms of the compact, officers of that state may apprehend the person in another state without any formalities other than establishing the authority and proving the identity of the person to be arrested. The states have expressly waived all legal requirements to obtain extradition of fugitives from justice in returning such persons, and the individual parolee or probationer is also required to sign a waiver of extradition as a condition precedent to his transfer to another state.

(d)   Rules, regulations, and forms designed to standardize procedures and foster efficient administration have been developed and are in use by the compacting states as they process out-of-state parole and probation under the compact.

Considerable interest has recently been shown in expanding the compact to include the District of Columbia and the territories and possessions of the United States. A bill granting the consent of Congress to such additional joinder was introduced toward the end of the 82nd Congress but could not be acted upon before adjournment. Subsequently, the administrators of the compacting states adopted a resolution unanimously favoring the inclusion of these additional jurisdictions as "a forward and necessary step" in the development of the compact.

Problems Under the Compact

An excellent job has been done by the states in making the compact an effective cooperative instrument. However, it would be less than candid to maintain that problems do not arise. A basic difficulty lies in the fact that parole and probation systems vary to a marked degree among the states. Despite the fact that lines of authority are delineated clearly by the specific language of the compact, there is bound to be some difficulty when two jurisdictions with differing policies both have certain authority and responsibility with respect to the same parolee or probationer.

Another problem arises because of the lack of facilities and personnel in some states. The addition of even a few interstate cases to an already heavy case load may prove difficult to the administrator who has two few tools and too few workers at his disposal. This, of course, is a problem that needs to be met basically and even if there were no interstate agreement operation. As a matter of fact, it may well be that the underlying obligation implicit in the compact—to do the job adequately in a spirit of co-operation—can serve well in bringing up the standards of all the states. Moreover, the interchange of information that occurs constantly by mail and frequently by means of regional and national meetings will help to iron out administrative difficulties.

Perhaps the major problem under the compact is related to decisions with respect to termination of out-of-state parole or probation. It is not uncommon for a receiving state to notify a sending state that a violation has occurred, only to learn that the sending state either cannot or will not return the violator. The reason may be that the sending state does not consider the violation to be so serious as to warrant a return, or again there simply may not be enough funds available to cover the cost of retaking the violator if the distance involved is great. In either case the result is unfortunate, for the only effective sanction in case of failure of a person to meet the conditions of his parole or probation is withdrawal of the privilege. The receiving state is put in the position of supervising a person who would be placed in jail if he were one of that state's own cases, or of letting the man go about without supervision.

The Compact and Probation

The compact has been less extensively used for probation than it has for parole. Several times as many parolees are under interstate supervision than are probationers. The reason for this is not hard to find. Parole as a governmental function is centralized commonly in some agency of the state. The compact administrator in most states is the person actually responsible for parole operations. Not so with respect to probation, which is administered most frequently on a decentralized basis through the courts. On occasion, some local probation officials have denied the legality of the compact on the grounds that their political subdivision had taken no action to ratify it! The compact obviously applies no matter what particular probation system is followed in any given state.

A partial solution to the weakness of probation supervision under the compact has been found by many states. In some instances there is an integrated parole and probation agency at the state level. In other states there is a separate state agency handling probation and the necessary coordination can be secured through the compact administrator and through the designation of one state official who will receive all out-of-state probation correspondence. Even in the case of virtually complete decentralization, the problem is not insoluble. California, for example, has enacted legislation requiring that all probation matters involving another state be channeled through the compact administrator and this system has worked reasonably well. In the final analysis, education is the prime necessity if the compact is to work effectively and to serve fully in the field of probation. The appropriate judicial and administrative authorities responsible for probation, though they be numerous and separate in any state, should be thoroughly familiar with the existence of the compact and should know what it can and cannot accomplish. A concerted effort should be made in every state to develop the required methods of intercommunication and the procedures which will properly carry out the provisions of the compact.

Constitutionality of the Compact

The constitutional validity of the compact has withstood many attacks and it has always been upheld when under court scrutiny. In such states as California, Arkansas, Washington, and New York there have been important decisions handed down by the highest state courts. It is perhaps unfortunate that no definitive ruling has ever been set forth by the United States Supreme Court, principally because no parole or probation violator has ever seen fit to carry his case that far. Because of this there will undoubtedly continue to be occasional court cases touching on the constitutionality of the compact. There is no reason to fear that they will successfully attack this well-tested interstate agreement.

The Compact Administrators Association

Since 1946, the official administrators of the compact have been formally bound together into a group known as An Association of Administrators of the Interstate Compact for the Supervision of Parolees and Probationers. All members of the Association meet together at least once a year to vote upon matters of policy and any proposals for revision in the rules and regulations that may have arisen. The burden of work for and on behalf of the Association is devolved upon the executive committee and upon a council of five members. The council acts as a standing committee on rules, regulations, and policies under the compact. In order to secure uniformity in procedure and practice, any administrator may request information at any time as to the council's opinion on the compact provisions, rules, and regulations, or on administrative practice. Upon recommendation of the Association's council measures may be submitted to the full membership during the year for a vote by written ballot.

During recent years, and at the request of the compact administrators, the Council of State Governments has served as secretariat to the Association. The secretariat maintains current rosters of state officials responsible for the operation of the compact, publishes reports and documents of interest to the administrators, arranges and services the annual meetings of the Association, drafts proposed language for compact amendments and rule changes, and perform such other services as may be requested.

In 1951, at the request of the administrators, the secretariat developed a looseleaf manual for the official use of those who administer the compact. It consists of separate pages indicating the specific arrangements that should be made with each individual state. A section is included which digests the interpretation of policies as determined by the Association's council and as laid down at the annual meetings, and containing tables which show state practices in certain areas of operation. Another section contains the text of all changes in, or additions to, the rules, regulations, and forms in use under the compact; amendments to the compact itself are also shown. A special appendix on legal references contains the text of all currently reported opinions of Attorneys General and important court decisions. Other appendices are used to insert various miscellaneous materials which may be of interest to the administrators.

Out-of-State Incarceration Amendment

The purpose of the basic parole and probation compact is to supervise persons in another state *outside* prison walls. An amendment to the compact has now been developed which would permit the supervision of violators *within* a prison. The problem of parole and probation violators is especially serious when such persons have been allowed to go out of state under the compact. Usually there are only two alternatives to follow—either leave the violator free of effective control or bring him back to the sending state. The former is of course undesirable and the latter may be quite expensive.

Because of this situation a number of administrators asked that provision be made in the compact to permit violators to be incarcerated in the receiving state rather than going to the difficulty and expense of returning them to the sending state. Such an amendment was drafted and is now known as the Out-of-State Incarceration Amendment. It is to be effective only among such of the states as may specifically ratify it. Under its terms, incarceration of a parolee or probationer may be had in the state where he violates the conditions of his parole or probation *if* the sending state wishes. Since states do not enforce the penal laws of other jurisdictions, the amendment makes the receiving or asylum state the agent of the sending state for purposes of such incarceration and provides that the sending state shall retain ultimate jurisdiction over the prisoner.

The Out-of-State Incarceration Amendment was prepared in 1951 and was considered by several legislatures meeting in that year. The states of Connecticut, Idaho, and Utah ratified the amendment during 1951 and at the present time it is effective only as between these states. Rules and regulations to implement the operation of the amendment were perfected during 1952 and it is expected that additional states will consider the enactment of legislation to ratify the amendment at their regular 1953 sessions. Since there has been such a limited amount of time elapsed since the development of the amendment, there is no record of experience to report as yet. It is felt, however, that the amendment will provide an additional instrument for the effective supervision of parolees and probationers by states which wish to adopt this approach. It is also felt that the amendment has been so carefully drawn, and the rules so drafted, that there is little danger of its being stricken down by the courts.

Conclusion

The Interstate Compact for the Supervision of Parolees and Probationers has now been in operation for some thirty-five years. From an initial nucleus of about twenty cooperating states, it has gradually grown to the point where every state has fully and officially ratified the basic agreement. The state officials responsible for the operation of the compact have developed their own Association which goes far toward smoothing out the rough edges that exist in any complex procedure involving intergovernmental cooperation. The administrators are increasingly interested in working out new and supplementary instruments to enhance the effectiveness of the compact, and in addition have done considerable work on related subjects which ramify beyond the strict operations of the compact. A current project has to do with cooperative returns of prisoners by one state on behalf of one or more other states. Efforts are now being made to expand the compact so as to include the District of Columbia and the territories and possessions of the United States. In spite of difficulties and certain gaps in the effectiveness of the compact, such as in the field of probation, the compact has proved its utility beyond question and should become an even more useful device in the coming year.

PAROLE AND THE DETAINER SYSTEM*

A detainer may be defined as a warrant filed against a person already in custody with the purpose of insuring that he will be available to the authority which has placed the detainer. Wardens of institutions holding men who have detainers on them invaria-

---

* Reprinted by permission of the Council of State Governments. From: *Suggested State Legislation Program for 1957*, p. 74-85. Footnotes are omitted.

bly recognize these warrants and notify the authorities placing them of the impending release of the prisoner. Such detainers may be placed by various authorities under varying conditions, for example, when an escaped prisoner or a parolee commits a new crime and is imprisoned in another state; or where a man not previously imprisoned commits a series of crimes in different jurisdictions.

While it would seem proper that authorities in quest of a violator of the law should have every assistance in returning him to their jurisdiction, nevertheless the detainer system now operates to the detriment of society all too often. The difficulties inherent in the existing detainer system affect the judge, the institutional officials, the paroling authorities and the individual himself.

The prison administrator is thwarted in his efforts toward rehabilitation. The inmate who has a detainer against him is filled with anxiety and apprehension and frequently does not respond to a training program. He often must be kept in close custody, which bars him from treatment such as trustyships, moderations of custody and opportunity for transfer to farms and work camps. In many jurisdictions he is not eligible for parole; there is little hope for his release after an optimum period of training and treatment, when he is ready for return to society with an excellent possibility of other detainers. A rather long sentence may be indicated, but the judge hesitates to give such a sentence if the offender is going to serve subsequent sentences, or if he stands to lose the privilege of parole because of a detainer. The incidental first offender may, and sometimes does, serve years in prison because he has violated the law in several jurisdictions, although only a short sentence or probation would accomplish the necessary rehabilitation. It seems obvious that proper sentencing, as well as proper correctional treatment, is not possible until the detainer system is modified. Ironically, society is the real loser in collecting its debt from the offender. Much money is spent in extra periods of imprisonment, and embittered offenders become recidivists, pyramiding the expense of law enforcement.

Recommended Principles

In 1948, the Council of State Governments served as secretariat for a group known as the Joint Committee on Detainers, upon which there was representation from the following organizations: Parole and Probation Compact Administrators Association, National Association of Attorneys General, National Conference of Commissioners on Uniform State Laws, American Prison Association, and the Section on Criminal Law of the American Bar Association. The Joint Committee's report included the following "statement of aims or guiding principles" which should govern the actions of prosecuting authorities, sentencing judges, prison officials and parole authorities to the end that detainers will not hamper the administration of correction programs and the effective rehabilitation of criminals:

1. *Every effort should be made to accomplish the disposition of detainers as promptly as possible.*—This is desirable whether the detainer has been filed against an individual who has not yet been imprisoned or against an inmate of a penal institution. Prompt disposition of detainers is a proper goal whether the detainer has been filed by a local prosecutor, a state prison, a parole board, or a federal official. Detainers lodged on suspicion should not be permitted to linger without action.

2. *There should be assurance that any prisoner released to stand trial in another jurisdiction will be returned to the institution from which he was released.*—An important cause of long-standing detainers is the presence of unsettled charges pending against a prisoner held by another jurisdiction. If the charges appear to be valid and if the individual is to be brought to trial before completion of his sentence, then it is essential that the institution holding him in custody be assured of his return after the trial has been completed. Unless there is such assurance, many jurisdictions will understandably hesitate to cooperate.

3. *Prison and parole authorities should take prompt action to settle detainers which have been filed by them.*—Prison officials and parole boards recognize that detainers create serious problems with respect to prisoners under their jurisdiction. Therefore, when such authorities file detainers against prisoners in other jurisdictions, they should cooperate fully to effect a prompt settlement of all detainers. They should promptly give notice as to whether they insist that the prisoner be returned at the end of his

present sentence, or whether they will agree to a concurrent parole. Every effort should be made to cooperate in planning effective rehabilitation programs for the prisoner.

4. *No prisoner should be penalized because of a detainer pending against him unless a thorough investigation of the detainer has been made and it has been found valid.*—It should be the duty of prison officials, parole authorities and judges to make such investigations before denying the prisoner privileges, probation or parole, or before imposing unusually heavy sentences upon the prisoner.

5. All jurisdictions should observe the principles of interstate comity in the settlement of detainers, and each should bear its own proper burden of the expenses and effort involved in disposing of charges and settling detainers. There should be full faith and credit given to the rights of any state or jurisdiction asserting them.

Recent Developments

During 1955 and 1956 the old Joint Committee on Detainers was informally reconstituted under the auspices of the Council of State Governments and the membership of the committee was augmented by representation from the National Probation and Parole Association and the National Association of County and Prosecuting Attorneys. Operating under the title of "Committee on Detainers and Sentencing and Release of Persons Accused of Multiple Offenses," meetings of the augmented group were held on June 30, 1955; November 25, 1955; and February 10, 1956.

The committee developed and approved three specific proposals dealing with disposition of detainers, and noted for information purposes an additional proposal with reference to merger of sentence. Then, on April 14, 1956, a larger group was convened to review the draft proposals. The conference was held in New York City and was attended by over sixty persons, representing the following areas of interest: state police; prison societies and correctional associations; bar associations; state legislators; members of commissions on interstate cooperation; state and local parole and probation officials (including administrators of the Interstate

Parole and Probation Compact) ; district attorneys; state corrections and prison officials; state attorneys general; and the United States Department of Justice.

Several draft proposals as acted upon and approved at the above mentioned conference. They cover the following subjects:

1. *Disposition of detainers within the state.*—This proposal, based substantially on statutes now operative in California and Oregon, makes it possible for a prisoner to initiate disposition of detainers which have been lodged on untried indictments, informations or complaints arising within the state where he is imprisoned.

2. *Agreement on detainers.*—This proposal, including an appropriate enabling act, carries into effect the right of the prisoner to initiate disposition of detainers based on untried indictments, informations or complaints arising in other states or from the federal government. It also provides a method whereby prosecuting officials may initiate such action.

3. *Parole to detainer.*—This proposed amendment to basic state parole statutes ensures that there is adequate authority for parole boards to release prisoners on parole to answer warrants from other jurisdictions.

Disposition of Detainers Within the State

The Intrastate Detainer Statute is designed for use within a single state. Since most state laws already provide methods whereby prosecutors can bring prisoners already under sentence to trial on other outstanding charges, no attempt is made to include such provisions in the suggested act. However, individual states which may not now give sufficient authority to their prosecutors may wish to review their present laws in connection with their study of the present proposal.

The suggested statute is intended to afford a means of permitting the prisoner to clear up detainers which have been lodged against him. It gives him no greater opportunity to escape just convictions, but it does provide a way for him to test the substantiality of detainers placed against him and to secure final judgment on any indictments, informations or complaints outstanding against him in the state. The result is to permit the prisoner to secure a greater degree of knowledge of his own future and to make it possible for the prison authorities to provide better plans and programs for his treatment.

The proposed statute provides that a prisoner, wishing to clear a detainer based on an outstanding indictment, information or complaint, may make a request for reasonable time as defined in the statute, the indictment, information or complaint ceases to be of any further force or effect and the detainer based thereon is removed. Other provisions of the statute are drafted to make sure that the prisoner does not frustrate the purpose of the law by escape from custody during part of the interval permitted for trial; to make sure that the prisoner has an opportunity to know his rights under the act; and to provide prosecuting officers with information concerning the prisoner's present status before proceeding to press for custody of the prisoner so that trial may be had on the indictment, information or complaint which forms the basis of the detainer.

Agreement on Detainers

The Agreement on Detainers applies the same principles embodied in the intrastate act to the interstate field. At the present time, there is no means by which a prisoner may initiate proceedings to clear a detainer placed against him from another jurisdiction. This is equally true on an interstate and a federal-state basis. In addition, the only way that a prosecuting official can secure for trial a person already imprisoned in another jurisdiction is by resorting to a cumbersome special contract with the executive authority of the incarcerating state. Because of the difficulty and red tape involved in securing such contracts they are little used.

The Agreement on Detainers makes the clearing of detainers possible at the instance of the prisoner. In this report it is the interjurisdictional counterpart of the intrastate statute. It also provides a method whereby prosecuting authorities may secure prisoners incarcerated in other jurisdictions for trial before the expiration of their sentences. At the same time, a Governor's right to refuse to make the prisoner available (on public policy grounds) is retained. Since the problems in the detainer field are both intrastate and federal-state, the Agreement on Detainers provides that the United States may become a party thereto. If this is done, the procedures provided in the agreement will be available on both an intrastate and a federal-state level.

Parole to Detainer

Parole contemplates release to the community and hence the term is not properly used for releases on warrants or detainers. However, authority is needed to release prior to expiration of term in the face of detainers. Some parole boards now deny parole when there is an outstanding detainer, sometimes on the ground that they feel they do not have authority to release. The practice should be to dispose of all detainers as early as possible. Using a detainer to deny parole to a prisoner ready for it not only penalizes him unjustly but also delays the pending proceeding and confuses its meaning.

PAROLE REVOCATION PROCEDURE*

The layman and most courts look upon parole as a gift to the convict, an act of leniency on the part of the executive, frequently given as a reward for good behavior in prison. But parole is actually much more than an act of leniency. It is one of a number of criminological devices, including probation, conditional pardon and parole, which, though differing in various details, have in common the goal of protection of society through the rehabilitation of the criminal. The parolee is required to live up to a rigid code of conduct which is intended to aid him in his readjustment to a socially acceptable and useful life. Revocation acts as a sanction to ensure that, if the parolee by violation of the conditions imposed upon him shows that he is either unwilling to cooperate with the effort to rehabilitate him or otherwise unready for release, he will be returned to the prison to serve the remainder of his sentence. At the same time, the threat of capricious or arbitrary recommitment does not encourage either cooperation or the success of the process of rehabilitation. The procedural steps in

---

* Reprinted by permission of the Harvard Law Review Association (copyright, 1951). Parole Revocation Procedures, *Harvard Law Review*, Vol. 65, Dec. 1951, p. 309-319. Footnotes are omitted.

parole must, therefore be analyzed with the objectives of simplicity, celerity and protection against arbitrary action in mind.

Constitutional Considerations

The existence of this sanction of revocation raises the question whether there are any constitutional limitations on its exercise. Several courts have specifically stated that the rights of the parolee are statutory only and are not protected by the due process provision of the Constitution. In stating this, the federal courts have relied upon the dictum by Mr. Justice Cardozo in a 1935 hearing where the Court required a hearing for the revocation of probation, basing its decision on a statute and refusing to accept the petitioner's contention that such a hearing was a constitutional right. But in 1941, the Circuit Court of Appeals for the Sixth Circuit, relying specifically on the Fourteenth Amendment, reversed a refusal of habeus corpus where the prisoner had been denied notice or opportunity to be heard in the revocation of a conditional pardon. The majority view that no constitutional problem exists has been justified by one or more of the following arguments: (1) that parole is a mere act of grace on the part of the executive, conferring no rights on the parolee and subject to withdrawal at any time; (2) that the parole is a contract between sovereign and convict in which the latter agrees to certain conditions, one of which may be revocation at the will of the grantor without hearing or notice; (3) that the parolee remains in the custody of the warden of the prison or the parole board and revocation is a mere change in the form of this custody which does not require special protection; and (4) that the parolee was given full constitutional protection at the time of the original trial.

The first of these theories has received the widest acceptance. But, while the actual granting of the parole may be an act of grace, the parolee is thus given a certain liberty which should be accorded some protection. The contract theory depends upon the power of the convict to accept parole or conditional release. The Supreme Court, speaking through Mr. Justice Holmes in *Biddle* vs. *Perovich* (274 U.S. 480) denied such a power to accept or reject a change in the form of his confinement. Since parole is a part of the reform system, it is difficult to find an option here when none exists with regard to accepting the sentence after conviction. The third theory seems to ignore the inherent difference between custody involved in imprisonment in a cell and "custody" as applied to a person who is at liberty in the world. A few courts have used a variation of the custody theory in saying that the violation is an "escape" from custody and that the parolee who has violated parole is nothing more than a fugitive from justice. This argument assumes that there has been a violation, which is the very question on which the parolee claims a right to a hearing.

The theory that the rights of the parolee were given full protection at the original trial is the strongest. Stated so boldly, the theory depends upon the postulate that revocation does not increase punishment. In fact, once his parole is revoked, the parolee may be forced to serve the maximum sentence undiminished by the time spent on parole. In addition, his conduct is considerably restricted while on parole: he must report periodically to a parole officer; he cannot leave the state to which he is sent on release without permission; he may be denied the privilege of driving a car; he may not use intoxicating liquors; he may be subject to a curfew; he may not marry without special permission from the parole authorities. This is not the freedom of the ordinary citizen. The addition of these years of restriction to the maximum punishment of the court sentence is thus potentially an increase in punishment. A few courts have met this objection by considering the risk of additional punishment without a contemporaneous hearing as being included in the original sentence.

Since the parole system is provided for in the statutes along with the specific penalties for crimes, these courts argue that the legislature and trial court intended it as a part of the punishment which can be imposed for violations of criminal statutes. Though the last argument might justify the statement that there is no constitutional right to protection of the parolee on revocation, there is some question as to whether the legislature or sentencing court in fact contemplated that the parole system with the risk of additional punishment would be included in the original sentence of the court. Certainly the legislature did not intend to give the parole board or executive the power to revoke and thus increase punishment on mere whim.

It may be plausibly contended that the interest in continuing the parolee's liberty is strong enough to require a regular judicial proceeding before revocation. Even if the circumscribed nature and penal context of his freedom reduces somewhat the constitutional protection required, the minimal protection against the danger of arbitrary or capricious action should not be eliminated. The question remains as to what specific procedure is required to give this protection.

Procedural Requirements

a. *Arrest.*—The first step is that of arresting the alleged violator. The federal law provides that the warrant for arrest may be issued by either the Board of Parole as a whole or by any member thereof. Before the 1948 codification and revision, the statute provided that this should be done only on the basis of "reliable information." It may be argued that the ommission of these words from the revised Section 4205 indicated an intent that the warrant may issue without such information. But since the avowed intention of the revisers was to codify existing law, eliminating inconsistent or obsolete provisions, such a substantial change seems unintended. Furthermore, federal courts have said that the issuance of a warrant without any information would constitute forbidden arbitrary action. There appears to be no constitutional right to have the arrest based on "reliable information." Although the Fourth Amendment requires that people "be secure in their persons . . . against unreasonable . . . seizures . . . and no Warrants shall issue, but upon probable cause, supported by Oath or affirmation," at the time of its adoption such release procedures as paroles were not recognized. The Amendment was therefore probably originally intended to refer to persons who were being taken into custody for the first time. The retaking of a person who is already under the obligation to serve a sentence may differ enough to prevent application of the Amendment, or, if the Amendment applied, to give unreasonableness and probable cause a milder meaning in this context. The due process clause would not prevent speedy investigations of alleged parole violations, but it should protect against arbitrary action.

The warrant may be issued at any time within the term of the maximum sentence of the parolee, for this purpose treating parole time as service of the sentence. The courts have interpreted this as meaning the absolute maximum of the sentence imposed, good conduct time being forfeited by violation of the parole conditions. The running of the maximum sentence is suspended during service of a sentence for another crime. Sometimes the warrant, although issued within the maximum term, is not put into execution by an arrest until after that term has run. Courts have generally upheld such action on the ground that upon violation of a condition and the issuance of a warrant for his arrest the violator becomes a fugitive from justice and cannot claim to be serving his sentence. Where the cause of such delay is action on the part of the parolee in absenting himself from the jurisdiction of the Board, the suspension of execution may be justified. But protection of society demands that there be no unnecessary delay in recapturing the violator. Also the parolee should be given a chance to exculpate himself as soon as possible. Delay may deprive him of evidence which would otherwise prove him innocent of violation. Since the period of delay does not count on his sentence, it increases the duration of effective restraint where the parolee materially complies with all but one condition of parole.

b. *Hearing.*—After the arrest, the next stop is to decide whether a violation has occurred. Here the federal statute provides that the parolee shall be given "an opportunity to appear before the Board, a member thereof, or an examiner designated by the Board." A large number of states have similar provisions. State courts have required hearings in the absence of provisions in the parole statutes or release instruments denying the right to a hearing. The federal court in *Fleenor* vs. *Hammond* (116 F. 2d. 982) went beyond this point to say that there is a constitutional right to a hearing which no provisions in a release instrument can take away. This statutory provisions would also be ineffective to deny a hearing is suggested by the Michigan Supreme Court in *People* vs. *Moore* (62 Mich. 496, 29 N.W. 80), which held unconstitutional a statutory provision allowing the violator of a conditional pardon to be held without preliminary examination before a magistrate or notice of charges pending a hearing on the question of violation. These cases represent the minority, but the preferable point of view.*

Some federal and state courts have said that the "hearing" need be only of the most summary nature. This hardly satisfied the demands of the situation. There is no requirement of a jury trial, except where there is in issue the identity of the parolee and the arrested person. Administrative convenience demands something less than a full trial with the attendant technical delays, for the Board could not give careful consideration to the many cases before it without resort to some informality in the hearing. Also in the informal proceeding, the Board may be able to get a clearer view of the true psychology of the parolee which will supply helpful clues to effecting his ultimate adjustment to society, and the parolee is able to discuss his problem and see for himself the error of his conduct. All of these advantages further the rehabilitation of the parolee.

But the undesirability of a formal trial on revocations of parole does not mean that some of the procedural requirements may not carry over into the informal hearing. The parolee should be entitled to notice of the charges against him so that he may meet such charges at the hearing without being required to prepare a full justification of every action and an accounting of every minute of time spent on parole. Connected with this should be the right on the part of the parolee to present evidence as to the truth of the charges, and perhaps as to the proper disposition of the case. While this may not involve the technical rules of a judicial trial, the parolee should be allowed to examine accusing witnesses either at the hearing or by interrogatories before the hearing. The right to representation by counsel was denied by the Fifth Circuit in *Hiatt* vs. *Compagna* (178 F. 2d 42, (340 U.S. 880), following a Board of Parole ruling excluding counsel from the hearing, but was recognized by the District of Columbia Circuit. The argument that counsel may unduly complicate the hearing and lead to

---

* The revocation of parole may be compared to the deportation of an alien. Although the alien is not entitled to a jury trial on deportation, he is entitled to a "fair hearing."

a variation from the desired information makes the unlikely assumption that the mere presence of lawyer would be sufficient to overthrow the established custom of informal hearings. It should be realized that the parolee may not be equipped to present all the facts of his case in the best manner, and presumably the Board can act most effectively in effecting rehabilitation when all of the facts are placed before it. The presence of a lawyer trained in dealing with facts and presenting them clearly should be of aid to both parolee and Board. Throughout the hearing the two objectives of speedy confinement of the violator and protection of the innocent parolee against unfair treatment must be balanced.

c. *Judicial review.*—The third step in the procedure is judicial review of the revocation. The question of revocation is one of discretion on the part of the parole board, which is presumably composed of men who as experts in criminology and penology are better equipped than the courts to determine whether return to prison is in the best interests of society and the parolee. Not every violation of parole need lead to reconfinement. A minor violation by one who is making an honest effort to reform may lead only to the imposition of a stricter code of conduct for some period. On the other hand, a minor violation by a parolee who gives no indication of attempting to cooperate with the parole authorities should be followed by immediate return to prison. In view of this situation the courts have wisely refrained from reviewing the facts or merits of the decision other than to correct abuses of discretion on the part of the parole board such as issuance of a warrant without any information to substantiate claim of violation, or the revocation of parole without any hearing or without some essential elements of a hearing. This limited type of review gives protection against arbitrary and capricious action and at the same time leaves the board free to make the ultimate decisions as to the question of policy involved.

d. *Application of the Administrative Procedure Act.*—It has been argued that since the Federal Board of Parole is an administrative agency it should be governed by the Administrative Procedure Act, which would require the elements of notice, right to present evidence and right to counsel discussed above and possibly judicial review. It would seem on the fact of the statute that the parole revocation hearing comes within the area of administrative adjudication under Sections 2 and 5. But Section 7 (a) provides that "nothing in this Act shall be deemed to supersede the conduct of specified classes of proceedings in whole or in part by or before boards or other officers specially provided for by or designated pursuant to statute." The Senate and House Judiciary Committees' reports say that the language was not intended to create a loophole for an agency to escape the requirements of the Act, but to exclude only those proceedings held before persons of a peculiar competence who would contribute something more than would the trial examiners provided for by the Act. Since Section 4207 of the Criminal Code provides for a revocation hearing before the Board of Parole, its members or examiners designated by the statute, it appears that the hearing is exempted from the application of the Act. In addition, the very nature of the question involved, the rehabilitation of the parolee and the protection of society, requires discretionary action by the specialized presiding officers. Furthermore, the need for a full understanding of the parolee and his problems may make it desirable to have the parole officer who has been closely connected with the investigation of the case sit as an examiner or advise the person hearing the case. Such procedure would not be possible under Section 5 (c) of the APA.

Conclusion

The majority of courts, rather than analyze the purposes of parole procedure and the requirements of due process, have merely relied on antiquated legal formulae in denying necessary protections to the parolee. Some have taken a more enlightened view, recognizing that the central purposes of the revocation of parole—protection of society and the rehabilitation of the parolee—can best be accomplished by a procedure which is speedy, sure, and fair to the alleged violator.

JUVENILE AFTER-CARE SERVICES*

The larger report, from which this selection was taken, presented an analysis of the types of aftercare services provided

---

* Reprinted in part by permission of the Florida Children's Commission and the author. Frank Manella: *After-care Services for Children,* Report No. 1, 1957, 66 pp., p. 1-9.

in each of the States. We give here the various types of services, omitting the state-by-state analysis. (Editor's note.)

* * * * * *

After-Care

The most important step in the rehabilitative process, for a child who has been adjudged delinquent and committed to a juvenile training school, is his step back into the community. Most of the child's problems can be traced to his home and the neighborhood in which he lives; therefore, successful rehabilitation of a juvenile delinquent will depend to a great extent on what happens to him when he returns to the environment from which he was taken. The need for supervision and assistance, by a trained person, during this transition period is paramount, if the child is to make the necessary readjustment to society. An inadequate or non-existent after-care program may be a contributing factor to recidivism on the part of these youngsters. This supervision and assistance after release from a state training school, by a trained worker, is referred to as *after-care.* . . .

There is no master plan for providing after-care to juveniles who have been released from training schools. The individual states approach this problem in a variety of ways. . . .

1. *AFTER-CARE SERVICE BY A STATE AGENCY:*
   After-care service is sometimes provided by a state agency which is specifically organized to provide supervision and assistance to children released from juvenile training schools. A number of states use this plan and if the state is large, regional offices are set up at strategic points for the purpose of providing continuous and close supervision of the children. This program has been recommended widely but its big disadvantage is that most states are unable to provide adequate financing.

2. *AFTER-CARE SERVICE BY THE TRAINING SCHOOLS:*
   Follow-up supervision and assistance would be given by the case worker or parole staff of the training schools. This plan is followed in some states.

3. *AFTER-CARE SERVICE BY THE JUVENILE COURT:*
   Supervision by the probation staff of the juvenile court which

commits the child to the training school. In Florida this is the plan that is generally followed.

4. *AFTER-CARE SERVICE BY A PUBLIC OR PRIVATE CASE WORK AGENCY:*
   After-care service is provided by a public or private case work agency upon request of the court of commitment or the authority responsible for the release of a child. Value of this plan is that it places emphasis on general child welfare rather than on correction or delinquency.

5. *AFTER-CARE SERVICE BY THE ADULT PAROLE AU-THORITY*

6. *AFTER-CARE SERVICE PROVIDED DIRECTLY BY THE JUDGE:*
   This happens throughout many states, especially in the small rural areas and in courts with limited probation staffs.

7. *AFTER-CARE SERVICE BY VOLUNTEER ORGANIZA-TIONS:*
   In many states the after-care program is provided by volunteer groups such as the Big Brothers and the Big Sisters. It should be borne in mind that programs of this type can only serve to supplement and assist juvenile courts and other agencies with this problem. They can never be expected to supplant or be a substitute for state responsibility to these children.

There are a number of other approaches to the providing after-care service to juveniles but the preceding classification embodies most of the programs that are now operating. In 1953 the United States Children's Bureau conducted a special study to determine the provisions of after-care or parole programs for children released from training schools. The following provides us with the results:

Agency Operating After-Care Program	No. of Training Schools
No program available	1
Training school itself	26
Probation Dept. of Committing court	14
State parole authority	9
State Dept. of which school is a unit:	
State Dept. of Institutions	5

State Board of Control	2
State Board of Training Schools	3
Youth Authority	9
State Dept. of Welfare	10*
Other:	2*
State Dept. of Public Welfare	2*
State Dept. of Public Assistance	——
TOTAL	83

The remaining 26 training schools that reported circled more than one answer, indicating that several agencies operated the after-care programs. (The relative degree of utilization of the different agencies for after-care services cannot be determined from the answers to the question.) The distribution of the various combinations of agencies operating the after-care programs is as follows:

Agency Operating After-Care Program	*No. of Training Schools*
Probation Dept. of committing court	1
State Parole Authority	
Youth Authority	2
State Dept. of Mental Hygiene and Correction	1
State Board of Correction and Training	1
Local Welfare Dept.	1
Prob. Dept. of court and State Welfare Dept.	1*
	3*
Probation Dept. of committing court and:	
State Parole Authority	2
State Dept. of Institutions	1
State Welfare Dept.	5*
Local Welfare Dept.	6*
State Board of Public Affairs and State D.P.W.	1*
State Parole Authority and State D.P.W.	1*
	——
TOTAL	26

The foregoing report emphasizes the variety of ways in which the administrative responsibility for aftercare is designated. An

---

* As indicated by the asterisks, State and local welfare department operated after-care of parole programs for 31 out of 109 training schools that reported—exclusively for 14 training schools and in conjunction with one or more agencies for 17 additional training schools. These figures might be slightly higher if data were available from the non-reporting training schools.

inter-agency cooperative program is used in some states; but other states place exclusive responsibility with one agency. No attempt was made to evaluate the effectiveness of any of the programs. A qualitative analysis would be very difficult, if not impossible, to conduct on a nation-wide basis.

COMBINING PARDON AND PAROLE ADMINISTRATION†

There is a growing tendency to combine the administration of pardon and parole in one board. About half the States now have in greater or lesser degree combined the two. Especially in recent years has this movement grown. In the year 1937 alone four States —Arkansas, Michigan, Missouri, and Tennessee—enacted laws which not only created such consolidated boards of pardon and parole but also combined probation administration.

Is This Tendency Sound?

What has been said in the preceding section about the proper function of pardon as distinguished from parole should help in answering this question. The main, if not the sole, argument in favor of such consolidation is that to have two agencies performing such similar functions means overlapping and duplication of efforts. But this assumes that the two functions are similar. It is true that as long as executive clemency is used to release persons on conditional pardon and other forms of release similar to parole, there is good reason to say that all these procedures should be handled by one board. But the sounder approach would be not to perpetuate the present misalliance of pardon and parole by throwing them together into one board, but to begin by defining the proper scope for each of them. Under present practice in most States there is no clear differentiation in nature and function between parole and conditional pardon. Yet the line between the two can be clearly and unmistakably drawn, as already stated; pardon should not be in any degree a regular release procedure, but should be restricted to the unusual cases of the types enumerated in the preceding section. All regular conditional releases should be under the parole law.

---

† Reprinted in part by permission. The United States Attorney-General, *Survey of Release Procedures:* Pardons, Vol. 3, 1940, p. 300-302. Footnotes are omitted.

If executive clemency would abandon the field which rightly belongs to parole, we believe the reasons for consolidation of the two agencies would disappear almost entirely. The field left for pardon would then be quite distinct from that covered by parole. The type of investigation and the training required of the investigators would be entirely different. Parole would depend upon the prisoner's personality, upon his prison record, the degree of his information, the environment into which he will return and his chances of getting a job. The investigators to determine these factors should have on its membership competent penologists, psychiatrists, criminologists, and social workers.

On the other hand, pardon in its properly restricted field would depend upon wholly different considerations and would have to be administered upon wholly different policies. The examples we have listed as properly coming within the scope of the pardoning power all depend upon political or judicial considerations. Whether political prisoners should be granted clemency is not a matter to be determined from the social worker's point of view, but from a statesman's. Whether a conviction is of a kind that popular opinion denounces is properly addressed to political officials. Whether a person is innocent though legally convicted is a judicial question which if too late to be reopened in the regular courts must nevertheless be decided by an investigation approaching as nearly as possible judicial fact-finding type of inquiry.

None of these are inquiries which a parole board is particularly fitted to determine.

Combining pardon with parole administration only tends to perpetuate the present muddled situation, in which no clear differentiation exists between the field properly covered by parole and that left to executive clemency. This is not only confusing but unfortunate in its results. In very few States are any officers provided to supervise persons released on conditional pardon, indefinite furlough, or any other type of executive clemency. The very definition of parole, on the other hand, assumes the existence of a staff of parole officers to supervise those paroled. And while in fact such officers are sometimes nonexistent even under parole statutes, two facts remain true: (1) There are more likely to be parole officers than conditional pardon officers (there are none of these in any State) ; (2) there is more possibility of reforming the parole law and obtaining an adequate staff of parole officers than of obtaining a staff to supervise persons at liberty on conditional pardon.

The goal to strive for then is not a consolidation of pardon and parole, but the utter exclusion of pardon from the field. Pardon should be restricted to special cases involving political or judicial considerations. The whole field of conditional release as a regular penal practice belongs to parole.

Chapter Eight

PAROLE PREDICTION METHODS

 W HAT IS the relationship between imprisonment and parole, or between imprisonment and any period of release after incarceration? Due to the extravagant claims of early reformers, a portion of the public has come to believe that prisons are established and equipped to rehabilitate prisoners as well as to keep them in safe custody. As a result, when prisoners are released on parole today the burden of proof is shifted from the correctional authorities to the convict since the latter is presumed to have been rehabilitated in prison. Even parole officials are often inclined to adopt this view and to assume that the parole period is a period of trial to determine whether the criminal has or has not been reformed in prison. Instead of approaching with the attitude that the parole agent is assisting the individual to make good, there is an inclination to watch and see if he fails. The effect is often a boomerang to both the prisons and to parole.

To evaluate the prison in relation to parole, it is essential to understand the functions of parole as well as of prisons. Parole is not, as often assumed, an exercise of executive clemency which permits complete return to normal society; it is a period of servitude under supervision just as is the time spent in prison. In anticipation of this later period, prisons do not complete the job; they merely prepare for another stage of the correctional process. Safe-keeping and isolation from society, diagnosis and observation, training for the future are the chief functions of the prison; rehabilitation, the chief function of parole.

In this chapter we consider the bridging point between prison and parole. What are the criteria for the selection of prisoners who are to be granted parole status? How effective are the various predictive techniques?

Selection for parole should be based upon the readiness of the individual to be returned to the community. This determination is developed from a thorough examination of all the best information from many sources close to the individual: the institutional classification service, personal history data developed by the probation staff prior to commitment, medical, psychometric, psychological, and psychiatric data, institutional progress reports, as well as recommendations from institutional diagnostic-treatment staff.

Due to the complexity and sometimes inconclusiveness of prediction methods, it is unlikely that many boards will base selections of potential parolees solely on actuarial techniques. This is not to minimize the necessity of continuing research into the factors which make for the success or failure of paroled offenders. It does suggest, though, that the day is still far off when we can feed punched cards into a mechanical sorter and determine the readiness of the individual for parole on the score which he records.

HISTORY OF PAROLE PREDICTION*

For over twenty-five years American social scientists have been involved in the effort to measure the prospect that a person will fail or succeed on parole. Their procedure has been very much like that of a life insurance statistician who, by tabulating the mortality experience of a given population, estimates the risk of death at different age levels. Analogously, the parole actuary calculates the relative frequency of failure within selected categories, and projects these rates into the future. It appears timely to review the published work on the subject of parole prediction, and also to evaluate its significance.

The approximately thirty year period covered by this research has been characterized by three phases: (1) initial efforts, (2) skeptical but constructive reaction, and (3) post-war studies, predominantly methodological. Hornell Hart was among the first, if not the first, to recognize the possibility of constructing an experience table with a view to predicting parole adjustment. In a 1923 paper he advocated that parole candidates be scored on the basis of items thought to be prognostic of parole success, and the risk of

---

* Reprinted by permission of the *Journal of Criminal Law, Criminology, and Police Science*. Karl F. Schuessler: Parole Prediction; Its History and Status, *Journal of Criminal Law, Criminology and Police Science*, Vol. 45, No. 4, Nov.-Dec., 1954, p. 425-431. Footnotes and tables are omitted.

violation be established for each score, or score interval. Not so long afterwards, this idea was applied by Burgess who, in what would now be called a pilot study, analyzed the records of 3,000 parolees drawn equally from three Illinois prisons. These cases were first cross classified according to outcome on parole and 21 items of possible significance, such as type of offense, number of associates, nationality, and so on. Then, by giving one point to each subclassification that had a violation rate lower than the over-all rate, a parole score was computed for each person. Finally, violation rates were determined for selected score intervals. The regular progression of rates according to the magnitude of prediction scores seemed to affirm the feasibility of prediction from an experience table.

As is true of many scientific accomplishments, almost identical work was going on concurrently in other quarters. In the late' nineteen-twenties, the Gluecks of Harvard developed a methodology of predicting post-parole adjustments rates for a group of something less than 500 prisoners discharged from the Massachusetts Reformatory in 1921-1922, which was very similar in form and significance to the table prepared by Burgess. Their procedure differed slightly in that persons were scored on 6-13 items and items were weighted according to their capacity to differentiate outcome groups. Although these differences appear rather trivial, they do nevertheless represent persistent problem areas, as indicated by continuing research on both topics.

Some intimation that these two pioneer efforts were to mark the beginning of a sustained research movement was provided by two studies that followed almost immediately. Vold's study of 1,192 Minnesota cases is significant primarily because of its attention to the problem of sampling variability in violation rates, and to the possible consequences of not weighting items in accordance with their discriminative value. By randomly dividing his entire sample into two approximately equal groups, he was able to illustrate empirically, what might have been expected *a priori*, that score-specific violation rates would differ somewhat between random samples of parolees just as a matter of chance. The major finding in the scoring experiment was that weighted and unweighted scores arranged parole cases from high to low in about the same way ($r = .92$), and Vold concluded that weighting had little influence on actuarial results, a conclusion which recent research has weakened but not repudiated.

Shortly after its appearance, the scoring procedure devised by Burgess was applied by Tibbitts to a sample of 3,000 persons released to parole from the Illinois Reformatory. The scoring was altered so as to eliminate from consideration those subclassifications in which the violation rates did not differ by more than five percentage points from the over-all rate; and several additional factors were analyzed. His results served mainly to confirm the point that parolees scored and ranked on items closely associated with parole adjustment will exhibit differential violation rates, an inevitable result whenever there is any correlation between prediction items and the criterion.

Middle Period

The initial group of studies, although modest in claim and scope, were followed by a run of somewhat critical studies. Sanders, for example, expressed skepticism as to whether an experience table, after Burgess, would persist relatively unchanged in the short run future. To throw light on this question, parole outcome and various items were correlated in a sample of 5,683 federal prisoners released; cases were scored in best items, and violation rates computed by score intervals to form an experience table. A follow-up sample consisting of 2,838 parolees was scored in the same way and violation rates computed, so as to make possible a check on the constancy of the score-specific violation rates in the two periods. Although the first set of violation rates showed a regular progression, the pattern of rates in the follow-up table was erratic and quite possibly a result of chance factors. This finding, as significant now as at the time of its discovery, high-lighted the possibility that items which rank persons reliably as to parole success in one period may be unreliable for that purpose in the almost immediate future.

The pioneer studies were also criticized on the grounds that they made use of whatever information happened to be on hand and that much of it was irrelevant. A corollary was that progress in parole prediction is tied up with the discovery of significant categories of information. This attitude is exemplified in the writing of Laune who contended that intimate personal knowledge about a man is likely to be, if not a substitute for, at least an important supplement to, the objective data obtained from a prisoner's record. To this end, he solicited the opinions (hunches) of several inmates in regard to the parole prospects of 150 inmates. It was impossible to check on the accuracy of the raters, as the prospects were still in prison. Inmate ratings acquired a semblance of validity, however, by reason of their fair correlation with Burgess scores ($.34 < r < .54$), and because of fair consistency ($.34 < r < .62$) among the several raters. A recent validation study of these inmate appraisals reviewed in a later section, revealed that inmate hunches are no better than objective scores.

The critical attitude of psychiatry toward the neglect of psychological data in previous efforts, and perhaps unconsciously toward the actuarial method itself, is reflected in a paper by Jenkins and his coworkers. A group of 221 boys paroled from the New York Training School for Boys were scored on 95 items, including 28 personality characteristics. Although these scores yield different violation rates, no demonstration was provided that psychiatric information did improve prediction significantly beyond what would have been achieved had objective items been used exclusively. This study must therefore be considered as principally suggestive in regard to the manner in which psychiatric material might enhance the accuracy of a prediction table.

Not critical in nature, but falling within the middle-period, is the work of the sociologist-actuaries in Illinois who scored 9,000 cases on 27 items, and computed violation rates for selected score intervals. These results, usually termed the 1938 Illinois Experience Table, represent not so much an application of the method devised by Burgess, but rather a continuation of his original work. The Gluecks, like Burgess, did not revise their original method in any significant manner during this period, but they did continue to apply it to the unfolding experience of their now-famous 500 reformatory cases. They acknowledged that in the absence of validation samples their results were important primarily because of their suggestiveness.

The Post-War Period

It seems fair to say that recent research has concentrated almost exclusively on methodological matters, rather than on conditions, personal or situational, which affect behavior on parole. These studies have concerned themselves with the relative efficiency of experience tables, the validity of the 1938 Illinois Experience Table, the validity of the inmate "hunch" method, the optimum number of items in a prediction battery, and the problem of weighting items.

It is almost axiomatic that an experience table in order to justify itself as a prediction instrument should make fewer errors than a blanket prediction based on the overall rate, i.e., the modal frequency. To evaluate an experience table from this point of view, Ohlin and Duncan have proposed an *Index of Predictive Efficiency*, defined as the percentage change in prediction error resulting from the use of an experience table instead of the over-all rate. The application of this index to twenty-two published tables indicated that these tables were not particularly efficient, the average reduction in error being only 16 per cent. This result, perhaps disappointing to prediction enthusiasts, is immediately due to the heavy concentration of parole candidates in score intervals in which the violation rates are very close to the average; in short, because relatively few candidates were characterized by actuarial risks close to one or zero. This feature of the score distribution is basically due to the inability of available prediction items to discriminate sharply between violators and nonviolators.

As a check on the validity of the 1938 Illinois Experience Table, Hakeem computed score-specific violation rates for 1,108 Illinois parolees of 1939 and 1940 and compared these results with the rates as projected from the 1938 Illinois Experience Table. His results were negative in that the observed rates were consistently smaller than the expected rates, the average difference being approximately 13 per cent. The experience table, equipped with memory but not foresight, reacted as if the violation rates would maintain themselves indefinitely, while in fact there was a marked decline in score-specific rates throughout the entire table. Therefore, even had the parole board selected only the most favorable parole risks, the estimated number of violators would still have been excessive, since as previously noted, score-specific rates were dropping over the entire table.

In a study of greater scope and refinement, but similar in orientation, Ohlin compared the parole experience of 8,013 consecutive parolees from 1936-1944 with the rates predicted by the 1925-1935 sample on which the 1928 Illinois Table was based. His major result, anticipated by Hakeem's earlier finding, was that the 1938 experience table was outmoded, as the observed rates were significantly lower than the expected rates. To meet this serious difficulty, Ohlin devised an ingenious method for adjusting the experience table on an annual basis, utilizing the parole experience of persons who had completed the first year of their five year parole period. This procedure utilizes the constant relationship, as it has been observed, between the number of parole violators in the first year and the total number who will violate in the entire five-year period. Application of this procedure to 1925-1944 Illinois State Prison series revealed that an experience table, if made to eliminate outmoded information, can be made to predict violation rates with reasonable accuracy, although such revisions in no way guarantee that an experience table is performing more efficiently than the over-all rate. The significance of these two validation studies seems to consist in their demonstration that an experience table may be outdated in a short period of time, due to major social changes which facilitate or hinder adjustment on parole, and that provision must be made therefore to keep the table up to date by continuous feed-back of the latest parole experience.

By 1950, it was possible to compare the inmate hunches solicited by Laune in 1934 with actual parole behavior of 110 of the 150 inmates who had been rated. This comparison, undertaken by Ohlin and Lawrence, revealed that the hunch method was not quite as efficient as the Burgess method, although neither method predicted much better than the over-all rate.

Another recent study by Ohlin has demonstrated that an experience table based on twelve items performs just as efficiently for prediction purposes as a table based on the 21 items originally used by Burgess. As a result of this analysis, the experience table now in use at the Illinois State Prison is based on 12 items. This type of analysis, although designed primarily to eliminate useless items, has a certain theoretical significance in that it directs attention to basic variables, presumably most influential in regard to parole success. Ohlin discovered, for example, that the six most efficient items defined an area of personal and group attitudes toward criminality. It is to be anticipated that the question whether several prediction items reflect the influence of a single common factor will be approached next by factor analysis as this method seems especially appropriate.

Kirby has recently completed an investigation of the efficiency of an experience table based on items selected and weighted in accordance with the principle of least squares. His table, representing the experience of 455 federal parolees, was slightly more efficient than a comparable table based on arbitrary weights, but not much more efficient (10 per cent) than a blanket prediction based on the over-all rate. Although an important demonstration of the power and advantages of the least squares method, this study nevertheless underscores the need in parole prediction for more meaningful data.

The research of Glaser represents an exception to the main trend of recent methodological studies, in that his search for factors was guided by a theoretical concept. He hypothesized that degree of identification with criminality as a way of life would distinguish prospective violators and nonviolators, and, in accordance with this idea, scored persons on seven items thought to be indicative of "differential identification" with criminality. The resulting experience table was somewhat superior in efficiency to the twelve-factor table prepared by Ohlin, tending to uphold the claim for theoretically oriented research as versus the statistical manipulation of available material.

Conclusion

It is evident from the foregoing review that parole prediction as a research movement has centered in the midwest and that this activity has been pursued mainly by Burgess and other sociologists in the Chicage area. Illinois is the only state that has thus far made provision for the tabulation of actuarial data and its continuous utilization in connection with selection for parole. That this method has not diffused rapidly to other states is due, as is true of most social inventions, to a wide variety of complex social circumstances: political, legal, economic, and ideological. Whatever social conditions have impeded its spread, it must be acknowledged on the basis of this review, that the application of actuarial methods to parole experience has thus far not provided data that greatly reduce the uncertainty attached to forecasting individual behavior on parole. The reasons for this seem to lie, not in the actuarial method itself, which is indifferent to the nature of the data, but rather in the unavailability of items that sharply differentiate outcome groups, and in the apparent sensitivity of parole adjustment to abrupt social changes which militate either for or against a good parole adjustment. The significance of parole research to date, therefore, seems to consist, not so much in the actuarial data produced, but rather in its delineation of the most troublesome problems in this field. These problems, as mentioned before, embody as their major theme, the need for improved knowledge concerning the conditions, both personal and situational, which determine outcome on parole.

ORGANIZING A PAROLE PREDICTION SYSTEM*

Parole prediction methods can be used effectively only when a routine system of applying the experience table, preparing prediction reports for the parole board, keeping the predictions up to date, and conducting research to improve the methods becomes an accepted part of parole administration. Improvements in prediction methods will increase as the advantages and limitations of the existing methods are tested in practice. Research development of prediction methods will be stimulated by the constant effort to make experience tables more reliable, informative, and accurate.

---

* Reprinted in part by permission of the Russell Sage Foundation. Lloyd E. Ohlin: *Selection for Parole: A Manual of Parole Prediction*, 1951, p. 99-102. Footnotes are omitted.

Personnel

The efficient functioning of a prediction system depends on its being administered by a person adequately trained to organize work, conduct interviews, prepare reports, and carry on the research necessary to the development of prediction methods. He should have sufficient knowledge of sociology, criminology, statistics, and research methods to understand clearly how to formulate and apply the experience table, how to readjust it, and how further research can improve the techniques used. Training in these fields also permits the prediction worker to make more accurate classifications of the various factors in that it enables him to understand the experiences implied by a parole applicant's responses during an interview. Thus the administration and development of a routine prediction system requires the constant application of a fund of social science knowledge.

In many states persons employed in the prison classification system are well qualified to carry on prediction work. Whether the prediction system is administered within the existing classification system or set up separately will depend upon the particular classification system. In some states it may be preferable to establish the prediction office as a separate unit under the immediate jurisdiction of the parole board so that the prediction office can also work as a research unit for the board. In any case close cooperation between the classification and prediction staffs is required to ensure complete and reliable information being available to the prediction worker.

If inmates are used to perform the clerical functions of the prediction office, close supervision is required to prevent them from altering reports in response to pressure from other inmates. Careful selection of inmate clerks will make it easier for the prediction worker to impress them with an understanding of the usefulness and objectives of prediction work, and to enlist their aid in preserving the confidential nature of the reports.

Interviews and Reports

Each parole applicant should be interviewed prior to the parole board hearing, and complete information obtained concerning the offender's criminal and social history, so that the prediction worker may secure a clear picture of the influences operating in his background. In addition, considerable attention should be devoted to his institutional adjustment and progress, outside contacts, and future plans. The information obtained in this interview will furnish the basis for the prediction classifications and for a social history report to the parole board. By preparing a topical outline of the general areas of information to be explored the interviewer will be able to secure complete coverage. The use of a questionnaire is inadvisable since it had a tendency to restrict the interview, instead of permitting a free-flowing discussion in which the unique aspects of the case may secure ready expression.

In interviews with previous parole violators an excellent opportunity is offered the prediction worker to explore the influences which lead to violation. A continuous search can be carried on for new factors which will reflect more accurately the basic differences in the experiences of parole violators and parole successes. Information on these new factors can then be secured routinely, after sufficient data have been accumulated, the new factors can be made part of the prediction device. The interview should thus be regarded not only as a source of required information on each case, but also as a source of new theoretical insights into the nature of parole violation and for new factors which will improve the accuracy and usefulness of the experience table.

Sources of Verification

Verification of the offender's story should be obtained from as many sources as possible. It can best be obtained from reports of actual field investigations, conducted either by a court probation officer at the time of sentence or by a parole agent prior to the parole hearing.

If field reports are not available, a certain amount of information on the offender's past life and his prospects for securing an adequate parole situation can be secured from letters directed to his family, friends, relatives, and former employers. The offender's criminal history can be checked against the FBI transcript of his record. The report of the state's attorney and sentencing judge may furnish information on the offense for which he has been incarcerated. A letter of inquiry directed to the armed forces concerning offenders with service experience acts as a check on the military record. Clearance of the case through a central bureau of records for social agencies may provide information on the extent of previous contact of the social agencies with the offender or his family. Specific transcripts of agency records will usually be furnished on request. Institutions to which the offender has been previously committed are generally able to supply transcripts of the classification report and institutional history. Many such requests for information may already have been made by the classification division of the prison. To avoid duplication of work, a check should first be made of the classification file. Follow-up letters or requests for new information may then be issued where necessary.

The institution provides the prediction worker with many informational sources regarding the official facts of the offender's adjustment in prison. The record office maintains a file on each offender, including all official correspondence and actions taken. From this source the prediction worker can obtain information which will clear up doubtful aspects of a case from an official standpoint. The bureau of identification can furnish a copy of the offender's criminal record. Disciplinary and assignment officers of the prison maintain records which provide an official statement of the various changes in work and cell assignments, and also of the number, nature, and reason for various punishments. The visiting and mail office can furnish an accurate list, identifying the vistors, the number of visits, the correspondents, and the number of letters written and received. The hospital office and the prison physician can furnish medical and health records, which are important in cases where there are physical disabilities. The classification unit maintains valuable files, including sociological, psychological, and psychiatric reports of diagnoses, progress, and adjustment. In many instances the classification file will also contain information from many other institutional and outside sources previously mentioned. For this reason very close liaison should exist between the parole prediction worker and the members of the classification unit.

Chapter Nine

PRERELEASE PREPARATION FOR PAROLE

IT IS GENERALLY agreed by authorities in the correctional field that preparation for parole begins the day that the inmate enters the institution. This means that the prisoner has to be prepared physically, emotionally, and socially for the day when ultimately he will return to the community as a free man. And for between 95 to 98 per cent of all persons who are committed to prison, that day of release will sooner or later become a reality.

One of the first steps in the institutional process is that of classification. Initially, classification serves to compile, organize and evaluate the social history of the inmate. Some of this data may be obtained from the pre-sentence investigation conducted by the probation department. Where such material is not provided by the court, the classification unit obtains the material to compile an admission study, the basis of which is to determine the institutional assignment of the prisoner. Moreover, the classification program makes provision for the periodic re-evaluation of the prisoner's progress and planning, so that changes in his assignments can be made, always with the view to preparation for release.

It can be assumed that by the time an individual is ready for favorable parole consideration, he will have progressed to a minimum custody status. As he is drawn closer to the outside world, the pre-release program will provide access to outside persons who will brief the inmate on employment and other conditions on the outside.

Some states have experimented with parole camps as a means of bridging the gap between institution and community. Other jurisdictions have provided special units within the confines of the prison to quarter impending parolees. Very little progress has been made in the direction of pre-parole furloughs to allow the inmate to find employment in the community prior to his absolute release, although, from a realistic standpoint, such a procedure might ultimately improve the adjustment of the parolee in the community once he makes his final departure through the prison gates.

Just as commitment to an institution is undoubtedly a traumatic situation in the life of the inmate, so it can be assumed that return to the community after a prolonged absence will be an anxiety producing experience. To the individual who has made the desired behavioral changes while in prison confines, there are always the questions of how the community will accept him, whether or not he will be able to go "straight," whether he will be exploited in his employment because of his previous status, or whether anything beyond the most menial tasks will be open to him.

The task of preparation for separation is not unique to prison environments. Hospitals for long-term patients have found it desirable to initiate such programs. The armed services, since World War II, at least, have found it desirable to send men to separation centers prior to their release from service, recognizing the transitional problems which are involved. How much more so, then, the necessity to prepare the inmate for return to community life? In this chapter, we consider prerelease preparation for parole.

RELEASE PREPARATION OF THE PRISONER*

In recent years studies of parole failures indicate that the largest percentage of failures occur within a period of 60 to 90 days after release. This would indicate something is lacking in both the institutional preparation of the offender for release and the community's acceptance of the release. Recognition of these facts has resulted in widespread efforts to improve release planning.

Obstacles to Effective Release Preparation

One of the chief obstacles to effective preparation of men and women for return to the community is the traditional custodial concept of prison administration. Admittedly a prison administra-

---

* Reprinted in part by permission of *Federal Probation*. Reed Cozart: Release Preparation of the Prisoner, *Federal Probation*, Vol. 16, No. 1, Mar., 1952, p. 13-16.

tor owes his first obligation to the public for the safekeeping of the prisoner committed to his institution. The second obligation is to attempt to provide a program that will assist the prisoner to improve his chances for adjustment while he is serving his sentence. In many of our prisons these two obligations are conflicting. Where the emphasis is placed exclusively upon custody, it is necessary that the men be regimented to the point where it is difficult to effectively employ any rehabilitative devices. Much of the training and orientation the average prisoner receives, particularly during the beginning of his sentence, is directed toward fitting him into institutional routines and toward readjusting his life to a pattern where he is thoroughly regimented. Consequently, when the time for release comes, the prisoner must make an about face when he enters the free world which is relatively free from regimentation.

Two examples of men with whom I am acquainted will serve to illustrate the problem.

Case "A"

"A" was a military prisoner, a Negro from a southern state who was convicted by a general court martial in France shortly after World War I and received a life sentence for taking part in a riot and mutiny. He was suddenly released from a federal penitentiary during World War II after receiving clemency from the Army. During this long period of time he had lived behind walls without any contact with the world outside except through employees of the institution and had never wore civilian clothing, handled any money, eaten in a restaurant or private dining room, had never had a social conversation with a woman or child, had never ridden on a bus, streetcar, train or automobile, was entirely unfamiliar with traffic regulations, and had no knowledge of how to even make a purchase in a store. No wonder he was bewildered when the news was given him that he would be permitted to return home immediately!

Case "B"

"B" had a life sentence for murder on an Indian reservation and was paroled at the age of sixty-seven after serving eighteen years. Twelve years had been spent in a penitentiary and six years in an open institution where he had an opportunity to see more of the outside world. The data of his release was known several months in advance and the institution officials attempted to help him orientate himself toward problems of the outside community by permitting him to take rides to town on the truck. He was taken out on two or three occasions for dinner, either in a restaurant or an employee's home and had an opportunity to attend prerelease meetings. Even so, he had been out of the community so long that he was totally unprepared to cope with the problems he faced and shortly after release asked to be returned because the free world was traveling at too fast a pace for him.

Release Preparation Should Begin on Admittance

Preparation really should begin when the man is admitted to the institution, particularly if he is serving a substantial sentence. Preparation at this stage can take the form of encouraging him to maintain close ties with his family, friends, and former employers or business associates and, at the same time, encouraging them to keep in contact with him. This can be done through liberal correspondence and visiting policies. Also, it would be ideal if the work assignment received by the man would be in keeping with the type of employment he would have upon release, in order that he may keep his hand in the trade, so to speak. Naturally, he should be kept aware of the importance of his trying to keep up with what is going on outside through reading, movies, and the radio so that he will not be completely out of step.

One of the most essential requisites of a release plan is legitimate, self-sustaining, and acceptable employment. Too often a man is released to accept a job which provides nothing more than a stopgap arrangement, in order to secure his release, and which does not challenge him in any way. A prisoner's employment should be of the type that he is looking forward to with enthusiasm and hope and the type that he would like to retain and make a go of upon release. Whenever it is necessary to secure temporary employment the man is likely to go out with very little confidence in his future opportunities. He is very likely to be discouraged unless he can very quickly arrange for suitable employment.

Another very important factor in preparing a man for release is developing the proper attitude on his part and on the part of the community toward his release. In other words, if it is his intention to just try to get by when he is released and to make no serious effort to adjust, all release planning will be to no avail. Many prisoners go out of our institutions with a defeatist attitude and many times prison employees let the men know they expect them to return. It would be well to concentrate on trying to encourage the men to make a sincere effort to adjust and to work toward building up the proper attitudes toward release, helping the men restore their own confidence in themselves and develop a feeling in them that they really will be given a real opportunity to make good so far as the public is concerned.

The Prerelease Program

Recognizing the importance of developing the proper attitudes of the men, many institutions have instituted prerelease programs from sixty to ninety days prior to their release date. These programs take on different forms but a typical one involves some five or six discussion meetings, led by representatives of the outside community.

1. *Role of the probation officer.*—One meeting is usually conduced by representatives of the parole authorities who supervise the men upon release. In the federal system this means the probation officers. The probation officer carefully goes over the parole conditions with the men, explaining and interpreting what parole means and informing the men what will be expected of them. Then an opportunity is given for questions concerning many problems they will face while under supervision. Not only do they receive a firsthand impression of what is expected of them by their probation officers, but they also have an opportunity to size up a probation officer, so to speak, and resolve some of their doubts concerning the sincerity and genuineness of the interest which probation officers may be expected to display.

2. *Meeting with representatives of employment services.*—Another meeting is conducted by representatives of the public employment services. Here the men have an opportunity to meet with representatives of the agencies which obtain employment for a large percentage of the workers in our country today.

They learn the steps followed in applying for jobs, how much of their record to reveal, and to whom and under what circumstances. They are also encouraged and discouraged, as the occasion warrants, to enter certain fields of employment. For example, the public employment agencies usually discourage men from going to clerical and white-collar jobs and try to encourage them to enter other fields.

3. *Meeting with representatives of large companies or corporations.*—The third meeting is conducted by the personnel director or other responsible representative of a large company or corporation. Here the men have an opportunity to receive firsthand information as to what business men expect of their employees in the way of performance, loyalty, production. The employers often inform the men that they have more to fear from their fellow workers than from the employers themselves because competition is likely to cause resentment on the part of the employees if they know a fellow worker is an ex-prisoner. Consequently, they are encouraged not to talk about their prison record nor allow fellow employees to learn about their background.

4. *Meeting with representatives of organized labor.*—Representatives of organized labor meet and furnish the men information on how to secure membership cards or permits, particularly in the skilled trades, how they go about paying off their initiation fees on installments, and just how to make contacts with local unions.

5. *Meeting with professional and business men.*—Finally, a professional or business man conducts a meeting which concerns itself with problems of human relations—how to budget their time and money, how to meet their civic responsibilities and obligations in the community, and many other things.

After attendance at five or six meetings of this type, the men have had an opportunity to rub elbows with successful business and professional men and to obtain information which gives them encouragement. They gain confidence in these representatives of the community and they feel they can rely upon their advice. This does much toward building up a proper attitude on the part of the men toward problems they will face on release.

Special Problems of the Alcoholic

A number of men who come to prison are known alcoholics. As a matter of fact, some of them are delinquent as a result of alcoholism. Certainly we should not overlook the contribution to release preparation of the organization known as Alcoholics Anonymous. Many of our prisons in this country have chapters of AA meeting regularly. It may be, however, that in some instances the restrictions placed upon these meetings prevent them from functioning efficiently. I believe that restrictions upon the activities of AA should be held at a minimum. In other words, there should be no screening of inmates who attend the meetings. The discussions should be open to all prisoners who are properly identified as alcoholics. Beyond that, staff members should not be present at the meetings. It certainly is stimulating to have frequent and regular visits from members of outside AA organizations to give inspiration, counsel, and advice to members of the prison chapter. In some instances even selected inmates are permitted to accompany one of the institutional personnel who is an AA member to meetings of chapters in the community.

The prisoner who participates in a program of this character feels that he is getting the same type of break or consideration that any other alcoholic receives. After all, these meetings are concerned primarily with problems of alcohol. One of the most noticeable results from these meetings is that many men, after accepting the principles of the Alcoholic Anonymous organization, stop rationalizing with respect to their offenses and begin to look objectively at themselves and accept sole responsibility for their own predicament. This certainly puts them in a good position to seek self-improvement. The effectiveness of this organization in this regard is felt within the institution when there is a lessening of disciplinary problems and frustrations and evidences of neurotic behavior.

The most important result of the program, however, is its carry-over value on the outside. Members of outside groups are willing to meet the prisoners when they are discharged, accompany them to their busses and trains, staying with them and helping them to overcome that great urge to drink as soon as they get out.

Also, arrangements are made to have them met at their destination where they will again be accompanied and befriended by sympathetic members, helping them to get established in their respective communities. Too much cannot be said about the great value of this organization.

Informing the Public

Perhaps one of the big weaknesses in our program is the failure to inform the public and secure its assistance in the way of preparing men for release. It is very difficult to say how this important problem can best be met. Prison officials can only reach a very small percentage of people living in the community at large. This is similarly true of the probation officer. Prison officials and probation officers give talks to service clubs, church groups, etc., interpreting their work and their problems and ask for assistance from representatives of these organizations. These groups usually are cooperative and it is not as important to meet them as it is the average citizen residing in the small town or the neighborhood where the prisoner is to be released. To date there has not been enough effort to acquaint the law-enforcement officials with the importance of assisting men upon release. Consequently, the average prisoner is released perhaps with feelings of hostility toward law-enforcement agencies in general. While there are some exceptions, many law-enforcement officers are equally suspicious of ex-prisoners. There are only rare occasions when there is a real understanding between the law-enforcement officer and the ex-prisoner. It would appear advisable to invite police officers and other agents of law-enforcement organizations to visit prisons and see for themselves what is being done toward helping prepare men for release in order that they may have a more sympathetic understanding.

A word should be said also about the approach the institutional staff should take toward preparing the men generally for release. Undoubtedly too often prison officials are not realistic enough. There is often a tendency to over-encourage prisoners to give them a false sense of optimism about their future adjustment. A conscientious attempt should be made to be very realistic and point out to the men the many pitfalls, the road blocks, the disappointments and letdowns they are likely to face. Most prisoners when they leave the institutions are concerned about how they will be accepted by an employer and how they will be treated by the police. Actually, however, they have the most to fear from their fellow workers and fellow residents in the community, the public with whom they are in daily contact. The average employer these days would be sympathetic toward a man with a prison record, but the average fellow employee who must compete with him on the job will not be so sympathetic. Particularly is this true where social contacts are made with fellow employees and the wife of a fellow employee hears about the prison record and gossips in the community about the ex-prisoner's wife. This leads to the point that the prisoner should be encouraged not to discuss his prison background with anyone except his personnel director, his employer, or someone who has a legitimate right to any information concerning that part of his background.

One of the main obstacles to a proper information program for the public, so far as prison administrators and probation officer are concerned, is that there are so few prisons in the country and there are so many communities from which the prisoners come and to which they are released. A fairly good job can be done in the localities where the prisons are situated and where the probation officers maintain their offices. It is extremely difficult, however, to reach thousands upon thousands of people throughout our country who have no contacts with a prison, no knowledge of prison life, and no conception of what a prisoner faces upon release. Perhaps the only way these countless thousands could be reached would be through dramatizations on the radio, television, and in movies. Even here the people who really understand the problems would not be the persons in charge of the dramatizations and there would be the danger of only a superficial job being done, with perhaps more to be lost than to be gained.

It is my view that the institution personnel and supervising probation officers will have to bear the brunt of release preparations since it is not practicable to really prepare society as a whole for the reception of release prisoners. In other words, those working in the field of corrections will have to intensify their efforts toward preparing the prisoners in every way for re-entering the community life, particularly emphasizing to them the realistic situation they are likely to face. It is encouraging to observe, however, that increasingly more thought and attention are being given to the prerelease preparation of prisoners to enable them to meet the varied problems and situations which will confront them when they return to their respective homes and communities and that a progressively greater effort also is being made to really acquaint society with these problems and needs and its responsibility to aid the prisoner in making the difficult adjustment from the rigid and unnatural environment of prison life to normal living in the community which is to receive him.

AN EMPLOYER'S VIEWS ABOUT HIRING EX-CONVICTS*

This section contains a verbatim account of a meeting at the United States Penitentiary at McNeil Island, Washington, of a prerelease group of fifty together with the owner of a drug firm who had been invited to discuss the attitude of employers toward hiring persons who had served time. The questions and concerns of the men and the replies of the employer are characteristic of those that come up for discussion at prerelease meetings. (Editor's note).

Employer.—"Fellows, let's get something straight to start with; I came here to talk to you, not to preach. I'm not much of a speaker, so if you'll all relax I think we'll get along.

"A few weeks ago I was asked to talk to you on how an employer feels about hiring a man that has served time and while you may not believe some of the things I say—they might not represent what a lot of other people would say or believe—I want you to know, here and now, that what I say, I believe.

"I don't particularly feel I am experienced enough in the ways of the world to give advice unasked, but you want to know how an employer feels and I'm going to do my best to tell you how *one* employer feels.

"First, perhaps I should make my position clear. It is that of the operator of a small drug firm. I know all the people who

* Reprinted by permission of *Federal Probation*. An Employer's Views About Hiring a Man Who Has Served Time, *Federal Probation*, Vol. 17, No. 4, Dec. 1953, p. 43-46.

work for me and know how much I depend upon them. If they were to quit I'd be out of business because I couldn't do all the work myself. Between me and my employees there is a relationship that grounds on mutual respect and understanding and this is also true of most of the employers I have met while I've been in the drug business. Regardless of what you may have heard of the hardheartedness and money-grubbing of businessmen, it just isn't so. No, I'm not trying to tell you the average businessman isn't there to make every dollar he can, but the longer you are in your own business, the more you find out that your biggest business asset is satisfied employees. The most important asset is not the store, not the merchandise, not the money I have in the bank, but my personnel. And how I learned it during the last five or six years when merchandise was hard to get, and good employees even harder!

"During those years when a person came in and wanted a job you looked up and asked the personnel man: 'Can they walk?' If he nodded his head you hired the person immediately. It's a bit different now. Our employees get a thorough checking before we let them come to work. We're in a position to pick and choose, and naturally we take only the best. Why? Because a good employee makes the most money for you and to keep a good employee you go to quite some lengths. At present we are encouraging our employees to buy a share in the company and make it easy for them to do it with small monthly deductions. And we do this because we want them to feel more than that they are just coming to work. We want them to feel they own part of every article they sell, and the better service they give the more goods they sell and the more money we'll all make.

"As I said before, we have passed the state where we had to take anyone. We can now pick and choose, and the basis of our selection is that we pick the person we feel is best fitted for the job. When we get that person the job is done better and we make more money. And how do you get the best person? You hire the best available and then develop him. And if he can't be developed, can't be improved, you fire him!

"When I was asked to talk to you my first reaction was to say, 'No.' I wondered what I could say that would matter. And then I was handed a list of questions you asked. I'll read it to you now, or perhaps I'd better just take the questions the writers proposed and answer them one by one. Now whether you like it or not, believe it or not, I'm going to answer these questions as I see the answer."

"Should I Tell My Employer of My Record?"

Employer.—"Put yourself in my place or any employer's place. What do you want? You want a man who can do the job and you want to know about the man that is going to work for you. You give him an application to fill out. It asks: 'Name and address; and then, previous employment: begin with the last employer first, fill out length of time you worked for employer, work you did, salary and reason for leaving.' If I filled out one for you and I'd worked last in 1944, what is the first question you'd ask me? You're damn right you would! 'Where have you been the last several years?' and I'd have to tell or you wouldn't give me the job.

"Put this in your mind and keep it there. If your employer fires you because you have a record, you didn't have a job in the first place!

"There is only one answer to the question. Certainly you should tell him. And if you don't tell him then every checkup, every bit of criticism, every heavy look you're going to feel is directed right at you, and you'd really get that if you worked for me. But how the devil are you going to do your job right if you're worried every hour of the day that you are going to lose your job? By not telling you're being unfair to yourself. You just cannot go to an employer with dirty hands and expect his hands to be clean.

"Don't think just going in and telling an employer, 'I've got a record,' is going to get you a job. You've got to have the qualifications the employer is looking for. If you haven't the qualifications, you're not going to get the job and that isn't being discriminated against.

"And you're not always going to get the job you want even if you have the qualifications. Sure you're going to have to walk up and down the street and take just whatever you can get, and while you're doing it don't think you're the only one that ever did the same thing. Shortly after the first World War, in 1919 that was, I walked up and down the streets of Vancouver, B.C., looking for a job. There I was, a college graduate, and couldn't get a job of any kind. Sure, I thought I was being discriminated against. Everybody in all the stores was busy and I couldn't even get anywhere near the kind of job I wanted. Yes, I found a job, at $18 per week. Nice salary for a college graduate, but it was a job I could do and that's why I was hired. And that's the only way anyone gets a job. Because the employer is convinced you can do that job and do it better than someone else. I say this in answer to the second question, which asks:

"Will the Employer Because of My Record Refuse to Start Me in a Position for Which I Qualify?"

Employer.—"Look, fellows, the average employer is damn glad to get a competent employee and he's going to try to keep this employee as well satisfied as he can, within reason. So if you're a topnotch salesman you're not going to make the employer any money sweeping the floor. If you want to work for me, you are not going to start in my job, but if you're good I'm sure going to do everything I can to keep you."

"Will My Employer Tell the Office Manager and Staff of My Record?"

Employer.—"You're here for a reason. You got out for a reason. And if you're made of the right stuff, you belong out and you stay out. And it's the way you conduct yourself that will give people your measure. I know that this sounds a bit like 'blarney,' but I don't think people pay much attention to what's happened in the past. So don't worry about what the other person thinks. Most people don't give your record a thought, and feeling they think about you is a condition largely created in your own mind. Your boss isn't going around to tell the staff whom he hires, or why. After all, that is his job, to hire people. If he hires you, you're going to be with the company until he gets ready to fire you. Don't worry about that record."

"What Are My Chances of Advancement if My Record Is Known?"

Employer.—"If you want one man's idea—and it may not be worth anything and I may be the only guy in the world that feels that way—you would be advanced as rapidly as it was possible if you worked for me. Actually I'd have more faith and trust and confidence in you simply because you told me about your record. I am naïve enough to believe you are a little smarter than the average fellow because of your experience and that you wouldn't let me down. If you did let me down, I'd just say you weren't half as smart as I thought you were. But if you made good, don't you see what a smart man you'd make out of me? People feel good when their judgment is substantiated. I could say: 'I gave him a place of trust and look at him now.' And everytime I pushed you up another notch my chest would swell out a little. Why shouldn't I advance you? You bet your boots I would, just as long as you warranted it."

"Did He Hire Me Out of Pity?"

Employer.—"If you had a job someone gave you out of pity you wouldn't be working for me. Maybe some philanthropic organization might hire you that way, but if I hired you, it would be because you could do the work and make some money for me."

"Will I Be Under Constant Supervision?"

Employer.—"Yes! That's how you get the most out of people. You keep prodding them. All of my people are under constant supervision. As an employer that's all I have to do and if I didn't do it the people who work for me would feel neglected and hurt. And incidentally, anytime you're working for anyone, make sure they see you. That's the way you get ahead, by someone noticing what you are doing. If you think I'm going to open your hand every time you take it out of the till—no. But I'll be around to know whether you're making money for me or not."

"If Something Went Wrong Would I Be Automatically Blamed?"

Employer.—"Get away from the persecution complex. The guys who ask these questions sound like they're scared to death something's going to happen to them. But there is no reason in the world to feel that way if you do your job, regardless of what goes wrong. It makes me think the guy feels that he is prone to accident. You know, one man can walk down the street through broken glass barefoot and nothing happens. And this guy comes along in high-top boots and gets cut. If something goes wrong, someone was negligent. Whoever was negligent is going to hear from me.

"How could I run a business under conditions other than that? You're not going to be blamed unless I'm damned sure you were to blame. You'd probably get more leeway than would an ordinary employee because I'd hesitate to accuse you wrongfully. Forget those thoughts. Come to work ready to look the world in the eyes. You're as good as any man on the job or you wouldn't have been hired. No employer has money to waste on worthless employees.

"When people hire people they try to get as much information as they can possibly get about them. The employer wants to find out everything he can. What they like; what they don't like; where they go to church; and where they spend their spare time. That's what application blanks are for. And this is why they are studied. The personnel manager doesn't just take your blank and toss it in a drawer. He studies it, and after he's talked to you he has almost as much to fill out as you did. Some of the important factors the personnel manager must consider are: appearance, dress and grooming, knowledge of the job, grasp of job principles, and familiarity of job.

"In my business when I hire a man I want him to look neat. He has to meet the public and scores of people look at him during the day and judge our store by him. We figure, too, if a man looks neat it also indicates character and habits. And knowledge of the job. Sure, some guy shows up and says: 'I have worked in a drug store all my life.' So I ask him, 'If a customer came in and asked for something for a cold what would you recommend?"

Answer from members of group: "Castor oil!"

Employer.—"You're fired, even before you're hired! In the first place castor oil isn't worth a damn for a cold, but more that that, we don't make a nickel on it. What kind of an employee are you. You've got to recommend something that will help the customer and at the same time make money for the store. You see, we're in a position to pick and choose. We look for a man with business acumen, with essential knowledge, and with qualities we can develop.

"This pamphlet I'm now reading from is developed to aid men in evaluating new employees or would-be employees. It's developed through the research of thousands of people who looked for jobs and a lot of employers use it.

"We employers look for self-assurance. Now that doesn't mean cockiness and playfulness. We look for men who look like they can take care of themselves and not be easily upset. We may even needle a would-be employee to get his reaction. I might even make some remark about your record just to see what you would do. I take a jab at you. I try to get you sore, just to see the reaction.

"Cooperation—ability and willingness to work with others. Now a lot of us think we're cooperative, but we aren't. I have seen a whole organization torn to pieces because some guy came in that wouldn't cooperate. He felt that someone wasn't doing quite all he should, so he didn't either. Result: pretty soon no one was doing his work.

"Command of language and handling of ideas are other factors. Naturally in my business, which is primarily selling, command of language is most important. So if you want to be a salesman you have to know how to use your language.

"Health, stamina, physical drive, and record of previous employment are also important. I'm going to read you part of a letter that came to the institution. It's from the Blank Company. 'We are glad to aid Mr. Inmate in his rehabilitation. We notice he has operated a jumbo-drilling machine and as part of our project is 4000 feet of tunnel drilling, he can join our tunnel crew.' "

"And there you have it. This man had something to offer. Something the Blank Company could use. He had experience with the drilling machine. Blank Company didn't care about the record, they wanted a man to operate a drilling machine. Experience! I have a dozen applications on my desk right now, all of them from people I would like to hire, except they don't have the right experience.

"And here's another letter the institution received. It's from a union in San Francisco and states: 'We cannot aid you in finding this man a job. At the present time several hundred of our own members are out of work.'

"So you see sometimes even when you have experience, you can't locate a job. So how much tougher it's going to be for the fellow without experience.

"Now fellows, I have given you the facts as I see them. I'm just one employer but what I've said, I believe. And I believe, too, that if there's a job open where you make your application, and you have the skill to fill that job, no one's going to give that record of yours much thought as long as you do a good job. If I've done you fellows some good I'm glad and I want you also to know it's done me some good to talk to you."

RELEASE PREPARATION: PAROLE CAMP*

A 1952 study of parole violations in Michigan showed, much to no one's surprise, that the majority of men who violated parole did so within the first six months after release. The inference drawn, again to no one's surprise, was that we were releasing on parole many men who had not been made ready for life outside prison walls.

Like most states we had some sort of prerelease program functioning in the penitentiary. However, we were not particularly proud of what we had, and the survey gave added support, not that any was needed, to our argument that the candidate for parole must be specially prepared for community life and that a parolee stood a pretty good chance of being returned to the institution in a few months unless he received some special attention before release.

We debated the issue of just what kind of "special attention" would best meet the pre-parolee's needs and ours, and came up with the idea of separating him from the general inmate population and placing him, before his return to the community, in an environment as nearly approximating a normal community setting

---

* Reprinted by permission of the National Probation and Parole Association. Gus Harrison: The Michigan Parole Camp, *Focus*, Vol. 33, No. 2, Mar. 1954, p. 37-42.

as possible. To fill the bill, we designed a pre-parole camp, which went into operation under the administration of the state parole division. It makes no claim to exciting originality (the practice of segregating men about to be released has long been used in the armed services, for example) and it won't lead all of us out of the correction wilderness, but there's no denying that segregation is a new idea as far as parole candidates are concerned. Nor is there any denying that parole departments need new ideas, and old ideas expanded and refined, at least as much as they need better budgets.

Our prison camp division constructed a 125-bed pre-parole camp, at a cost of $37,500, about a half mile from the main prison building at Jackson. The site, surrounded by a thick growth of tall trees, already had on it an attractive brick cottage, which was remodeled into offices. The construction crew erected a long, one-story white clapboard barrack to house 108 inmates. The beds are double-deckers and the windows have curtains. The building includes washrooms, a barber shop, and other small service rooms. One wing of the dormitory contains the classroom; another, the lounge. Close to the dormitory the men put up another long, white building containing the dining room and a spacious kitchen. Near the mess hall are quarters for seventeen trusties (for operation and maintenance work) on loan from the Prison Camp Program of the Department of Corrections.

The walls of the lounge are painted and the windows have drapes. The blond wood furniture is arranged in conversational groups; there are library tables and a small collection of varied reading material. In the dining room, which is approximately 100 feet long, the men sit at small tables in groups of four, six, or eight. The food is served in cafeteria style, on dishes, not the conventional institutional trays. The kitchen, large, airy, and equipped with the latest in cooking, refrigeration, and storage equipment, is staffed partly by trusties and partly by pre-parolees. The food is well prepared, varied, and plentiful.

Undoubtedly there are persons—including some in the corrections fields itself—who sneer at the type of environment we have provided as "too good for a bunch of cons," but most of us agree that people are influenced by their surroundings and it was that principle which justified our spending a good deal of time and effort, plus $37,500, toward making the camp buildings and grounds as attractive as possible.

Regulations and Routines

We try to orient the newly-arrived inmate as soon as possible after his entry into the camp. We find that giving him a rundown on his prime concerns at the moment—his prospective release date and our regulations about laundry, purchases, mail, and visits— makes him more receptive to instruction in the educational phase of the program.

The men wear regulation prison clothing except on Sundays and holidays and during visits, when they are permitted to wear their "going home" clothing.

Each friend or relative on a man's visiting list can make one four-hour visit or two two-hour visits a month. Prospective employers may visit at any time.

Pre-parolees spend an average of three and a half weeks in camp before receiving a certificate of parole. The law in Michigan, as in most states, requires that a man eligible for parole must have, before he is released, assurance of gainful employment; issuance of a parolee certificate is held up if a camp inmate does not have a job by the time his release date rolls around. Prospective parolees who for this reason cannot leave the camp after the customary twenty-five day "cushioning" period are detailed fulltime thereafter to various work crews around the camp grounds. Sometimes this presents a problem. Men who have gone through the pre-parole school feel that they should be given preferential treatment, not be assigned to just any trivial task that happens to be lying around loose, and they tend to become more and more restless with every day spent on the "overdue" list. We try to allay their fears and anxieties by making special efforts to find employment for them.

The men in the camp never return to the main prison, except in the case of serious misconduct. They are dressed out, cleared medically, etc., without further contact with the big institution. Their availability in one spot for interviews and counseling on their parole programs is an important advantage of the parole camp.

Custodial personnel assigned to the camp consist of one sergeant and four officers. Sometimes the men chafe at what we consider light restrictions. They feel, for example, that they should be permitted greater freedom about the grounds. There are no fences, and movement within the camp boundaries is not restricted. But we do not want to endanger the program and we have to be realistic. We know that if we don't take certain precautions, some overdue men, as well as some who are subconsciously fearful of their return to the community, may be impelled to take flight. So far we have not had any runaways.

Mornings are taken up with gardening, working in the mess hall, and various other jobs about the grounds. Lunch is followed by a short interlude for rest and relaxation, after which the budding parolee attends the day's lecture and discussion session in the classroom, which lasts most of the afternoon. There is another relaxation period before chow, after which the men may pitch horseshoes or play baseball, softball, or volley ball. The less actively inclined watch television (the set was donated to the camp), listen to the radio, or play cards or checkers.

Pre-parolee School Program

We are proud of our physical setup, but not dominated by it. Far more important than the trappings—and I am not decrying their value—is our educational program, which is designed to help men make the transition from the regimentation of prison existence to the individuality of life in a free setting.

The men who give the lectures and lead the discussions in this program—college professors, law-enforcement and parole officers, clergymen, psychologists, etc.—are experts in their fields. They receive no compensation for their work. Obtaining the service on a voluntary basis was not as difficult as you may suppose. Our appeal for help practically sold itself. The most important part of promoting assistance from the experts consisted of making clear to them just what we wanted to achieve in the educational program. Once they understood this they were impressed and interested, and proof of their belief in the work lies in the fact that they have stayed with us. So as not to impose too heavily upon any one guest participant we rotate the assignments; rarely do we call on any individual to lead the program at the camp more often than once every two months.

We do not believe in "programing down" and have found that topnotch lecturers raise the sights and self-esteem of the students. Whatever small fears we may have had originally that speakers of the high caliber we were obtaining would prove too tough for the group to handle were pleasantly dissipated by experience.

The lectures, supplemented by carefully chosen films, cover the following subjects:

Getting along with people. Relationships with spouse, others in the family, employer, landlord, work associates, law-enforcement officers.

Role of the police in the community.

Mental and emotional health. How to recognize and control tensions.

Religion as a way of life.

The necessity of regular and steady employment; how to apply for a job, and the benefits of good work habits. Budgeting.

Physical and mental effects of the use of alcohol; control of drinking habits.

Use of leisure time.

Interpretation of parole; the role of the parole officer; conditions of parole; assistance offered by parole supervision.

Usually the guest speaker for the day talks for about forty-five minutes, trying to put across several points to open the way to general discussion. During the planning stage we were a little concerned that the men would be reluctant to speak up in groups, but we saw, after the program got going, that they participated in an uninhibited manner. Nothing is sacred and sometimes we parole officials emerge a bit bruised, but we think it's healthy to let the men air everything.

So convinced are we that the active participation of the students is essential to the success of the program that we have set aside a definite part of each school session to encourage the men to "sound off." In informal preliminary group discussions, our parole supervisor "warms up" the men for the speaker of the day.

Aside from the immediate objective, this has the value of giving the supervisor a good opportunity to spot the "problem children" for later individual attention.

The questions most frequently asked during the discussions after the lectures are those that touch on general community resistance to parolees, projected fears of ostracism because of a prison record, police attitudes toward parolees, and projected mistrust of the parole officer.

As in other situations where experiences are shared by a group under the leadership of a capable person, the individual inmate finds that the anxieties which have been looming so large are not unique to him. As he discovers the many ways in which he is similar to his fellows, his problems diminish and fall into proper focus. Many of the apprehensions of the prospective parolee are disposed of in some measure by the constructive comments of those in the group who had been on parole before and now admit their failure and the reasons for it. Moreover, the group experience enables the prospective parolee to seek and accept help more readily than before.

We know that we are violating some of the principles of guided group interaction, but we know why and how our situation forces us to do so and we are not at all dismayed by factors which make ideal group work impossible. For example, we cannot select our students with fine discrimination, although we do screen out medical cases, men with detainers, and a few others whom we feel would not be good camp material for obvious reason. These inmates, who make up 5 per cent of the total scheduled for parole, are released directly from the penitentiary under the same procedure that was in practice before the parole camp was established. The other 95 per cent of the men who make parole at Jackson are transferred to the parole camp. They are heterogeneous in age, intelligence, and educational level.

Sometimes, when our camp population gets uncomfortably high, our turnover is rapid; nevertheless we are sure that on the whole something good is being accomplished by the lecture-discussion sessions. While it may be expected that some men will retain only bits of the instruction, we believe that the over-all impact of the pre-parole program serves to improve the attitudes of the men toward the free community and toward themselves as members of it.

Most of the men are proud of their role in the camp and are cooperative and serious. The impression the camp has made on relatives, friends, and prospective employers is lasting and salutary. These people are convinced that we are interested in our parolees and, consequently, give us their wholehearted cooperation.

Between the end of last April and December 31, 739 men were released from the parole camp. Not enough time has elapsed for us to arrive at valid success and failure rates for these men, but the signs are promising and we feel we have made a good start on doing a better job of parole preparation. Our field officers state that graduates of the parole camp are much more relaxed, friendly, and informed than were parolees released under the old system. They note a diminishing of some of the tensions classically found among new parolees and consequently a multiplying of the chances for success.

We are convinced that sooner or later all of us will prepare men to "bridge the gap" between prison and home through programs which are similar to ours but which no doubt will go beyond our present limitations in Michigan. And we look forward to the day when such programs, working deep into the recesses of our institutions, will accomplish what we have been inching toward for years—a system under which "individual treatment" and "rehabilitation" will be actually practiced, not merely professed.

REORIENTATION TO EMPLOYMENT*

Satisfying, steady employment is probably the most significant deterrent to delinquency and crime. This being true it is surprising that more has not been done to incorporate a strong voca-

---

* Reprinted in part by permission of *Federal Probation*. Charles E. Odell: Job Adjustment for Probationers and Parolees, *Federal Probation*, Vol. 15, No. 2, 1951, p. 12-15.

tional guidance service as part of every prevention and reform program.

Program of the United States Employment Service

Staffs of correctional institutions and probation officers necessarily must do much of their own vocational guidance. They can get assistance in their work from local offices of the employment service. The employment service is the largest public agency next to the schools which touches the problem of job adjustment. Its primary function is job placement—a service to get the right workers for employers and the right job for workers. The USES, through its affiliated State agencies, provides free employment services in nearly 1,800 local offices throughout the country, but the employment service also has several other valuable services. Among these are employment counseling, selective placement of the handicapped, special service to veterans, and occupational and labor market information.

Since the prime purpose of the employment service is job placement, its staff members contact thousands of employers each month to assist them in filling openings in their firms. At the same time, it registers millions of workers, getting a record of their experiences, training, and vocational interests. In the course of its registration, placement, and employer-visiting work, the employment service naturally gathers a wealth of occupational information. Some of this information is developed and published for use in employment counseling and placement. Much additional knowledge of job, their conditions, requirements, and rewards is also available, although unrecorded, in the minds of employment service interviewers and counselors.

Among the many publications relating to employment which have been developed by the employment service, the best known is the *Dictionary of Occupational Titles*. It contains definitions of about 22,028 jobs. This is the standard classification tool of the employment service. It also is used by the military and other government agencies, as well as by industry, for selection, occupational filing systems, and as a general reference tool. Other publications of nation-wide significance are *National Job Descriptions*,

The Labor Market, a monthly publication, *Job Family Series, Selective Placement for the Handicapped, Physical Demands Analysis, Physical Capacities Appraisal, Occupational Guides,* and several on labor market information. In addition, many states and localities develop and distribute material which is prepared locally.

Aptitude Tests Prove Useful

The General Aptitude Test Battery developed by the USES is now used in more than 575 of its local offices. This battery of tests for ten basic vocational aptitudes relating them to nearly 2,000 specific occupations in twenty fields of work. The abilities measured are general learning ability, word discrimination, numerical ability, form perception, finger dexterity, manual dexterity, spatial, clerical, aiming, and motor speed. This tool has proved of great value in the counseling of those who are confronted with problems of vocational choice.

A careful analysis, through the interview, of a person's work experience, educational record, physical capacities, leisure time activities, interests, and goals can tell the experienced interviewer much about his abilities, but tests often give additional clues as to undeveloped aptitudes. Besides the practical value of discovering these potentialities and their use in making vocational plans, test results have proved a great morale builder. It is a very reassuring experience for a man to know that objective tests indicate abilities which he has never had an opportunity to exploit through actual work experience. These tests could be used with profit for men leaving institutions.

Reorientation to the Job

Psychological preparation of inmates for reentering work—discussion of right attitudes, the variety of jobs open, development of work-mindedness—and giving of information regarding the requirements and differences in circumstances of various jobs all help orient the parolee. Parolees should be prepared too, for giving considerable time to job hunting. They need to be prepared for some failures. Discussion as to ways of presenting themselves to employers and putting the best foot forward is important.

Here again, some of the materials and personnel resources of the employment service should be helpful.

When jobs are scarce both the employment service and probation officers will have difficulty in getting jobs for men on probation. Special programs of solicitation will be needed. The selling to an employer of one individual parolee at a time on the basis of his ability to perform is the best long-term approach. The employment service can be useful in helping overcome some of the employer resistance and hostility to those with crime records. When competition for jobs is great, the probation officer also may wish to consider counseling with his clients as to the possibilities for self-employment.

Probation officers working on vocational rehabilitation of parolees should insure that all necessary credentials are available as men leave institutions for work. For example, working certificates are necessary in most states for people under 18 years of age. Boys should have all necessary papers such as proof of age and their school records before they start out from the institution. Otherwise there is a delay in their employment. Employers may turn them away unnecessarily. These frustrating experiences may needlessly set them back. Parolees need help in meeting these routine paper requirements.

Easily discouraged people, as many parolees are, need special help in order not to feel they are getting the run-around. In referring parolees to the employment service, probation officers will help their clients most by making all useful information about the man available to the employment service interviewer. The more the counselor or interviewer knows about the man, the more helpful he can be. The man's institutional record with an evaluation of his success and failure in work assignments is useful. Recommendations by social workers regarding the best environment for the individual should be taken into account. Also the more the employment counselor knows of the man's life story, the more interest he is likely to take and the more likely he is to place him in suitable work.

The practice of not releasing a man until he has promise of a job seems an unrealistic one. Most employers will not hire a person without a personal interview.

In referring men to the local employment service office, it is usually better to give them the name of a specific individual after telephone arrangements have been made for the interview. This is particularly important in large cities where the impersonal atmosphere may be discouraging. It is important that all data about the applicants reach the local office before the man gets there. It is usually considered desirable to tell employers something of the man's background and the circumstances which brought him into legal custody. This saves questions later, and gives the man a greater sense of ease and acceptance.

*Chapter Ten**

PAROLE SUPERVISION AND TREATMENT

T HE SUCCESS or failure of parole as a practice can be decided to no small extent by the effectiveness of the prison program which precedes it. Parole, it is worth repeating, is a part of the total correctional experience, rather than a segmented, isolated, entity. The classification unit of the prison, the vocational, social, educational, and psychological education and training which the inmate receives as part of the retraining program, *as well as the benefits which undoubtedly accrue from the custodial aspects of a controlled living environment*, contribute to the remaking of the citizen.

The parole board, through its careful selection of parole candidates, attempts to discover which inmates are most ready to serve the balance of their sentences in the community setting. It must be recognized, however, that the vast majority of inmates are ultimately released, and that, in spite of the desirableness of selecting only the best parole risks, the practical reality of the situation is that, *with* or *without* parole, most inmates return to the community. Hence, supervision and treatment following institutionalization becomes a necessity for all. While this idea has gained some acceptance from the professional community in parole, it is questionable whether the larger community which frequently continues to regard parole as nothing more than an *act of clemency*, would accept the idea of parole supervision for *all* inmates. Where commitments are made on the basis of indeterminate sentence, however, there would not be any particular problem involved since, on failure, the parole could be revoked, and the inmate returned to prison until such time as a true change in his behavior can be detected. Thereafter a new parole period could be initiated.

As in probation work, the task of parole supervision and treatment is to fulfill a dual goal: the protection of society from re-

*See also, Chapter VI, on probation supervision and treatment.

peated transgressions by the offender, and the culmination of the treatment and reorientation of the inmate in the community setting.

In some instances, neither of these goals is achieved, nor will they ever be so long as we continue in our thinking that custody, *per se*, alters character, nor, in the community, that only strict surveillance will eliminate recidivism. Certainly as long as prisons continue to go "through the motions" of rehabilitation with "window-dressing" programs, it cannot be hoped that the less-secure community environment will effect the necessary changes, when the parole counselor contacts are, at best, periodic.

The elements of good supervision in parole are the same as those in probation. The issue of whether probationers and parolees should be supervised by the same officer is an academic one, for with practical reality, there are sufficient cases in most jurisdictions to allow an officer to supervise either one group or the other. Admittedly, there may be differences in the experiences of the probationer and the parolee, but it does not necessarily mean that the probationer has not had institutional experience, perhaps as a juvenile, or on a previous conviction.

As in public assistance, there is a tendency to group case loads with one of the various forms of categorical assistance (such as Aid to Dependent Children, Old Age Assistance, and so forth) for administrative convenience. So it may be argued that probation and parole case loads should be separated. In those States where probation and parole services are not amalgamated into a single administrative unit, the question of joint supervision does not occur. (Probation has developed as a court function within the separate jurisdictions of a state, while the history of parole, in the United States at least, has been marked by initiation on a state-wide level.)

The purposes and objectives of parole supervision and treatment can be simply stated: to provide the individual with the setting and guidance he needs in working out his problems subsequent to institutional release. Certain conditions, rules, and restrictions are placed upon his behavior to assure that he will not become exposed to the situations which are presumed to be causative in etiology of criminal behavior. The function of the parole officer is two-fold: to assist the individual with his problems, and to protect the parolee against himself and the community through surveillance. The former involves the use of counselling and case-work skills to diagnose and *treat* the underlying social and emotional problems. The latter, surveillance, involves the skillful use of authority, ascertaining the parolees' conduct, activities and whereabouts, to control the parolees' behavior in such a manner so as not to impede the treatment process. It is important to remember that the prognosis in every case is not equal, and thus, we must expect a certain number of parole failures. The essential element is to discover those failures before they do the maximum of harm to themselves and the community.

PAROLE TREATMENT AND SURVEILLANCE*

Parole supervision is the final phase of the correctional process. In this continuation of the treatment program, the effectiveness of the two other aspects, preparation for release and selection for parole, is realistically tested in the laboratory of community living. Parole supervision is commonly viewed as a two-sided endeavor—surveillance and treatment. The surveillance aspect connotes a close, watchful scrutiny of the parolee's conduct with power to arrest and detain. The treatment side suggests professional guidance in meeting everyday problems as well as emergencies. Many observers feel these two tasks of the parole agent are incompatible and irreconcilable, that he cannot be at once a policeman and a caseworker. The serious question posed for us today is which of these two phases of parole should dominate the efforts, attitude and philosophy of the parole agent.

Several factors may have influenced the parole agent to look surveillance as the more important part of his work. Public opinion, generally adverse to parole, seems to regard the parole agent as society's only protection from paroled prisoners. The importance of watchfulness over parolees is often emphasized by the press and law enforcement officials. Legislative bodies commonly clothe the parole agent with peace officer powers and often desig-

* Reprinted in part by permission of the American Correctional Association. Ervis W. Lester: Parole Treatment and Surveillance—Which Should Dominate? *Proceedings*, 82nd. Annual Congress of Correction, 1952. p. 53-56.

nate him officially as parole officer. Much of his work after a serious violation of parole, is of an investigative nature. Board reports must set forth the exact cause of revocation, together with sufficient legal evidence to support each charge. The emergency character of much of this aspect of the work, plus case loads that are universally too large, incline the supervisor to rely, to a large degree, upon the more negative or surveillance phase of supervision. It is unfortunate that the positive factors involved in guidance therapy are more easily neglected than the less effective negative ones.

The usual reaction of parolees to surveillance is one of fear and distrust. Yet most criminologists and penologists hold little hope that fear of consequences will prevent many inmates from committing new crimes after release from prison. Perhaps something positive can be said about the deterrent effects of arrest and imprisonment, together with the attendant disgrace as it operates upon the conduct of persons who have never committed crimes.

On the other hand, there seems to be no justification for the belief that it will be very effective in modifying the conduct of a parolee who is so depressed and frustrated that he has abandoned the good fight—who is so defeated by life's pressures that again he thinks a solution for his social or his economic problem may lie in the commission of some offense. At the moment, when he is thus tempted, he usually looks about him and, seeing no policeman, takes a chance in the firm belief that he will not be caught. At the same time he rationalizes that with the emergency vanquished by his deviate act some benevolent fate will surely reveal a brighter yet honorable course that can be pursued toward rehabilitation. Yet it is never quite so simple and, after the first offense on parole, it seems a little easier for others to follow, since there is always the chance that an earlier one will be somehow traced to the offender and it appears to him that one more will make but little if any difference.

Of course, this generalization greatly oversimplifies the problem. It is quite possible that it misses the mark completely. If so, how else can we explain the masses of parole violators who, in their clumsy but earnest attempts to assess their parole experiences, so frequently give voice to this statement: "I don't understand it myself. I know I had the best of intentions when I left the institution. I thought I had solved my problems and life would be different and I would be happy; yet, when I was released, I was not happy, I was worried. Everything seemed to go wrong. Pretty soon I didn't seem to care what happened. I had already lost my job. The next thing, I was broke and needed money. I tried to get another job. I guess I didn't try very hard. Then I thought if I just had enough money to hold me over for a few days until I could find a job, things would still come out all right, so I took some stuff. But things didn't seem to get any better so I just got more disgusted and kept on until I got caught and now here I am and I still don't know just what went wrong because I sure had good intentions when I went out."

After discussing these experiences with thousands of parole violators, it is my personal belief that fear of consequences is of small value in helping a parolee steer a true course. Fear is a negative factor and, as such, it has little if any influence upon the parolee who is full of hope and whose efforts are winning social and economic acceptance in his community. On the other hand, for the man or woman who is slipping, who is beginning to feel frustrated, fear is already present. Surely it is not more fear that is needed—rather it is hope that might conceivably turn the tide.

This brings us to the other, and perhaps the more important, aspect of parole—the sphere of treatment. To be really effective, the parole agent must be able to fully understand the parolee—his assets, his liabilities, his culture patterns, his motivations, his interpersonal relationships, etc. With a full knowledge of the parolee's background—his social history, intelligence, personality factors, medical history, his skills, aptitudes and interests, as well as his habits, vices and police history, the parole agent will usually know far more about the parolee than the latter knows about himself. Because of this, he is in a position to give guidance in every contact. Guidance is only worthy of the term if reception is assured on the same basis as it is given, namely, mutual respect and understanding. Therefore, even the methodology of carrying out the guidance program is dictated by this vast and intimate knowledge of the parolee.

The initial interview offers the first opportunity for the parole agent to lay the groundwork for a successful treatment program. When the parolee enters the parole office after many long months in detention, he is surcharged with mixed emotions—exhilaration that the day of freedom has finally arrived, joy that the dull routine of prison existence is ended, blissful anticipation of going places and doing things so long denied him, misgivings about his appearance and the fit of his clothing, uncertainty about domestic relations and the attitude of old friends, doubt as to his ability to please his new employer, worry about the treatment he may receive from society, fear that it will be his luck to draw a harsh, unsympathetic parole agent, guilt feelings, which he never expected, about his being an ex-convict. These currents of happiness, crisscrossed by twinges of anxiety, create a state of excitement with overtones of severe nervous tension. Men who have experienced this sensation call it the "release jitters."

With so many confused thoughts and mixed feelings, it is understandable that full attention cannot be given to detailed parole instructions. However, definite impressions will be carried away from this interview. The questions most likely to be uppermost in the parolee's mind are: Will I be able to get along with my parole agent? Will he be interested in me? Will he understand me? Will he help me and give me a break? Will he be warm and friendly? Or will he be cold and indifferent? Will he be tough and hardboiled? Will he lay down the rules and give the old police routine —"break the law and go to jail?"

At this point the parole agent must be alert to the necessity for objectivity. This frequently requires the exercise of his full professional capacity. As a matter of fact, he has just completed a careful and detailed study of the parolee's case history which, as we all know, is highlighted with every known mistake he has ever made. The assay of assets and liabilities, as reflected by the cold record, may easily incline the parole agent toward a pessimistic mood in which he finds more fault with the selectivity of the parole board than inspiration to assist the parolee in effectuating an acceptable social adjustment. However, any such gloomy reverie must be dispelled before the interview if the treatment process which was started in prison is to be continued successfully on parole. This is the beginning of a relationship which, if it is to be fruitful, must accentuate the positive.

THE NATURE OF PAROLE SUPERVISION*

The obvious implication of the title of this paper is that parole supervision is not a one-way process, but involves both parties to the business of rehabilitation. This concept is not new, but at one time is would have been the cause of a startled silence. At that time, I think, we were comfortably wrapped in our cloak of authority and thought only in terms of a parole agent issuing orders and a parolee obeying them—or else.

It must have been rather pleasant to be a parole officer in an era when one was not expected to engage self-consciously in a "relationship" with the parolee, and then to record what happened and its significance for his development. Because this paper is not a historical survey of the change in the philosophy of supervision, we shall not try to trace the development of our present thinking but rather to look at supervision today and see what is in the case relationship for both agent and parolee.

We probably can agree on "authority" as the starting point for our discussion. What we do as parole workers is possible only because legislation has created the agencies in which we operate and has given certain powers to these agencies. While the powers differ from agency, rather broad base of uniformity makes parole supervision an entity. The work of each agency is limited in extent by the law creating it. Administrative heads are not free to do just anything they may wish with the parolees or parole agents over whom they have jurisdiction. Whatever the authority, much of it must be delegated to subordinates, including supervising agents, whose job is in turn more limited in scope than that of the top level administrators. This important point must be kept in mind as we continue our inspection of supervision.

The relationship between the parole agent and the parolee is not a spontaneous association of two people or even a consciously

---

* Reprinted by permission of the National Probation and Parole Association, Richard G. Farrow: The Give and Take of Parole Supervision, *Focus*, Vol. 32, No. 1, Jan. 1953, p. 1-5.

sought acquaintance for the benefit of either party. It is an imposed relationship in which neither party has complete freedom. The agent is compelled, by the terms of his employment and by the operating rules of the agency, to follow a certain course of action. These requirements may be at a minimum level, and indeed should be for best professional operation, but nevertheless they define and limit the relationship for the agent. The parolee is similarly restricted by the terms of his parole compact, by the agency rules, and by the sentence or special laws affecting him. To think of the supervision relationship as anything but a created compulsory thing is to think in unreal terms. It is true, of course, that the agent may turn to other work and that the parolee may choose to remain in jail or to abscond, but short of these debatable alternatives, it seems true that each party accepts the relationship rather than selects it.

Such a relationship would be completely sterile were it not for the purposefulness which is basic to the situation. The purpose of supervision, from the parolee's point of view, is to permit him to live in the outside world with somewhat restricted freedom. For the agent, the purpose is to permit his entry into the parolee's life, with power to regulate certain aspects of that life. I use "regulate" rather than "control" because it has seemed to me that we deceive ourselves when we think of "controlling" human beings. Nor should we desire to do so. We influence, we speed up or slow down, we have an effect on other people, but we do not control them. The word "regulate," I think, better describes what we do. The phrase "certain aspects of that life" is used to point out that our power is not all inclusive but operates only in designated areas.

Compared with other authoritative relationships, we find that ours is not unique but that we are in an upper bracket in amount of authority given to us. We lack the near total rule of military power or of prison administration, but have more authority than have schools, industry, or even parents. This weight of authority is both ballast and burden in the relationship.

Some new parole workers have trouble in coming to terms with their authority. Some try to deny it and seek to make of the relationship a too friendly, personal thing. Thus by playing down the rules and regulations, by granting unearned and unjustified privileges, they make the parolee grateful to them or at least pleasantly disposed so that he will respond favorably. Sometimes this approach leads even to lending money and exchanging social amities. Others, unable to see beyond authority limit their work to the issuing of orders and the routine writing of reports. The experienced parole agent, with help and training, has usually worked through both of these cul-de-sacs to a clearer understanding of his job. He is aware of his purpose in making contacts, aware that he is seeking not so much to make a profound impression on a parolee as to represent to the parolee the agency, the rules, and the laws of society. By this I mean that the agent does not set out with the idea of reforming the parolee. Instead, he goes out to follow the procedures set up by the agency for his job. His helpfulness to the parolee will depend on *how* he does his job more than on *what* he does. The experienced worker knows that he is paid to participate effectively in this relationship. He knows that what he does must have some purpose which must lie within the agency's limits. For example, he is not domineering in his approach to a parolee, because there is nothing in the parole law which allows him to assume that attitude. He does not immediately adopt a familiar attitude with the parolee because the law does not strip the parolee of his personal dignity and his right to ordinary courtesies. Such thinking precludes an immediate use of the parolee's first name, for example, just as it precludes the agent from permitting use of his own name. The agent is aware that his relationship with the parolee does *not* give him the *right* to swear at the parolee or even to get angry with him. Ideally and theoretically, there is no reason for an agent to get angry, because he has no personal stake in what happens to the parolee. Practically, of course, there is a human interest that at times causes exasperation with and a genuine concern for the parolee's behavior. This can result in a display of anger but it will be different from the anger of an agent issuing orders as if from his own personal authority and seeing these orders disobeyed. It is part of the agent's knowledge of his job that the authority he has is not personal and that the relationship it initiates cannot be personal. He confines what use he makes of his authority to what he is empowered to do. He does not threaten a parolee with reprisal or use of force. He does not say, *"I'll send you back,"* when this is a matter solely for the agency heads. Instead, he explains the alternatives of action and what the parolee should know about the consequences of his own behavior. In short, the experienced and trained agent achieves a *professional* relationship.

The concept of professionalism is based on knowledge, skill, objectivity and responsibility. One of the weighty aspects of the job to a new agent is his sense of responsibility for the good or bad behavior of his parolees. This feeling goes hand in hand with a personal approach to the job and to parolees. Thus when a parolee makes good and the agent has had a close personal relationship with him, the agent feels a sense of accomplishment. When the opposite outcome ensues, the agent feels bad or even guilty. Perhaps some of this feeling in either event is inevitable, but the professional agent knows that he cannot be responsible for the total behavior of a parolee. Such a charge on an agent would be an impossible burden. I think we can agree that no one could accept so much responsibility for another person.

If a parolee makes good and the supervising agent can see how he helped in that progress, certainly he can feel happy about his work. He cannot take total credit, however, for the parolee's development; most credit will belong to the parolee himself and perhaps to some other person who has a stake in his success. Paradoxically, an agent may well be proud of work he has done with an unsuccessful parolee. He may have contributed everything possible to the job, but not have been able to stem the tide of adverse influences for the parolee. Since we cannot control parolees there will be times when they choose not to cooperate. If this were not so, supervision would be unnecessary. Parolees will always be able to deceive an agent and to conceal some violations from him, despite his best efforts in checking and investigating. It would be naïve to assume otherwise.

An agent is responsible for meeting the minimum requirements of his agency insofar as contacts are concerned. Beyond that, he is responsible for making each contact fulfill its purpose—that is, to contribute to the regulation or channelization of the parolee's life. He must *know* the parolee and know *about* the parolee. From his information, he must make reports and recommendations, and occasionally he must take prompt action. He is not omnipotent and he cannot be expected to prevent all further crime by parolees or to keep all of them under his thumb. He should not be assigned an impossible task.

What then goes on in this authoritative, limited, nonpersonal relationship that fulfills society's purpose with parolees? As stated first, there is more to it than issuing and obeying orders. We have seen that the agent is there to see, to counsel, to analyze, to report and to act. The parolee is there to establish a pattern of living that will exclude criminal activity and be generally acceptable to society. The two roles intermingle through the operation of the rules and procedures of the agency. In an early interview, for instance, the agent asks questions about the parolee's status, his plans and his feelings. These facts he is required to know about and to report upon. The parolee, whose life is restricted by the rules applied to him, answers the factual questions and then tries to obtain additional privileges. The agent explains the basis on which these may be granted, but the parolee, with his negative feelings about the concrete situation, shows hostility and evidence of an uncooperative attitude. If the agent were to react personally, if he were to fall into the trap unknowingly set by the parolee, he would resent this resistance to his authority, he would reply indignantly, and the interview would degenerate into a bickering squabble. If he is well-rooted in his job, its power, purposes, and limits, the agent sees the response of the parolee as a test of those limits, an attempt to gain some control in the relationship. The agent acknowledges the feeling that is shown by the parolee and doesn't belittle it. But by further questions and discussions, he aids the parolee to see himself in the situation. The agent reflects the parolee's feeling in a way that gets the parolee to discover his own motivation. Similarly, when a violation occurs, the agent discusses the offense with the parolee rather than scolds him for it. Only to the extent that parolees are aided to see themselves in operation and to discover truths about themselves is supervision successful. Ordering, advising, scolding, forbidding—all may be used and at times show positive results, but I incline to the belief that the results are more durable when they are rooted *within* and not outside.

I would not want to limit a parole agent in the supervisory relationship to a passive role, nor do I believe that this would be possible under most parole laws. The agent is required to take an active part in the total process, and strongly to represent the agency in contacts with the parolee, but this does not mean that he talks endlessly. The best agent draws out the parolee while he himself listens and observes. The parolee who at first seems to be chiefly on the "taking" end of parole thus shifts to the "giving" side. He gives of himself when he feels free and confident with the agent. He gives his compliance with rules, and he gives his cooperation in procedures. These are desirable products of parole, but they are obtained only voluntarily; they defy compulsion.

The agent's contribution to the relationship consists of his understanding, his skill in dealing with emotions and with parole machinery, his knowledge, and the indefinable "atmosphere" that surrounds him. He is the authority to the parolee, but he is authority humanized. He is not raw force but potential power that can be set in motion only by the parolee himself. The parole agent is seeking to do an effective job with the parolee as demanded by his agency. The helpfulness of this approach lies in its freeing of the parolee from fear and resistance as he comes to sense that the agent is not threatening him either by constant display of authority or by inept efforts at psychotherapy. The agent is not trying to do something *to* the parolee, not trying to remake him. Change in the parolee can and will result from such relationship, but it will be the parolee's own change, not the agent's handiwork. The parole process, not the agent alone, is the instigator of change.

The obvious limitations in such a position make for strength, not weakness. The agent knows what he is doing, has confidence in his authority and his training and is not trying to do the impossible. When necessary, he initiates disciplinary action such as restriction of privilege, more frequently reporting, or actual confinement, but he does this because of the parolee's behavior, not because of his own outraged feeling. The final test of the validity of a process is whether it functions well under positive and negative conditions.

The parole officer's stake in the whole process is not the behavior of the parolee but his own job, for which he is responsible.

It is impossible for him to do more than implement the regulatory structure created by the agency, the rules, job requirements, prohibitions, restrictions, reports, interviews and investigations. Within this process there is help for the parolee and ultimately for society. The help comes from the extent of the "give and take" between agent and parolee.

The process of supervision is restless and moving; it is characterized by upheaval and subsidence, flurry and calm, but it is always dynamic rather than static. Its success in individual cases depends on the security within it for both participants. Limit it to an arbitrary, personal, volatile encounter and it will soon be counted among the unsuccessful social ventures of mankind. Expand it so that it holds trust, self-control, free discussion, and a reciprocal feeling of purpose and goal, and it can lead the way to better understanding and method in the field of correction.

INTENSIVE PAROLE SUPERVISION*

The rising social and financial costs of a steadily increasing prison population led the Department of Corrections in the early 1950's to explore programs of treatment in the community rather than in institutions. One of the first of these programs combined earlier release from prison with intensification of parole supervision.

In 1953, the Adult Parole Division inaugurated the Special Intensive Parole Unit (SIPU) to study the relationship between size of parole agent caseload and amount of parolee criminal activity. With the March (1963) publication of its latest report, SIPU has completed three separate phases of this project. All tested the hypothesis that the release of inmates to smaller, intensively supervised caseloads would result in lower parole violation rates.

In the first two-year phase beginning in February, 1954, fourteen SIPU parole agents distributed over the state, carried caseloads averaging eighteen parolees, in contrast to the usual ninety.

Parolees whose release dates had been advanced three months, and those whose release dates had not been advancd were assigned

---

* Reprinted by permission of California Department of Corrections, Joan Havel: Special Intensive Parole Unit Reports on Phase III, *The Research Newsletter*, Vol. 4, No. 1-2, March & June 1962, p. 14-18.

randomly to both kinds of caseloads. After three months, those in the SIPU caseloads were transferred to the regular ninety-man caseloads.

Phase I did not show any consistent difference between SIPU and ninety-man (control) caseloads in number of suspensions or of major arrests at the end of the first six months of parole. It did demonstrate, however, that:

1. Parolees whose release dates were advanced did as well as those whose dates were not advanced, in both SIPU and control caseloads, and
2. The parolees released to intensive supervision without a pre-arranged employment program did as well as those who were released to a definite job.

In Phase II, which ran for eighteen months beginning in January, 1956, the SIPU caseloads were increased to thirty and the period of intensive supervision was extended to six months. Results were similar to those in Phase I, for both a six and a twelve months follow-up period. Neither study supported the hypothesis that small caseloads would reduce the number of parole violations.

It was felt that this failure may have been a consequence of the temporary nature of the SIPU caseloads. Because of rapid caseload turnover, SIPU parole agents became, in effect, intake workers. The agents themselves felt they were not given enough time to develop meaningful relationships with their parolees. The increased caseload size in Phase II, which afforded the parolees a longer time with the same agent, had been intended to offset the possibly damaging effect of disrupting the relationship of parolee to parole agent at a crucial period of parole. In Phase III, the requirement of transfer to regular caseloads was dropped, and SIPU caseloads were raised further to thirty-five men. Regular caseloads at this time numbered about seventy-two. Findings of other investigators suggested that the effectiveness of intensive supervision might vary with different types of parolees. The development of a Base Expectancy measure by the Research division offered a way of testing this impression. By means of Base Expectancy scores, computed from information about the inmate's background known at time of entry to prison, parolees were classified into poor, medium, and high parole risk groups in the Phase III study.

The parole performance of the Phase III subjects (911 SIPU and 2,806 control) was observed at the end of the first and second year on parole. At both times, parolees released to the smaller caseloads performed significantly better than those released to regular caseloads. A greater percentage of SIPU subjects had experienced no arrest of any kind than had control subjects, and a smaller percentage had been returned to prison. The difference, however, was not the same for all types of parolees.

It was larger for the medium risk parolees than it was for either the best or poorest risk groups. It was also larger for parolees in the northern region of California than it was in the southern region, and for those released in the middle of the time period covered by the study for those released earlier or later.

The difference between reduced and regular caseloads found in Phase III, compared to those from Phase I and II, suggest that intensive supervision should be continued at least through the first year of parole. We do not know, however, whether it was continued reduced caseload supervision or continued supervision by the same parole agent that made for this difference.

The finding that reduced caseloads were more effective with the medium-risk parolees than with poor or best-risk groups poses further questions. The Base Expectancy score by which parolees were classified into risk groups was based on only a few background factors — prior record, offense, race, and history of escape. We know nothing of the social, psychological or economic dimensions in which the men in one risk group differed from those in another. Other studies on the outcome of correctional treatment suggest that further attention to the nature of differences among parolees will be a productive avenue for future research.

Differences in effectiveness of reduced caseloads in different areas of the State are also difficult to interpret. Differences in the environmental situation, such as employment opportunities, may have been a factor in this. Seasonal differences in employment opportunity may also have been responsible for the findings that SIPU parolees released in the middle of the study did better than those released earlier or later.

In asking more questions that it answers to date, the SIPU program has defined problem areas and opened the way to further research objectives. In Phase IV, effort is turned toward defining types of parolees and the kinds of intensive treatment to which they may best respond.

PAROLE OF THE NARCOTIC ADDICT*

The Division of Parole is an administrative agency in the executive department of the state of New York, whose specific supervisory goal is the rehabilitation of adult offenders committed to state prisons and reformatories by the judicial system of the state, for violations of law, and who have been released to the community with part of their sentences still to be served under supervision.

Throughout the years of its existence, the Division of Parole has always had under its supervision some offenders who had been addicted to illegal narcotic use. Some of these offenders had abstained for years from the use of narcotics while on parole, and some had relapsed. However, the number of such parolees addicted to narcotics was small, and there was no particular awareness of their constituting a special problem as contrasted with other more sizable or more urgent areas of consideration.

The Division of Parole has always been concerned with developing its services successfully to meet longstanding or emergent problems by a certain degree of functional specialization within the organization and operation of the agency. Examples of such development to meet needs included establishment of specialized caseloads of mentally defective delinquents, and of youthful offenders, with parole officers specially selected and assigned, and given the opportunity to develop appropriate techniques and methods of approach.

In recent years, the epidemic horizontal spread of illegal narcotic use, with the lowering of the age of infection down to

---

* Reprinted by permission of the American Correctional Association. Paul Travers: An Experiment in the Supervision of Paroled Offenders Addicted to Narcotic Drugs, *American Journal of Correction*, Vol. 19, No. 2, Mar.-Apr., 1957, p. 4-7.

the adolescent level, has created difficulties for all the agencies engaged in social control, including the Division of Parole.

The rapid increase in numbers, the justified fear and alarm in the community, the demands for action matched only by the lack of knowledge of what to do, the frustration brought about by the seemingly vicious circle of arrest and relapse, repeated over and over again, the increasing demands upon the parole officer's time required by the supervision of parolee-addicts, had elevated the problem of the supervision of the narcotic parolee to a level requiring the consideration of further specialization of services in an attempt to find ways of more effectively helping such parolees.

The desire of the Division of Parole for a further development of its specialized services within the framework of its regular organization and operations was reflected, last year, in the recommendation of the governor of New York for "the development of a comprehensive rehabilitation program for addicts with adequate follow-up services." He called also for enlistment of an experimental drug addiction treatment center whose patients would include but not be limited to parolees. In addition, he requested funds so that "the Division of Parole may assign specially trained parole officers to work intensively with addicts released on parole from the state correctional institutions. In New York City these parole officers will, of course, work closely with the professional personnel engaged in the hospitalization outpatient treatment and follow-up program."

The Division of Parole was alloted $30,000 in the 1956-57 budget to conduct an experiment in the supervision of parolee addicts in the New York area. This fund was to provide specifically for the supervision of parolee addicts by means of the addition of four parole officers, a senior parole officer and a stenographer, in addition to conducting studies and analyses of the results of the experiment, and a limited amount was made available for the purchase of services not otherwise available when the need was acute.

The primary long range goal of our helping relationship with the parolee-addict is the abstinence of the parolee from the use of narcotics. The actual experience of the Division of Parole, prior to the formation of the experimental project, is that this has been accomplished in some cases. It is possible to achieve, however difficult, however rare.

Another goal reflects our refusal to be discouraged or to give up, because of anything short of abstinence. We have found that prior to the project, and during its operation, the helping relationship between parolee-addict and parole officer (as representative of the whole parole team) can serve a useful purpose even when it does not prevent relapse. Experience has shown that a number of parolee-addicts reverting to the use of narcotics, either in a short time after release, or after many months, will surrender to the parole officer, voluntarily inform him of their renewed addiction, and request treatment and help. This action on their part, in the fact of their fears and anxieties is attributable to the relationship patiently developed by the parole officer. It accomplishes the excellent parole goal of preventing crimes by the parolee-addict to secure money to feed his habit.

Obviously, we do not work in a vacuum and the use of the parole officer by the parolee as a support or a resource person is influenced by the availability of services in the community. A recent situation within the narcotic project points up our position of dependence upon the community and its resources. A parolee had reverted to narcotic use but had developed sufficient trust and confidence in his parole officer to telephone to him and inform him of his relapse. He wished to surrender and avoid the commission of further crimes, but he had a great fear of the withdrawal illness. He wanted assurance that he would not be given coldturkey-treatment in detention or elsewhere, but would be given medical help during withdrawal.

The severity of the withdrawal illness varies with conditions and with the individual, but it is said to be a true physiological illness. Therefore, this was a legitimate request, but the fulfillment of the request was dependent upon the community's resources and not upon the cooperation of the Division of Parole. The senior parole officer, attempting to comply with this request, was refused assistance by the public hospitals of the city as a matter of policy. The state mental hospitals are unable to accept such patients, unless they are psychotic, and this particular parolee was overage for Riverside Hospital.

The senior parole officer, through individual initiative, managed to secure a two-week period of hospitalization in a public hospital, not in keeping with the hospital's regulations, but as a personal favor. This exception to the rule secured the parolee's surrender, prevented crime, gained the confidence of the parolee and his family, and further sold the idea to the parolee and the inmate population that the Division of Parole is sincere in its desire to help.

The development of this parole officer—parolee addict relationship, in addition to providing the parolee with a nondisappointing human relationship, has a teaching function in that it provides a prototype of recurring, consistent and friendly contacts to show the parolee that his relationship with others outside his own limited group, need not be hostile or frightening.

Concurrent with and following the supervision work done in the project we will make case studies and analysis in order to extract from the individual cases common elements which may enable the construction of usable propositions as guides for future treatment in such cases, and, if possible, in other parole cases.

We will experiment, and are experimenting but not by arbitrarily using parolees to test various categories. Our responsibility is to select that available form of treatment which appears most advantageous in an individual case, regardless of categories. If that fails, and risk permits, we will try what next seems best of available possibilities, keeping track of what has been done in each situation, and the relative effectiveness of each approach. In other words, our responsible relationship is with the individual parolee, and he will not be used arbitrarily to serve the purpose of advancement of knowledge.

Our basic purpose remains the same in terms of our responsibility to the parolee, but within the frame of reference and limits necessarily set by our responsibility to the community, we will attempt to find what combination of parole relationships and available community resources will yield the best results.

Our ability to form effective parole relationships in these cases, and to have time to study the results of our work, has been enhanced by the funds, enabling us to limit our narcotic caseloads to a manageable size, a maximum of 30 per caseload.

As all sincere workers in the field of narcotic addiction treatment will admit, no one has as yet found the answer or answers to the problems involved. For that reason we are attempting to be as flexible as possible within the limits of public risk. We intend to avoid the position of those who assert that they never examine, physically, the arms of their clients or patients, relying solely on trust and confidence. We will equally avoid the position of those who insist upon always examining for physical evidence of narcotic use, routinely and out of context. We examine or refrain from examining depending upon the situation, our purpose during the interview and the individual parolee. We are not wedded to any preconceived methods except the general case work method which has always been individually based and as flexible as the need to be served.

A large part of experimentation in method is concentrated in the area of relapsed cases. Experience has shown that relapse is to be expected in the vast majority of cases. Relapse is, *de facto,* a violation of parole, and, as such, cannot be condoned. However, this, like all other violations, is properly evaluated, measured as to community danger, and proper disposition selected. It is a simple matter, administratively, and a legally justifiable matter to return relapsed parolees to the institutions from which paroled. This is done when the degree of danger to the community and to the man demands that disposition. But experience has demonstrated that, while such a procedure protects the community temporarily during the period of return, it does not change the parolee-addict to the point of reducing his likelihood of relapsing. It is asking too much of the institution to expect it to effect such a change when it is basically a problem of living in the community.

When we are faced with a relapsed parolee we must first estimate the degree of danger to the community. If the risk is too great, the relapsed parolee is ordered returned to the institution by the board of parole.

If risk permits, the program followed is determined by the parolee's attitude, degree of addiction, age, availability of resources, family situation and other relevant factors. The relapsed parolee is, usually, but not always, detained in the city prison pending a complete investigation of parole, with a recommendation as to the disposition. Detoxication is completed, together with withdrawal, either in the City Prison or at Riker's Island penitentiary (hospitalization is not available). During this period, the cooperation of the family is sought, and, if the parolee is ordered restored to parole by the board of parole for further supervision, the parolee is so informed and an attempt is made to convince him of our sincere desire to help him. Surprise is a heady wine but enjoyable when it goes against every expectation. Pleasant surprise—astonishment—is a common attitude experienced by such parolees and it provides us with the opportunity to prove by action what we have preached by words. He is shown that, despite his relapse, the entire parole team, including the parole board, is ready to exert all its efforts to help him if he will cooperate. He is usually passively willing to be helped, but this is not enough. He must be motivated to help even if he is helping only himself.

This type of detoxication in detention falls far short of rehabilitation but provides an opportunity for determining if such rehabilitation can be done under supervision in the community. The other alternative, rehabilitation within a hospital setting, is provided for some of our younger cases in Riverside Hospital. Experience will point to the relative effectiveness or ineffectiveness of one, the other or both.

This kind of disposition of relapse requires a uniformity of knowledge, expectation and approach on the part of all members of the parole team. The Board of Parole cannot risk restoration to parole supervision following relapse unless it can depend upon the parole officer to give intensive, patient, alert and understanding supervision and to keep the kind of case record that will permit administrative study and review. On the other hand, the Board of Parole knowing that the assigned parole officer will give the kind of supervision that will enable restoration to supervision, can with greater confidence, make such decisions, while the case record will permit periodic review as an administrative safeguard.

The parolee, thus restored to parole supervision, is in a state of mind that has changed from partial indifference, suspicion or antagonism to a willingness to cooperate with his parole officer. While relapse may again occur, such a parolee will tend to surrender when it occurs and avoid the commission of further crimes.

This situation is complicated, frequently, by conditions of ignorance, lack of moral training and similar limiting conditions. This has raised a question in some cases. Should we not be more selective in choosing cases for restoration following relapse? Why not return the more difficult parolees (long history of addiction, poor work habits, ignorance, etc.) and give our time to the better parolees. It may be, that after prolonged experience, we may come to that conclusion. However, at present we prefer to include such allegedly difficult cases in our supervision experiment and allow the facts to determine the adequacy of the hypothesis.

Thus far, our experience has taught us that a change in attitude is possible to develop despite relapse. While this change in attitude does not insure abstinence it is a necessary prerequisite for it. We have also learned that this change in attitude, by persuading the parolee to make his future condition known to his parole officer, prevents the commission of repeated crimes to feed the habit. This much is experience; the achievement of abstinence is still ahead.

While in the process of our supervision work we have cooperated with the police and other agencies of social control. The particular configuration of such cooperation is still being worked out but the goals are fixed and definite. We seek to reeducate the parolee addict to live in peace with his fellows, within the law, as a participating member of our republic.

Wishing to produce an educated enlightened citizen (within the limits of his abilities and situation) in terms of law, we have to aim at the active self-development of the powers and abilities of the parolee, and we must help him to develop an interest in things worthwhile. The value of the self-control of thoughts, words and actions must be revealed to him. His personal values, attitudes and aims must be brought within the limits of acceptable behavior. Our aims in this regard include the development of a constructive home membership, the increase of the parolee's ability to participate in the functions of a family and of his capacity to share in the values of home life. We aim also at his social membership in his neighborhood, teaching him how to get on with his fellows. We try to overcome his hostile relationship to the next larger social membership, society, in order to awaken his sense of membership in the state, his duties regarding the state and the values of good citizenship through cooperation with the community's laws. We try to show him that he mustn't wait for home, neighborhood and society to be perfect before he will cooperate.

These are but a few of our goals and they raise the question: Should a parolee reveal the previous or present source of his narcotic supply, and should his parole officer actively seek this information? The parolee, as a resident of the community has the responsibility to help prevent the illegal importation, sale and purchase of narcotics as far as he can. As an active participant in the drug traffic he has the information to contribute to help the difficult job of law enforcement. However, in practice this clear-cut situation becomes more complex. At this stage, these parolees have no such sense of civic duty or sense of obligation. Furthermore, fear—the most selfish of emotions—prevents easy cooperation.

We recognize that the parole officer, where possible, should obtain this information and reveal it to the police. The *where-possible* we interpret to mean that this is a goal that we approximate in stages. When the parolee volunteers this information, or reveals it willingly when asked, we turn it over to the police and this has aided enforcement and prevention in that it has been the basis for some gratifying arrests. We do not, at this stage attempt to force such information. This would be impractical as the parolee would simply claim ignorance or lie, and treatment would be precluded. We rather recognize such active citizenship participation as a desirable goal and seek actively to develop it, but in accordance with the dictates of practicality. We would, however, be negligent in responsibility if we ignored it.

COMBINED PUBLIC AND PRIVATE AFTER-CARE*

It is a truism that rehabilitation starts at the time of arrest. A man's chances of success or failure on release are to a great extent determined long before the gates clang shut behind him and he meets the free world again at the termination of his institutional experience by discharge or parole.

Broadly speaking, his whole life experience has brought him to the point of arrest and conviction and the problem of all those concerned with the process of correctional rehabilitation is to understand and deal with his failure to adapt in personal, family or community life.

The scope of our influence, however, begins only at the point of arrest and most of us will agree that the man's attitudes towards his own rehabilitation are shaped by his individual experience with the local police lock-up, the trial and sentencing procedure, the institutional experience, and the parole and pre-release regulations and practices.

In essence we sent a man from society for a period of incarceration to learn how to live within the law when he is returned to society. Hence we rightfully expect his experience with the process of law enforcement and correction to play a positive part in influencing his potential for later societal adaption and all of us must be everlastingly vigilant to secure and maintain this objective.

The problems of those working in the institutional area are manifold and not the least of these, effecting the man's future after-care, concerns his attitudes: He comes to the institution often bitter and hostile as a result of the experience of arrest, detention and conviction in which he was not able to "get away with it" and beat the law. The guard in the institution, being the only available person, is usually the one whom he vents his feelings. Driven by his own emotions he has to get mad at someone and the guard is available. It is little wonder that for years the "get tough" policy was adopted to bring the "fish" down to size.

---

* Reprinted by permission of the American Correctional Association. A. M. Kirkpatrick: After-care in the Canadian Correctional Treatment Plan, *Proceedings*, 83rd. Annual Congress on Corrections, 1953, p. 225-232.

It is most encouraging to note the efforts being made to use other methods of discipline such as segregation during an orientation or reception period as a means of letting him "cool off." By such ways can we convince him that authority is and wants to be helpful rather than moralistic or retaliatory? Can we meet his hostility with understanding in the framework of discipline? Can we help him by individualized treatment to see that he is essentially responsible for his own rehabilitation, that his problem is in greater or lesser degree within him, and that he himself is part of his own problem? Can we in addition by a constructive program of training and education help motivate him towards the building of some reasonably hopeful plan for the day of his release?

(It is a truism, too, that a man's real punishment begins when he returns to society and all of us in law enforcement, institutional treatment and after-care work are actively concerned about the kind of climate society maintains for the ex-convict. There are undoubtedly a number of men who do not seem to care much about their future return to society. But in most cases the man judges our efforts by the answer to his supreme question—"How will society accept me on release?" He has paid his debt, he has made his time, he wants to go straight. Will he be given the chance? Our main efforts in after-care are directed to this man.)

Eventually he confronts his community again and immediately becomes aware of certain needs common to all human beings. As a biological organism he must exist and to this end needs food, clothing and shelter. Federally he is provided with a minimum issue of clothing and the relatively meagre results of this prison earnings. Provincially he may receive a small discharge gratuity with further monetary assistance in some provinces towards his rehabilitation. But there is little question that the amount of his "gate money" is inadequate, in modern terms, to provide him with subsistence and necessities to last him till he has found a job and secured his first pay. In essence he is all too often to all intents and purposes insolvent the day he is released.

This is one area of need to which I would draw your attention. Efforts should be made to secure better gratuities based not on a relationship to time served, which may be a proper one to be observed in regard to prison earnings, but on a realistic appreciation of the need for physical survival faced by any man leaving prison. The material needs of a man who has been in prison for only three months are largely the same as those of longer sentence men. It is not so much the length of time served which is the important factor here; but rather, even for a short-sentence man, the dislocation from home, job and community relationships and the stigma of being an ex-convict. If reasonable provision is not made for his needs at this point we may well be leaving him in circumstances conducive to his return to crime.

In Great Britain the man finds himself immediately, as any other citizen in need, within the scope and provisions of an assistance program of some sort. In Canada this is not so and the Prisoners' Aid Societies are placed in the position of attempting to bridge the gap from institutional maintenance to self-maintenance in the community. Our efforts, because of lack of funds are, to say the least, minimal and we find ourselves all too frequently providing "flop-house" accommodation, inadequate meals, and cast-off clothing; but this is not in keeping with the objectives of the institutional treatment program, the needs and aspirations of the man, or the kind of circumstances and surroundings to hold on the straight path men who have known the lure of easy money and easy living. We know from studies on parole violation that men who return to stable residential quarters violate much less frequently than those who return to live in the transient, semi-slum life of the cities.

We should work for nothing less than an adequate minimum gratuity payable to all men and, in addition, a realistic rehabilitation grant budgeted to make up the difference between the man's available resources including prison earnings and the needs of his individual rehabilitation plan. It is rehabilitation that is the goal and a slightly higher economic cost at this point may well save untold future institutional and community costs. We are spending millions for institutional care and pitiful thousands for after-care.

Such a rehabilitation grant should be planned with the man while in the institution as part of the pre-release program. This grant should be made available to him under supervision and adjusted as necessary either through institutional field officers, where they are employed, with governments assuming the costs directly or, alternatively, through co-operation with the Prisoner's Aid Societies with the cost charged back to the government jurisdictions involved. Such a charge-back arrangement for specific direct assistance should be carefully distinguished from general governments grants to Prisoner's Aid Societies for administrative and developmental purposes. We are just scratching the surface of the job that needs to be done and it is suggested that governments should be urged to consider their responsibility for financing in greater measure after-care of this nature.

It is generally recognized that pre-release preparation within the institution should begin the direct process of after-care. Hence if the work is done by a voluntary agency it is most desirable that the institutional staff and the institutional representative of the voluntary agency work in close partnership to interpret the function of the after-care agency and to assist those men, who wish help, to develop a plan for their return to community of their choice.

This may well involve a reaching out to the local community through the facilities of the after-care agency to check the reality of home, family, employment, community acceptance and readiness to help. There would follow the interpretation of these to the man so that, if necessary, he may rebuild his plan. Another step would be preparation of a pre-release report covering his background and plans to be forwarded to the Local Prisoners' Aid Society in readiness for his reception into the community. Ultimately there would be the receiving of progress reports from the after-care agency which might help the institutional staff assess their planning and treatment of the individual man.

Where, for any reason, it is not possible for the Prisoners' Aid Society to maintain such a representative within the institution, it is most essential that a close liaison be developed with the institutional staff. To this end it is hoped that the Prisoners' Aid Societies may be regarded as extensions of the institution into the community with direct referral of the man and consultation regarding him prior to and following release with a free interchange of essential information regarding him and his progress.

Such direct referral is contingent, of course, on the man's willingness to accept it and to plan for after-care assistance through a Prisoners' Aid Society on his release; but no material distinction need be made in the case of men released by outright termination of sentence or on parole. It should be noted, however, that the parole function is an official one so that, while the institutional representative of the Prisoners' Aid Society may be the one to help the man develop a plan and the Society may agree to accept his supervision on parole, the plan should be worked out in collaboration with the institutional and/or parole board staff, presented by them with their recommendations to the parole board, and the decision regarding parole made entirely by the appropriate official agency. Similarly, objective reports may be made by the Prisoners' Aid Society as to the man's co-operation on parole; but any recommendation or decision to revoke should be made by official action of the appropriate authority.

The work of the local Prisoners' Aid Society is greatly helped when such planning takes place prior to release and the man can be shepherded, as it were, from the institution to the community. But many men do not accept this service in the belief that they can make it alone and, in the case of short-sentence men, because there is often insufficient time for anyone to build up such a relationship.

Hence, we encounter the problem of the self-referred men. Many of these are anxious for advice and counsel and are willing to try to make some kind of a plan even at a belated date and these we should reach out to help. However, many are frankly interested in nothing but emergency assistance to tide them over night. These latter present a problem more in the nature of emergency relief than of prisoner after-care and may have been discharged for months or years but still choose to regard themselves as ex-convicts for purposes of securing assistance.

The problem of the man seeking only such direct assistance becomes that of determining the real focus of his needs. These may well have changed from those related to his having been at one time an ex-convict to those related to his presenting himself now as a transient unemployed man. Thus he may well have passed from the field of responsibility of the Prisoners' Aid Society into that of those organizations concerned with hostel service or direct relief. Our best function may be not to try to work with these men or render them the direct assistance they seek; but rather to direct them to the appropriate agencies in the community for assistance.

Our communities will soon be obliged to face squarely the problem of these single, unemployed, transient men who seek assistance from every conceivable social agency or individual. They are able to secure enough help that, by going from city to city or living on "skid row," they can eke out an existence of sorts in between sporadic and ineffectual employment. How much we as social agencies are making possible such a way of life needs to be examined and some determination made of the most helpful way of meeting the needs of these men who represent both a sickness and an unmet need in our social organization.

This problem should be discussed frankly with officials in those Government Departments which make grants to the work of the Prisoners' Aid Societies and also with Community Welfare Councils to the end that some planning may be undertaken to solve this broad social problem. We in the after-care agencies should clarify the nature of the intake policies we set up that there may be understanding and recognition of the waste of money and time entailed in our attempting to work with this type of man when so many more hopeful opportunities demand more time than we can presently give under the best of circumstances. Interpretation should also be made with the men in the institutions and the institutional staffs so that they may be made aware of the nature, limitations and scope of the services we are prepared to render. We should exercise some measure of selection so that we may best utilize our limited staffs and funds.

The work of after-care would clearly seem to be best done under conditions of referral or at least within the framework of the man's willingness to co-operate to the extent of developing a plan even though this be tentative and short-term. The provision of direct assistance in the form of lodgings, food, clothing or tools should be contingent on such subsidies being constructively essential to some purposeful plan in which they become a means of reconstruction and rehabilitation rather than ends in themselves.

When direct assistance is used in such a way it becomes obvious that it is not regarded as a matter of right to which a man becomes entitled by identifying himself as an ex-convict. Rather it becomes part of the total case work process and the price expected of the man is that he be willing to make some sort of plan which hopefully will bring him to a self-supporting status. This cannot always be accomplished in practice as we well know; but is a goal which we should keep in mind in our interviews. The use the man makes of direct assistance provided in small amounts at the initial stages of a relationship may prove a valuable index of his capacity and willingness to plan constructively and to co-operate in bringing his own resources of self-awareness and skill to focus on his own problems. His abuse of it also becomes an index of the necessity for termination. While many men have been helped most effectively in the case work or counselling relationship without the provision of direct assistance of any sort, it would be quite inappropriate to counsel a hungry man. His physical needs must be met in order that he may be helped to deal with and resolve his fears, hostilities and insecurities.

One of the most important problems facing the man is the securing of employment and an important function of the Prisoners' Aid Society is in the area of employment counselling. It is in everyone's interest that the man speedily secure the employment which relates to his plan for rehabilitation; but it should be no reflection on him or the employment agency if he accepts a non-demanding unskilled job on an interim basis. He needs employment not only to become self-supporting; but also in order to regain his self-confidence and obtain a reference by which he may upgrade his job and income and reach into the area of whatever training, skill or experience he may have.

In this connection we should use the facilities of the National Employment Service for the actual job placement and do all in our power to co-operate with this agency in developing its job resources in industry and placement skills in working with ex-convicts. Our task is to help get the man to accept and use these services in addition to his own efforts. Where the Prisoners' Aid Society has job contacts of its own they are best used not to place the top grade men leaving the most difficult for the National Employment Service; but rather holding its own job contacts in reserve to help the men who may prove difficult to place through these other channels. We have been in an era when job placement has been relatively easy and we may have done rather well in this regard; but in the long view we should use, support and help develop the services available in our communities for job placement and recognize that our part is largely that of counselling the man regarding employment and making the proper referral.

A major function of an after-care agency is that we know our communities as the ex-convict cannot know them and acquaint him with the resources which can be mustered to help him if he will accept and use them. We need to interpret the needs of ex-prisoners among the health and welfare agencies of our communities and enlist their goodwill so that they will only be willing to render their appropriate services to our men, but may achieve, where necessary, some perspective regarding the way in which they render them. Where needed services are lacking we need to play our part, through interagency co-operation and community planning, to help bring about their development. We should accelerate our developing relationships with these agencies operating in the whole range of individual treatment—medical, psychiatric, social work, psychological and sociological—and should bring into our considerations in the correctional field the best practices we can find from these or other sources. We cannot do this job alone and need to involve in our communities all the agencies which can make a helpful contribution to the social reconstruction of our men.

The phrase "social reconstruction of our men" begins to indicate the nature of our task which has its roots in the correctional institutions and its branches in many agencies and personal relationships in our communities. We are in an enabling or facilitating role bridging gaps which the man cannot himself bridge; providing him with knowledge of the community which he may not have; helping him see opportunity where he may face frustration and hopelessness; providing him with his immediate creature needs of food, clothing and lodgings; helping him to understand the nature of his own problems and supporting him in the developing role he must play in his own behalf.

Essentially this involves a partnership between government departments and private agencies in which the institutions see the Prisoners' Aid Societies as extensions of their treatment program. There should be the utmost co-operation between the Prisoners' Aid Societies and the field officers of the institutions, whether concerned with parole or rehabilitation, and frank discussion of the ways in which the facilities and contributions of all concerned can be meshed into an effective service in the interest of the man. The institutions cannot do the job without the help of Prisoners' Aid Societies mustering community and citizen support and understanding. Neither can the Prisoners' Aid Societies do the job without the information and co-operation available from the institutions.

This should be a partnership not only in service but in financing. The history of our correctional institutions shows that when left to themselves they suffered from lack of citizen understanding, support and, when necessary, informed criticism. The private citizen is anxious to play his part not only in the provision of funds for after-care; but in the whole correctional program regarding which the Prisoners' Aid Societies must always keep a watching brief. But the private citizen should not be seduced by human sympathy into footing the entire bill for after-care. Government grants and payments for services on an agreed basis are essential to ensure the proper discharge of the total social responsibility. These grants, however, should never be allowed to assume so great a proportion of the income of the Prisoners' Aid Society that the Society feels obligated to or dependent on government either in the partnership by which services are rendered or in the important function of promoting the individualized treatment of prisoners throughout the entire correctional process. The voice of citizen participation may well be a soft one; but it must be effective in expressing convictions which are built up from our knowledge of the needs and problems of the men we serve in Prisoners' Aid work.

USE OF VOLUNTEERS IN PAROLE WORK*

The parole adviser is primarily and essentially a volunteer in the field of rehabilitation. As such he has a long and honorable

---

* Reprinted by permission of *Federal Probation*. Edwin B. Cunningham: The Role of the Parole Adviser, *Federal Probation*, Vol. 15, No. 4, Dec. 1951, p. 43-46.

lineage. John Augustus, that celebrated Boston shoemaker who is often regarded as the father of probation, was of this group. Of course, he was functioning as a volunteer or unpaid probation officer, but essentially he was a nonprofessional counselor, adviser, first friend, and sponsor to the offenders released under his supervision. The fact that they were technically probationers rather than parolees probably did not alter the relationships established or the techniques attempted.

Aid societies, sometimes subsidized by government, typically were interested in parole cases. However, it is generally considered that parole as now understood originated at the Elmira (New York) Reformatory in 1876. The parolee was required to report to a sponsor known as a guardian. The guardian apparently combined the functions of adviser and parole officer.

Development of casework and the use of professionally trained workers naturally combined to relegate the untrained, unpaid volunteer to a lesser role. Furthermore, professional and volunteer workers sometimes failed to appreciate each other or to realize that one may be complementary to the other. In many cases the role of the parole adviser has been reduced almost to the vanishing point. One might question whether an adviser belongs in a well-developed parole system. There may also be the suspicion that an overzealous amateur in some cases might actually disturb the adjustment of the parolee. This might logically bring up the question of whether the whole system could not well be scrapped. Objections implied by these considerations do have a certain degree of validity. Others could easily be raised. It may be readily conceded that the adviser relationship is frequently not very meaningful to the parolee. What then is the role of adviser?

Opportunities for Interpretation

Much has been said and published on the premise that parole is a failure because so many parolees are arrested. From time to time editorials in the daily press criticize parole systems for releasing men who commit new crimes. Too frequently parole may be considered merely as a device for relieving criminals from punishment rather than as a phase of a rehabilitating program. Actually the citizen who criticizes the system may not have considered the alternatives of parole. Would such a critic advise capital punishment for all offenses; would he prefer life terms for all convicted felons; or would he rather see all inmates released without restriction of any kind? The citizen who has had the experience of having served as a parole adviser is more likely to appreciate these considerations.

In a typical case the applicant for parole will try to suggest a rather representative member of his community as his adviser. This suggested adviser may be interested in the inmate. In most cases he may not have been aware of parole as a system, but he will usually have a number of questions to ask about his duties and his responsibilities. If the relationship with the parolee turns out to be successful it may be a matter of gratification and inner satisfaction to the citizen who has had a part in this process. Even if the parolee does not respond the adviser will usually not begrudge the efforts he made. Nearly always his attitude toward parole and rehabilitative efforts in general will be more sympathetic because of his experience.

Prerelease Planning

It has been suggested that the requirement of the parole adviser in parole planning offers a useful device for interpreting parole to the public. This is not to suggest that the adviser should not have a vital position in the rehabilitative program. If his help is to be utilized the field officer will need to cultivate consciously some kind of a working relationship with the adviser. In practice, the most favorable opportunity for doing this will usually be in connection with the normal prerelease investigation. The adviser may be well acquainted with the prospective parolee; he may have known him only slightly; or his interest may have been enlisted by relatives. In any case the fact that he has consented to serve is evidence of some interest and good will. It is up to the officer to make the most of these associations. Certainly the adviser is more likely to exert constructive effort if he understands that his offer of assistance is appreciated and recognized by the professional worker. This interview with the adviser under favorable conditions can be productive and helpful throughout the ensuing parole period.

Selection of Adviser

Obviously the prerelease interview is part of the required parole report. Does the person suggested impress the probation officer as a suitable counselor for the parolee. Presumably he is qualified by reputation, citizenship, and standing in his community. If there is any doubt further investigation may be indicated. Ideally, an effort might be made to match advisers and parolees on the basis of what is known of their personalities, characters, experience, and interests. In practice this is hardly feasible. Actually it will be found that almost any applicant for parole, as well as his friends and relatives, will avoid suggesting anyone whose reputation would not bear investigation. In the writer's experience the only exceptions have been in cases of inmates probably not eligible for much consideration in any event. There are, of course, exceptions to this rule. Some inmates are unable to secure help from the usual sources and are compelled to appeal to the field officer. A probation officer who has worked in a community for a few years will have accumulated almost automatically a sort of pool of public-spirited citizens available for such cases. These may come from the ranks of former parole advisers, educators, clergymen, and social service agencies, public and private. Nevertheless, it would seem advisable whenever possible for the applicant to suggest his own adviser. The need of doing this for himself may have the effect of placing some responsibility on the applicant. If he realizes that his entire plan will be investigated he is not likely to suggest anyone objectionable from a moral standpoint. If he selects a sympathetic individual, so much the better. The inmate is made to feel that parole is something more than a routine reward for doing part of his sentence.

Working with the Adviser

Ideally, the field officer and the adviser should function as a team. In actual practice this may not be realized as frequent contacts are not always possible. However, even a few contacts between the two can be productive. As hinted above, the probation officer will do well to express in some manner his sincere appreciation for the assistance of the volunteer worker. Such an expression may mean to the volunteer a form of recognition.

Most experienced workers would agree that advisers differ widely in their interests in the particular cases in which they are active. One may feel that by a monthly meeting with the parolee and the act of signing report forms he has adequately discharged his obligations. Another may feel constrained to offer a variety of services. Perhaps it is in the area commonly classified as executive casework that a volunteer aide can often function to best advantage. In rare cases an excess of zeal or misguided effort may disturb the adjustment of a parolee, but such situations can usually be controlled with reasonable use of tact and good will. One may recall advisers who knew too much, saw too much, and reported more problems than a busy worker might care to have brought to his attention; but such assistance can usually be turned to good advantage. If that is not possible the parolee can usually be oriented away from the overzealous adviser without undue friction or disturbance. In short, the adviser relationship has a high potential value with negligible risks.

[*The Adviser in Rural Areas*)

These observations apply to parole supervision in general. In rural communities at a distance from the office the role of parole adviser usually assumes a larger significance. Parolees near the field office will normally see their probation officer frequently and can ordinarily look to him for guidance and counsel. Problems that arise can usually be investigated promptly.

In outlying areas there is greater need for assistance. Some problems demand attention which cannot be immediately given by the probation officer. These considerations make it almost imperative that the adviser have some conception of the case in which he is interested; for the parolee may have to look to him for a certain amount of counsel and advice. These considerations probably justify more attention to the matter of enlisting the services of competent advisers than is true in urban areas. Furthermore, the officer may have to depend on the adviser for reliable information regarding the parolee's conduct, as well as his adjustment. Sometimes it may be advisable to encourage correspondence from the adviser. Here again the volunteer worker is more likely to accept responsibility if he feels that he has the confidence as well as the appreciation of the professional worker.

There is another important consideration in the supervision of parolees living in remote areas. Visits of the probation officer may necessarily be infrequent. This makes it almost imperative to have some kind of a contact on any given visit. In rural communities, even more than in urban neighborhoods, the parolee may be very sensitive about neighborhood gossip. If no one is home when the probation officer calls, an adviser with some understanding of the case can usually supply more accurate information than would be secured from a chance contact; and this information is secured with a minimum of disturbance to the parolee and his family. Incidentally, certain advisers in outlying sections are often of great service as resources of information in investigative assignments aside from the case in which they are directly interested.

Delegating Responsibility

Sometimes considerable responsibility may well be delegated to the adviser. Assuming that the adviser is an individual of intelligence, good will, and insight the parolee can be encouraged to look to him for assistance and counsel. Such procedure is time-saving to the officer and may be satisfying to the adviser. Such an adviser, because he understands his neighborhood, may also be in position to interpret the parolee's point of view to the probation officer. Intelligent efforts to meet special problems may strengthen the constructive influence of the adviser.

The following cases illustrate the role that the adviser may play in certain situations:

Case No. 1

Clarence was a twenty-six-year-old man of borderline intelligence, unstable work record, and emotional immaturity. The prognosis for his adjustment was necessarily guarded at the time of release. About the only evident favorable factor was an exceptionally devoted wife who enlisted the help of an active and able adviser.

In this case the adviser performed a variety of services beyond what a probation officer could have been expected to attempt. In the face of discouraging failures he found jobs for the parolee who, incidentally, was not very employable. Furthermore, this parolee had little vocational training or experience, and he was not well motivated. Most of the services performed by the adviser would be in the category of executive casework. The parolee's borderline intelligence and personality defects rendered him virtually inaccessible to counseling of the nondirective type. Furthermore a probation officer with a heavy caseload would probably not have felt justified in spending more than a fraction of the time and effort the volunteer invested in this unpromising subject. Without this assistance Clarence would almost certainly have been returned as a violator. Probably the net gain to society was small but at least failure was averted for a season. Whatever gain was made could be credited almost entirely to the adviser.

Case No. 2

Leonard was sentenced as a juvenile. Poor institutional adjustment led to transfer from the training school to a reformatory. The parental home was maintained under submarginal economic circumstances in a rural neighborhood far from the probation office. Leonard was of dull normal intelligence. The parents who obviously had little to offer were unable to assist in release planning. Much counseling and close supervision were indicated in this case.

It proved difficult to find anyone in the community who was willing to work with Leonard. The reluctant citizen who was finally induced to assist would hardly qualify as an ideal choice. He was a very religious person, lacking a sense of humor but with keen awareness of the existence of sin and crime and definitely on record as opposed to both. However, he knew Leonard and his family and was aware of their limitations; he probably regarded his sponsorship as a sort of unwelcome Christian duty.

This parole adviser took his responsibilities seriously and somewhat surprisingly acquired a sympathetic insight into some of Leonard's problems. A degree of wholesome restraint was tempered by some exceedingly frank but sympathetic counsel. Some rather amusing conferences involving the parolee, members of his family, the adviser, and the probation officer were held. There was also considerable correspondence between the adviser and the probation officer.

In this case the influence of a zealous adviser was probably a decisive factor. Leonard has had no conflicts with the law in more than four years since his period of conditional release expired. This alone is a remarkable gain in the light of the juvenile record. A more intelligent, sensitive, aggressive youth would probably have rejected the counsel and assistance of this adviser who by chance proved to be well fitted for the task at hand. Incidentally, this adviser has been of assistance several times since Leonard's case was closed.

Case No. 3

This was also a case in which the prognosis was dim. The home situation was poor and there was little prospect for improvement. Apparent personality defects and an unsuccessful marriage were a few of many unfavorable factors. It was hoped the adviser, who seemed unusually well fitted for this case, might counterbalance some of the unfavorable elements. After a few weeks crowded with many complications and problems the sympathetic, realistic adviser sent in a resignation with the observation, "You can have him. I'm through!" In this case a competent adviser was not enough to tip the scales, but at least more of a program had been attempted than would have been possible without volunteer assistance since this was another case in a remote community.

Case No. 4

Alfred's capable and sympathetic wife had joined a religious sect distinctive in its tenets and, therefore, somewhat clannish and group conscious. As the parolee was believed to be interested in the church of his wife's choice no objection was made to the pastor as parole adviser. However, the parolee actually rejected this form of religion much to the distress of the sincere and zealous pastor. In this case it was necessary to re-interpret the situation to both the parolee and the religious leader in terms of diverse and personal viewpoints. This was apparently accomplished without serious disturbance to the parolee. Naturally the relationship became a nominal one but it was not considered necessary to wound the adviser's sensibilities by formal termination.

Advisers for Probationers

The foregoing considerations also apply to some extent to probationers. In most probation cases, however, the presentence investigation will have revealed a potential sponsor or adviser. Often this relationship has developed on an informal basis and can well be left there. Frequently, especially in cases involving youthful probationers, a referral to a social agency or civic group is indicated. In such situations the appointment of a sponsor or adviser, whether on a formal or informal basis, is usually left to the agency or organization to which the referral is made.

In many probation cases the role of the adviser appears less significant because the probation officer has made recent contacts with individuals and organizations interested in the probationer. In some cases it will seem advisable to attempt to establish a closer relationship between the probation officer and the probationer and to subordinate multiple or conflicting influences.

Frequently I have had occasion to solicit assistance from local probation workers, particularly in rural counties. In some cases it has seemed advisable to request probationers to visit a local probation office frequently. Of course, the co-operating official should not be expected to do a lot of reporting or investigating. This arrangement so far has seemed to be especially useful in cases where alcoholic tendencies appear to be part of the problem and where referral to an Alcoholic Anonymous group has not been feasible. Naturaly the value of such an arrangement is largely dependent on the personality of the co-operating official. In my experience, officers of local juvenile courts and common pleas courts have apparently been very willing to assist. This would appear to be a useful arrangement to be used sparingly when there is evident need of more casework and more personal contacts than can be given by the supervising probation officer without assistance.

With probationers as well as with parolees an important consideration is the matter of securing assistance from unofficial sources; in other words, drawing on available community resources. There are surprising reservoirs of good will in almost any community that can be drawn on to real advantage. One problem of the probation officer is to try to utilize these potential resources to the advantage of his clients.

Summary

1. Parole advisers offer opportunities to interpret parole to the public.

2. Parole advisers often serve as a key to other community resources that may be utilized profitably.

3. Some sort of a volunteer aide is almost indispensable in areas remote from the home office; a parole adviser can fill this need. Whatever risk may be encountered in the use of an untrained volunteer in an advisory role can usually be controlled by the probation officer.

4. It is usually easy and profitable to establish a working rapport with the adviser.

5. While the adviser relationship in some cases remains a nominal one with little real influence on the parolee there is often the possibility that the help of an adviser may prove to be a vital, favorable factor in any given case.

Chapter Eleven

PAROLE: INTERNATIONAL ASPECTS

As we have seen in the previous chapters, to maintain success-ful parole and after-care programs, there is a need for sound selec-tion and pre-release preparation. Here and there, earnest efforts are being made to achieve this goal, but in the main, most juris-dictions release to parole without adequate preparation for it.

It seems clear, moreover, that policy and practice in parole vary from country to country, and frequently, within the various jurisdictions of a single country, as in the United States. The ex-tent of these variations was brought to light by a recent United Nations study, a portion of which is presented in this chapter.

In some areas, parole services are carried out wholly or in part by lay participation, much in the practice of such early reformers as John Augustus. Elsewhere, as in the United States, parole supervision is generally carried out by paid, public personnel. In some countries, however, private agencies, with governmental subsidy have responsibility for after-care services to released of-fenders, as well as those assigned to parole.

We are frequently prone to regard the ideal of parole concept as the actuality of practice. However, the scope of supervision, the length, and flexibility of parole regulations vary from area to area. In some instances, parole is no more than formal control through surveillance. Elsewhere, it is constituted by well-defined individ-ual treatment programs. The parole period may be fixed by statute and not subject to modification, or it may be defined on an in-dividual basis. As we saw the great variation of parole regulations among the various American states, so it is with those countries around the world which use parole as a penological practice. Thus, parole *is* clemency in those countries which have not made it an extension of the period of incarceration through community supervision and treatment. It is only under those latter circum-stances that *parole* truly becomes parole.

PAROLE AND AFTER-CARE IN CANADA*

Both parole and after-care have a long history in Canada. Perhaps the progress in both has at times been much too slow to satisfy the desires of some forward-looking people but progress has nevertheless been achieved.

Bridging a Gap

Canada's parole legislation was first introduced into parliament in 1898. The Prime Minister of that day in speaking to the new bill recognized the problem of readjustment to the free community which faces an inmate of a penal institution when he is discharged. Conditional liberation or parole was an obvious device to bridge the gap between the control and restraint of institutional life and the freedom and responsibilities of community life.

I have been using the word parole to describe this procedure because it is the word in common use today. The legislators of 1898 chose however to use the then current English term, "Ticket-of-Leave" and so our act is known as the Ticket-of-Leave Act. Whatever the term or name used I should like to make it quite clear that Canada's Ticket-of-Leave Act is a Parole Act. *It provides for the conditional liberation of a person under sentence so that he or she may continue to serve his or her sentence at large in the community rather than within the confining walls of the prison.* This needs to be emphasized because there has been some misunderstanding in the past due to the confusion in the terms "Ticket-of-Leave" and "Parole." Ticket-of-Leave is Parole.

In the early days of this century, the Salvation Army Prison Gates Section was the one active organization in the field of after-care. The good people of the Salvation Army undertook to provide supervision for some of the persons released on Ticket-of-Leave and one of their officers, Brigadier Archibald, joined the staff of the Department of Justice in 1905 as the first Dominion Parole Officer. This was a precedent later to be followed in 1949.

Canada was a new country sparsely settled across its vast areas and it was not easy to develop a system of close parole supervision. Consequently the parole policy was conservative down

---

*Reprinted by permission of *Canadian Welfare.* Frank P. Miller: Parole and the after-care agency, *Canadian Welfare.* Vol. 9; No. 5, Dec. 1956, p. 213-217.

through the years. This was only natural—any parole authority must consider above all else the protection of the public.

Unfortunately, the failures of people released on parole are likely to be magnified out of all proportion. The whole system and philosophy of parole is always in danger of attack and no responsible official can afford to ignore this. It would be a poor parole system indeed that released unreformed criminals before the expiration of their sentences only to have them resume their criminal activity. Parole is not mere sentence-shortening.

Foundations for Parole

During recent years there have been great developments in both after-care work and institutional treatment of offenders. In our penitentiaries today and in several of our provincial institutions you will find many new facilities for rehabilitation. Vocational training and educational courses are fitting many inmates to become producing citizens.

Classification officers and other trained specialists help the inmates to understand their personal problems. Group activities such as Alcoholics Anonymous have given the inmate opportunities for self-expression and mutual sharing of experience.

Along with this there has been during the post-war years a great expansion in the services of the after-care agencies in Canada.

The after-care society is a voluntary private society—not a government department nor an adjunct of the government. This is as it should be. From the day of the great penal reformer whose name your Society bears,* there have been private citizens deeply concerned to redeem the prisoner and ex-prisoner.

Private citizens so concerned, and banded together as independent private agencies, can ultimately lead the public to accept its responsibilities in the rehabilitation of the offender. This function of social action has been ably discharged by John Howard Societies and other after-care societies in Canada throughout the history of the movement.

Now the other function of the after-care society which I wish to stress is the direct assistance and guidance given to the individual offender.

---

* John Howard Society.

Today many societies, including your own, have professionally trained social workers on their staffs, using their special experience and skills to help ex-prisoners, and there are now many more societies, giving better and better service.

Remission Service and After-Care Agencies

You can see how these improvements in institutional and after-care services have enabled the Remission Service to expand in the field of parole. As the institutions have produced better prospects of conditional release and the John Howard Societies have offered better facilities for assistance and guidance it has been possible to release more persons on Ticket-of-Leave.

The trend was recognized by the Remission Service first in 1949. At that time it was decided to open two regional offices, one in Vancouver and one in Montreal.

During recent years more and more the John Howard Societies have recognized the contribution they could make in offering guidance to the person released to Ticket-of-Leave.

Let me give you some figures to make clear the increase between 1949 and 1955 in the number of parole cases in which it was possible to arrange for qualified supervision through an after-care agency or a provincial probation or parole agency:

In 1949, there were 89 cases in which special supervision was arranged. In 1955 the number had risen to 768.

For several years the After-Care Societies had been receiving grants-in-aid from the Penitentiaries Branch for their assistance to discharged prisoners, but by 1954 the department felt that the special services rendered in Ticket-of-Leave work needed recognition. Consequently funds were appropriated for distribution, as a grant-in-aid, in proportion to the actual service rendered.

How It Works

The John Howard Society of Ontario deals primarily with men released on Ticket-of-Leave from Kingston and Collin's Bay Penitentiaries. Of course they deal with some men coming to Ontario from penitentiaries in other parts of the country.

In the Remission Service we receive certain documents from the penitentiaries routinely, and of course, our own representative visits the institutions periodically to interview inmates at their own requests. At this time he discusses with them their plans and submits a report.

The Wardens also submit periodically lists of inmates who, in their opinion, appear deserving of favourable consideration for Ticket-of-Leave. However, it is usual for an investigation to start off with an application from the inmate himself or from someone applying on his behalf.

I may say at this point that it is unnecessary for any elaborate application to be presented on behalf of an inmate. We have a simple form which the inmate uses himself, in which he is asked to indicate clearly his plans. A simple request from a mother asking for the release of her son will start off the same complete investigation as the formal application from some prominent person.

We already have on record the report of the Finger Print Section of the R.C.M.P., which disclosed the detail of previous convictions. We immediately proceed to obtain a report from the police officer who investigated the case, to obtain some information about the offender's background and the circumstances of the offense.

We also obtain the views of the Trial Magistrate or the Trial Judge. Sometimes reports are obtained from social agencies or governmental departments, that may be in a position to give us special information.

We look to the Warden of the penitentiary and his senior officers to advise us on the inmate's progress in the institution. The Classification Officer submits a comprehensive report and if the inmate is, for example, taking vocational training, we receive a report from the Chief Vocational Officer, giving an assessment of the man's skill at his new trade.

If at this stage it appears that there is some prospect of a favourable decision, we direct an enquiry to the casework supervisor of the John Howard Society, asking him to have the Kingston representative of the Society interview the prisoner and discuss with him thoroughly his plans for release.

At the same time if the case were an Ottawa case, for example, we would write to the executive secretary of the Ottawa branch, giving him information on the case and asking him to make a community investigation. He would then visit the home of the inmate and discuss the plans with the parents or the wife, as the case might be. He would also attempt to confirm any offer of employment that may have been made.

This community investigation may raise new problems which make it necessary for us on the John Howard Society person to communicate further with the Kingston representative of the Society to have a further interview with the inmate.

This period of pre-release preparation is exceedingly important. Frequently the inmate, however well intentioned, is not fully aware of the problems he will have to face on release and it may take several interviews with either the Classification Officer or the John Howard Society worker to bring him to face his problems realistically.

Finally, however, the John Howard worker may conclude that he is willing to accept supervision of the case and advise us accordingly.

The case is then brought down for a final review by the Remission Officer handling the matter and he prepares a precis of the relevant facts, concluding with the advice that a release on Ticket-of-Leave appears appropriate.

The file then comes to one of the Assistant Directors, who examines the whole matter as a reviewing officer and, if he approves the course of action advised, he passes the file to the Director. At any stage in the procedure, of course, there may be case conferences with the Director, the Assistant Director and the Remission Officer handling the case.

The Solicitor General is the Minister responsible for making the recommendation to the Governor-General, and all documents are passed to him for his consideration.

Once the Governor-General has signed the authority for the release on Ticket-of-Leave, official notifications are then sent to all persons concerned, including applicants and persons who have reported to us in the course of the investigation.

The Warden has a thirty-day period in which to effect the release. He will have the man released as soon as arrangements are made to his satisfaction.

A New Life Begins

Now we have an ex-prisoner who has served some time in the penitentiary coming out on parole to start a new life. There will be a special condition on his license that he immediately report to the John Howard Society worker and accept his supervision and guidance. No restrictions are placed on the superior, who will use his own judgment about the assistance and counsel which are needed. Of course the need varies from case to case.

Sometimes serious problems arise, such as sickness or loss of employment, which necessitates the man's moving to a new locality. On such occasions the supervisor gets in touch immediately with the Remission Service to obtain sanction for the move.

At the same time the parolee is required to report once a month to the local Chief of Police. His failure to report to the police or his failure to abide by any other conditions of his license can bring about a revocation of his license and a return to the penitentiary. However, if there is careful selection in the first place, there is likely to be little cause for revocation. The commission of a new indictable offense, however, brings about an automatic forfeiture of the license and the parolee is re-committed to the penitentiary to serve the balance of his original term, plus any new sentence he may have received.

The supervisor continues to give guidance until the satisfaction of the parole period is over. In the cases of men on very long periods of parole, however, it has been found unnecessary to continue this supervisory relationship for the full length of the parole period.

The parole period, particularly the first few months, is a critical time for the ex-prisoner. Without the guiding hand of an experienced supervisor, he may easily become discouraged and revert to his former way of behavior to solve his social and emotional problems.

GENERAL CHARACTERISTICS OF PAROLE ABROAD*

Parole Conditions

Generally, refraining from criminality is an obligation that is mandatory upon the parolee. In some countries the law states this specifically. In those countries where progress in the field of parole and after-care has been greatest the law usually allows

---

* Reprinted by permission of the United Nations, Department of Social Affairs. *Parole and After-Care* (1954) p. 76-80. Footnotes are omitted.

the parole-granting authority much latitude in imposing additional obligations on the parolee. Such is the case in the U.S.A. (as far as Federal Parole is concerned, which is organized on more progressive lines than the analogous services in many states of the Union), Belgium, England, the Netherlands and Switzerland (federal legislation).

Where, however, the idea of parole and after-care did not gain influence until more recent times the legislator is rather prone to adopt a more stringent system of parole conditions. A series of conditions may be laid down which the paroling authority simply has to impose in pursuit of the law as in Argentina and France, or from which the paroling authority is allowed to make a choice as in South Africa in respect of ordinary prisoners. In a number of states the law orders the imposition of certain conditions and next to that, allows the enforcing agency to fix additional conditions for the parolee to live up to on an individual basis, mostly to be devised by the agency itself (Belgium, Portugal, Sweden and Tasmania).

Although there are different methods employed for imposing conditions, the conditions themselves actually show a certain similarity. It is commonly deemed of great importance that the parolee will find a job, that he won't associate with bad companions or change his address without permission, that he will abstain from the use of liquor and follow the instructions given to him by the parole authority. In Chile and Victoria the parolee is still bound to report regularly to the police, but as far as Chile is concerned this practice appears to be in disuse.

In none of the countries examined is there a channel open to the parolee to appeal against the conditions imposed upon him, but in some of them the law makes the validity of conditions dependent on their acceptance by the parolee (Belgium, France).

As for the period of conditional freedom, it is common policy that it should not extend beyond that part of the sentence left at the time of parole (U.S.A., Argentina, Chile, England, the Netherlands, Punjab and Sweden). The Swedish law, though basically sharing this view, allows for lengthening this period, while the Swiss federal legislation provides that conditions obtain during a term equal to the remainder of the sentences but neither less than two years nor more than five years.

There are exceptions to this policy, however. In Australia (Tasmania, Victoria) and South Africa the authorities fix the length of the parole period. In Belgium the length of this period ranges between set limits: a minimum of twice the remaining period, but never amounting to less than two years, nor more than five years. In France parole conditions obtain for ten years after expiration of the sentence. In Portugal the term lasts at least two years and at most five years, but periodical lengthenings are allowed with a maximum of ten years.

No special arrangements for female parolees have been made. South Africa has set up particular regulations for youthful offenders and inmates of Work Colonies. Argentinian law provides that aliens who have been granted parole are allowed to leave the country instead of accepting the parole conditions, but in that case a permanent ban is placed upon their return.

Supervision

In a number of states, public functionaries, especially trained to this end, are charged with supervision (Federal Parole in the U.S.A.; Belgium and England partly; South Africa for the greater part; Switzerland in some cantons and Victoria, but for repeated offenders only).

Where private organizations have been created to work in the field of parole and after-care, these orginizations have been charged with supervision wholly or partly: Argentina, Portugal and the Netherlands wholly; Belgium for a small part; Chile wholly with the exception of the capital; England, France and Switzerland partly, Sweden wholly, but with institution boards maintaining top supervision.

The degree of independence of these private associations is not the same everywhere. They are never financially self-supporting; nearly always they receive subsidies from public funds to cover their expenses entirely or partly. Consequently governmental authorities often exercise considerable influence upon the activities of the associations and the composition of their boards.

In Argentina the private association of Buenos Aires apparently works almost independently. In England the Central After-Care Association was set up in 1948 on the basis of a partnership between the State and private benevolence to co-ordinate the efforts of the existing associations.

In Portugal public authority maintains a strong influence. In South Africa and the Netherlands the private organizations have to be approved by the State. In Sweden the supervisory work is done by private persons, who do not have to be members of an organization. In the Swiss cantons no uniform regulation exists. The private associations, some of which have a long history, are in a greater or lesser degree linked to the government machinery.

The scope of supervision is also very divergent in the various states. In some of them supervision has gradually developed into a many-sided responsibility requiring the supervision to concern itself both with aiding the parolee and maintaining public security. In other countries supervision has not yet outgrown the stage of mere control. Still others that did not organize supervision until recently, have approached with progressive concepts profiting from the experiences gathered from other countries. Policy, however, has not yet fully been implemented in all cases.

It seems to occur repeatedly that in spite of the acknowledgement that supervision implies procuring aid and support in the broadest sense, this aid does not actually go beyond job-finding and relief allowances. Such is the case in Argentina, Chile, and Portugal. However, there is a universal trend towards emphasizing the personal elements in the relation between supervisor and parolee and towards limiting material aid to urgent cases. Particularly in the U.S.A. this idea has gained ground in the last few decades. In the recent South African regulations a declaration on the scope of supervision has been laid down. Supervision is broken into eight elements to begin with control which should harmonize with the friendly relation between supervisor and parolee.

It is well known that there was formerly a rather strong tendency to have parolees, particularly repeated offenders, checked by the police. As data from the various countries clearly show, police supervision is generally disapproved nowadays; a view based on the unsuitability of the police for this kind of work.

In the U.S.A. supervision by the police is rejected almost all over the country but in several states supervisors have been granted such extensive police powers that they have been practically put almost in the position of police officers in respect of the parolees.

In Argentina the after-care agencies have ended police participation in their supervisory work.

In Belgium the police had formerly been charged with supervision but this situation caused such grave discontent that another course was chosen at the end of the first World War. In France a similar development took place after World War II.

In Chile, Portugal, South Africa and Victoria the parolee is ordered to report to the police only when the situation excludes any other mode of supervision.

No police interference with supervision exists in England, the Netherlands, Sweden and Switzerland, or in South Africa in respect of Work Colony inmates and juveniles. The Swiss Federal Penal Code formally prohibits the introduction of the police into supervision by cantonal legislation. Though police supervision is no longer used, police authorities often exercise some influence as members of Parole Boards, etc.

In all the countries examined supervision and after-care are wholly or almost wholly financed from public funds. Voluntary contributions received in some countries do not amount to more than a fraction of the large sums needed for this work.

It seldom occurs that supervision is exclusively in the hands of officials. If so, lack of interest on the side of the population sometimes urges toward such a solution, as in the case of Tasmania and Victoria.

Very often both private persons and officials are included in supervisory work, but it is doubtful whether in all those cases a system of supervision by professional officials of the co-operating laymen has been deliberately aimed at. A form of collaboration between both groups of supervisors is theoretically provided for in the U.S.A. federal parole system, but in practice the officials carry out the bulk of actual supervision. An analogous state appears to exist in France. In Sweden this theory of expert supervision over lay-supervisors seems to be realized in practice to a greater extent. A certain tendency can be noted to emphasize the official element in supervision.

Eligibility

a. Common Offenders

The portion of the sentence which must be served before parole may be granted, is as follows:

1/3 in the U.S.A. (fed system) and a maximum of 15 years. in Belgium	with a minimum of 2 months with a minimum of 3 months;
1/2 in France and Portugal in Chile	with a minimum of 6 months; with a minimum of 1 year and in any case, after 3 years;
2/3 in the Argentine Republic	with a minimum of 8 months, imprisonment or 1 year reclusion.
in the Swiss Federation	with a minimum of 3 months;
in Sweden	with a minimum of 8 months;
in the Netherlands	with a minimum of 9 months.

The term is equal to the minimum term of the indeterminate sentence in some jurisdictions of the U.S.A. The term is not specified and is left to the direction of the parole authority in Australia (Tasmania and Victoria), South Africa and a number of jurisdictions in the U.S.A. No provisions for the parole of common offenders are in force in England. Offenders who committed certain specified crimes are excluded from parole in some jurisdictions of the U.S.A.

b. Young Offenders

Special provisions for young offenders were enacted in the following countries, fixing the term after which parole is possible on 3 months, provided 2/3 of the sentence have expired for young prisoners in England; on 6 months for sentences of less than $1\frac{1}{2}$ years, or 1 year for other sentences in the Netherlands; on 9 months in case of Borstal training in England; on 1 year for lesser and 2 years for more serious crimes, provided $\frac{1}{2}$ of the sentence has expired in Portugal; on 1-3 years in the Swiss Federation.

In the Swiss Federation parole of those interned as inebriates is possible as soon as they are well, and in any case, after 2 years.

In England parole under corrective training is possible after the expiration of 2/3, under preventive detention after the expiration of 2/3 or 5/6 of the sentence. In the Argentine Republic, Mexico and some jurisdictions of the U.S.A., recidivists are excluded from parole.

d. *Life Termers*

These prisoners may be paroled after 10 years (recidivists 14 years) in Belgium; 10 years (recidivists 15 years) in Chile; after 10 years in England (practice, no legal provisions) ; 15 years in the Swiss Federation and the U.S.A. (federal system) ; and 20 years in the Argentine Republic

They are excluded from parole in Australia (Victoria), France and a number of jurisdictions in the U.S.A.

e. *Obligatory Parole*

In England young prisoners are to be paroled after expiration of 2/3 of their sentence, offenders under Borstal training after 3 years (i.e., 3/4 of the fixed term). In Portugal young offenders, abnormal but criminally responsible offenders, vagabounds and those put on a par with them are paroled only when their sentence or term of internment expires. In Sweden parole is obligatory when 5/6 of the prison term has been served.

Initiative

The initiative for the petition for parole is, or may be, taken by the prisoner himself, his relatives or counsel in the Argentine Republic, Belgium, England, Sweden, the Swiss cantons, Bern, Luzern, Schwyz, Zurich, most of the jurisdictions of the U.S.A.; the management of the penal establishment in Belgium, the Netherlands, Portugal, some cantons of the Swiss Federation (Basel, Zurich,) South Africa and the U.S.A.

Parole Authority

The ultimate decision of granting parole is made by the governor or the government in Australia (Tasmania), Belgium, Chile, England (Borstal training), some cantons of the Swiss Federation (Bern, Luzern, Schaffhausen, Schwyz), South Africa (Prisoners and convicts), some jurisdictions in the U.S.A.; the minister of justice in Australia (Victoria, in case of release on probation), Belgium, Chile, England (life termers), the Netherlands, some cantons of the Swiss Federation (Aargau Vaud, Zurich); the minister of social walfare in Mexico and South Africa (work colonies); the tribunal which pronounced the sentence in the Argentine Republic and the Swiss canton Thurgau; a special tribunal in Portugal; a special board in England (Borstal training, young offenders preventive detention), Sweden, some cantons of the Swiss Federation (Basel, Geneva, Vaud); the federal system and most of the other jurisdictions of the U.S.A.; the institutional management in South Africa (statutory institutions) and some jurisdictions of the U.S.A.

SELECTED BIBLIOGRAPHY*

Allen, R. M.: Problems of parole. *JCLC, 38:*7–13, 1947–48.

American Correctional Assoc.: *Correctional Officers Training Guide,* 1962.

————: *A Manual of Correctional Standards,* 1960.

————: (formerly American Prison Association): *Handbook on Pre-release Preparation in Correctional Institutions,* 1948.

Arluke, N. R.: A summary of parole rules. *JNPPA:* 6–13, Jan., 1956.

Ashley, P. D.: Group work in the probation setting. *Probation* (Great Britain): 6–7, March, 1962.

Barneberg, G. E.: The board of trustees: duties and responsibilities. *APA:* 221–224, 1947.

Barry, J. V.: An Australian experiment in probation and parole. *Probation* (Great Britain): March, 1961.

Beattie, R. N.: Measuring the effectiveness of probation. *Calif. Youth Authority Q., 10:*33–36, Summer, 1957.

Bell, M. and Chute, C. L.: *Crime, Courts, and Probation,* MacMillan, 1956.

Benton, F. M.: Supervising the adult parolee. *NPPA:* 202–210, 1948.

Bissell, D.: Group work in the probation setting. *British J. Criminology,* 229–250, Jan., 1962.

Brewer, J. L.: The clerk also has an important part in probation. *Fed. Prob.,* 6–9, July, 1955.

Bridges, F.: The personal interview. *NPPA:* 34–37, 1953.

Burbank, E. G.: The place of social casework service in the pre-release program of the correctional institution. *APA:* 252–260, 1948.

———— and Goldsborough, E. W.: The probation officer's personality: a key factor in rehabilitation. *Fed. Prob.,* 11–14, June, 1954.

Burkhart, E. A.: Interstate Cooperation in probation and parole. *Fed. Prob.,* June, 1960.

Chappell, R.: The federal probation service: its growth and progress. *Fed. Prob.,* Oct., 1947.

Chute, C. L.: Probation versus jail. *Jail Assoc. J.:* Jan., 1940.

Clark, R. E.: Size of the parole community as related to parole outcome. *Amer. J. Sociol., 57:*43–47, 1951.

*Key to abbreviations of page 339.

Class, N. E.: Qualifications: a realistic approach to personnel requirements. *JNPPA:* Apr., 1957.

Cooper, H.: *Probation.* Shaw (London) , 1949.

Council of State Governments: *Suggested State Legislation Program, (especially materials on detainers),* 1957.

Cozart, R.: Release preparation of the offender. *Fed. Prob.,* Mar., 1952.

Crihfield, B. E.: The interstate probation and parole compact. *Fed. Prob.,* Dec., 1951.

Crime and Delinquency: Issue devoted to parole prediction tables. July, 1962.

Cunningham, E. B.: The role of the parole adviser. *Fed. Prob.,* Dec., 1951.

Dalton, R. H.: Value and use of counseling techniques in the work of probation officers. *Fed. Prob.,* Dec., 1952.

Doyle, R. F.: Conditions of probation. *Fed. Prob.,* Sept., 1953.

Dressler, D.: *Parole Chief.* Viking Press, 1951.

————: *Probation and Parole.* Columbia Univ. Press, 1951.

————: *Practice and Theory of Probation and Parole.* Columbia Univ. Press, 1959.

Dwoskin, S. I.: Jail as a condition of probation. *Calif. Youth Authority Q.,* Summer, 1962.

Evjen, V. H.: Current thinking on parole prediction tables. *Crime and Delinquency,* July, 1962.

Farrow, R. G.: The give and take of parole supervision. *Focus,* Jan., 1953.

———— and Giardini, G. I.: The paroling of capital offenders. *Annals,* Nov., 1952.

Federal Probation: A symposium on sentencing alternatives in the federal courts. June, 1962.

Fenton, N.: The psychological preparation of inmates for release. *APA:* 100–110, 1949.

Fink, A.: Parole supervision—a case analysis. *Fed. Prob.,* Sept., 1951.

————: Authority in the correctional process. *Fed. Prob.,* Sept., 1961.

Finsley, F.: Who gets parole. *Fed. Prob.,* Sept., 1953.

Fishman, J. F. and Perlman, V.: In the name of parole. *Yale Rev., 28:* 1939.

Fitzgerald, E.: The presentence investigation. *JNPPA,* Oct., 1956.

————: A critical review of probation and parole. *NPPA:* 3–23, 1953.

Floch, M.: Mental hygiene in parole work. *Focus,* Jan., 1955.

Flynn, F. T.: Parole supervision—a case analysis. *Fed. Prob.,* June, 1951.

Fuller, J. K.: Extension of group therapy to parolees. *Prison World,* July, 1952.

Giardini, G. I.: Evaluating the work of parole officers. *NPPA:* 38–42, 1953.

————: *The Parole Process.* Thomas, Springfield, 1959.

Gibbons, D. C.: Some notes on treatment theory in corrections. *Social Service Rev.,* Sept., 1962.

Gillin, J. S.: Parole prediction in Wisconsin. *Sociol Soc. Res., 34:*407–414, 1950.

Glaser, D.: The efficacy of alternative approaches to parole prediction. *Amer. Social. Rev.:* 283–287, June, 1955.

————: Testing correctional decisions. *JCLC,* Mar., 1955.

————: A reconsideration of some parole prediction factors. *Amer. Social. Rev.:* 335–341, June, 1953.

Galvin, J.: Planning a pre-release unit program. *APA:* 144–149, 1950.

Glover, E.: *Probation and Re-education.* Routledge & K. Paul (London), 1949.

Glueck, S.: *Probation and Criminal Justice.* MacMillan, 1933.

Goodman, L. A.: The use and validity of a prediction instrument. *Amer. J. Sociol., 58:*503–512, 1953.

Graham, M. R.: *These Came Back.* University of Alabama, Bur. Pub. Adm., 1946.

Grygier, T.: Education for correctional workers. *Canadian J. Corrections, 4:*137–151, 1962.

Gurman, I.: Community discrimination against the parolee. *Focus,* Nov., 1953.

————: The relationships that should exist between prisoner aid societies and probation and parole department. *APA:* 43–47, 1952.

Hakeem, M.: The validity of the Burgess method of parole prediction. *Amer. J. Sociol., 53:*376–386, 1948.

————: Glueck method of parole prediction applied to 1861 cases of burglars. *JCLC, 36:*87–97, 1945.

Hannum, R. R.: Employment problems of ex-offenders. *Focus,* Nov., 1954.

Harrison, G.: The Michigan parole camp. *Focus,* Mar., 1954.

Hartman, H. L.: Interviewing techniques in probation and parole-building the relationships. *Fed. Prob.,* Mar., 1963.

Harvard Law Review Assoc.: Parole Revocation procedures. *Harvard Law Rev., 65:*309–315, 1951.

Havel, J.: Special Intensive Parole Unit Reports on phase III, Calif. Dept. of Corrections. *Research Newsletter,* Mar., 1962.

Hayner, N. S.: Summary of discussion-NPPA. *APA:* 326–328, 1952. *(A summary of discussions on parole hearings, policy, etc.)*

Head, W. J.: Job finding for prisoners. *Fed. Prob.,* Mar., 1952.

Hendrick, E. J.: Basic concepts of conditions and violations. *JNPPA:* Jan., 1956.

Hiller, F.: Adult probation laws in the United States. *NPPA:* 1933.

——: Methods of appointing probation officers. *JNPPA:* Apr., 1957.

Hink, H. R.: Application of constitutional standards of protection to probation. *Univ. of Chicago Law R.,* Spring, 1962.

Hyman, E. C.: Holding the promiscuous girl accountable for her own behavior. *NPPA:* 189–201, 1948.

Huffman, A. V. and Meeks, W. M.: A statement of principles of treatment in preparation for parole. *Fed. Prob.,* Dec., 1954.

Illinois Dept. of Public Safety: *Rules and Statutes Governing Restoration of Citizenship Rights to Discharged Probationers and Discharged Prisoners.* 1949.

Ives, J. K.: The essential task of the probation-parole officer. *Fed. Prob.,* Mar., 1962.

Jacks, W. L.: *A comparison of parole agents' salaries, caseloads, and supervision duties.* Pa. Board of Parole, 1957.

Johnson, A. R.: Recent developments in the law of probation. *JCLC,* June, 1962.

Jones, M.: The treatment of character disorders. *British J. of Criminology, 3:*276–282, 1963.

Keve, P.: *Prison, Probation, or Parole.* Univ. of Minnesota Press, 1954.

——: *The Probation Officer Investigates.* Univ. of Minnesota Press, 1962.

——: The professional character of the presentence report. *Fed. Prob.,* June, 1962.

Killinger, G.: The federal government's parole program. *Fed. Prob.,* June, 1950.

——: The functions and responsibilities of parole boards. *NPPA:* 121–129, 1950.

Kirby, B. C.: Parole prediction using multiple correlation. *Amer. J. Sociol.,* May, 1954.

Kirkpatrick, A. M.: After-care in the Canadian correctional treatment plan. *ACA:* 225–232, 1953.

Lejins, P.: Criminology for probation and parole officers. *JNPPA,* July, 1956.

——: Parole Prediction—an introductory statement. *Crime and Delinquency,* July, 1962.

Lester, Ervis, Ervis: Parole treatment and surveillance—which should dominate? *APA:* 48–60, 1952.

Lippman, H. S.: The role of the probation officer in the treatment of delinquency in children. *Fed. Prob.,* June, 1948.

Loveland, F.: Financial and material aspects of release planning. *Fed. Prob.,* Mar., 1952.

McCord, W., McCord, J., and Verden, P.: Family Relationships and sexual deviance in lower class adolescents. *Int. J. Social Psychiatry 83:*165–179, 1962.

McDivitt, C. B.: Reintegration of the offender in the community. *APA:* 126–131, 1949.

McHugh, T. J.: Requirements for parole selection. *APA:* 170–174, 1954.

————: Practical aspects of casework in parole supervision. *NPPA:* 158–169, 1950.

————: Parole from within the institution. *Focus,* Jan., 1948.

McMinn, E.: The institutional parole officer. *Focus,* Jan., 1954.

Meacham, W. S.: Conditions of probation and parole—do they help or hinder? *NPPA:* 40–59, 1947.

Meeker, B. S.: Federal Probation Training Center exemplifies agency responsibility for training. *Social Work Education,* Sept., 1962.

————: Relationships of probation staff and the guidance center. *Progress Report,* July–Sept., 1962.

————: Probation is casework. *Fed. Prob.,* Mar., 1948.

Meyer, C. H.: A half century of probation and parole. *JCLC, 42:*707–728, 1952.

Miller, F. P.: Parole and the aftercare agency. *Canadian Welf.* Dec., 1956.

Monachesi, E. D.: American studies in the prediction of recidivism. *JCLC 41:*268–289, 1951.

National Council on Crime and Delinquency: *International Bibliography on Crime and Delinquency* (periodical) .

————: *Current Research Projects Reported to National Research and Information Center* (periodical) .

————: *Crime and Delinquency* (periodical) .

————: *NCCD NEWS* (periodical) ; Employment Bull.

————: Standard Probation and Parole Act.

————: *John Augustus, First Probation Officer.* (Reprint of the original with an introduction by Sheldon Glueck) .

Newman, C. L.: Casework in Adult Probation and Parole. *Indian J. Social Work* (Bombay) , Mar., 1959.

Newman, C. L.: Concepts of Treatment in Probation and Parole Supervision. *Fed. Prob.*, Mar., 1961.

——: The sexual offender: criminological enigma. *Alabama Correctional J.*, Nov., 1962.

——: Foster care in the treatment of juvenile delinquency. *Quarterly J. Pennsylvania Probation and Parole Assoc.*, Feb., 1963.

New York State, Division of Parole: *Parole Officers Manual.*

——: An approach to the study of delinquency among parolees. *Correction*, New York, Nov., 1953.

New York State, Division of Probation: *Manual for Probation Officers.*

Odell, C. E.: Job adjustment for probationers and parolees. *Fed. Prob.*, June, 1951.

Ohlin, L. E.: *Selection for Parole.* Rusell Sage Foundation, 1951.

——: The routinization of correctional change. *JCLC, 45:*400–411, 1954.

——: *Sociology and the Field of Corrections.* Ruseell Sage Foundation, 1956.

—— and Duncan, O. D.: The efficiency of prediction in criminology. *Amer. J. Sociology, 54:*441–451, 1949.

Oswald, R. D.: Community discrimination against the parolee—a second look. *Focus*, May, 1954.

Panakal, J. J. and Dighe, K. G.: Probation. *Indian J. Social Work* (Bombay) , Sept., 1961.

Pennsylvania, Board of Parole: *Sex Offenders Released on Parole.* 1962.

Pigeon, H. D.: *Probation and Parole in Theory and Practice. National Probation & Parole Assoc.*, 1942. (Now, the *National Council on Crime and Delinquency.*)

Plummer, E. C.: An honor cottage experiment. *APA:* 124, 1950.

Podair, S. and Tabb, B. I.: Group education with parolees. *Fed. Prob.*, Sept., 1954.

Prigmore, C. S.: Surveillance or treatment—the supervisor's decision. *Focus,* Jan., 1955.

——: The role of the supervisor in achieving a balance between surveillance and treatment in probation and parole. *APA:* 175–180, 1954.

Ray, J. M.: Scientific parole—a proposal. *JCLC, 37:*384–389, 1947.

Reckless, W. C.: Training of probation and parole personnel. *APA:* 100–105, 1947.

Reinemann, J. O.: *Parole and Probation,* Phila. Jr. Chamber of Commerce, 1953.

——: Principles and practices of probation. *Fed. Prob.*, Sept., 1950.

Remington, F. J. and Newman, D. J.: The Highland Park Institute on Sentence Disparity. *Fed. Prob.,* Mar., 1962.

Resko, J.: *Reprieve.* Doubleday, 1956.

Richardson, S.: Parole and the law. *JNPPA,* Jan., 1956.

Rikelman, H. and Weiss, M. H.: A cooperative effort in finding jobs for prisoners. *Correction,* New York, June, 1953.

Root, M. B.: What the probation officer can do for special types of offenders. *Fed. Prob.,* Dec. 1949.

Rubin, S.: A legal view of probation and parole conditions. *JNPPA,* Jan., 1956.

Rumney, J. and Murphy, J. P.: *Probation and Social Adjustment.* Rutgers Univ. Press, 1952.

Sanson, D. R.: Probation and Parole for Misdemeanants. *NPPA:* 186–192, 1949.

Schnur, A. C.: The validity of parole selection. *Social Forces, 29:*322–328, 1951.

Schuessler, K. F.: Parole prediction: its history and status. *JCLC, 45:* 425–431, 1954.

Scott, A. W., Jr.: The pardoning power. *Annals,* Nov., 1952.

Sharp, J. L., Inservice training in probation and parole. *Feb. Prob.,* Dec., 1951.

Silverman, E.: Surveillance, treatment, and casework supervision. *JNPPA,* Jan., 1956.

Smith, A. B. and Bassin, A.: Research in a probation department. *Crime and Delinquency,* Jan., 1962.

Smith, E. R.: Supervision of field personnel. *NPPA:* 79–85, 1953.

Smith, P. A.: Principal criteria for evaluating parolee progress. *NPPA:* 38–42, 1953.

Stanley, F. G.: Attracting employer interest in parolees. *Focus,* July, 1950.

Stern, L. T.: Popular or scientific evaluation of probation and parole. *NPPA:* 55–70, 1948.

Sterne, R. S.: *Outcome of Parole as Related to Pre-Parole Prognosis.* Pennsylvania Committee on Penal Affairs, 1946.

Stone, W. T.: Administrative Aspects of the special intensive parole program. *ACA:* 126–131, 1956.

———: New concepts in release procedures. *APA:* 233–244, 1953.

Street, T. G.: Canada's parole system. *Amer. J. Correction,* Mar.–Apr., 1962.

Studt, E.: Worker-client authority relationships in social work. *Social Work,* Jan., 1959.

Studte, E.: Education for social workers in the correctional field. *Council on Social Work Education,* 1959.

———: An outline for the study of social authority factors in case-work. *Social Casework, 35:231–238,* 1954.

Sullivan, K.: *Girls on Parole.* Houghton, 1955.

Tappan, P. W.: The legal rights of prisoners. *Annals,* May, 1954.

———: *Contemporary Correction.* McGraw-Hill, 1951.

———: *Juvenile Delinquency.* McGraw-Hill, 1949.

———: *Crime, Justice, and Correction.* McGraw-Hill, 1960.

Timasheff, N. S.: *One Hundred Years of Probation.* Fordham Univ. Press, 1941.

———: *Probation in the Light of Criminal Statistics.* Declan X Mc-Mullen, 1949.

Travers, P.: Experiment in the supervision of paroled offenders ad-dicted to narcotic drugs. *Amer. J. Correction,* Mar.–Apr., 1957.

Trecker, H.: Social work principles in probation. *Fed. Prob.,* Mar., 1955.

United Nations: *Parole and Aftercare.* Dept. of Social Affairs, 1954.

———: *Practical Results and Financial Aspects of Adult Probation in Selected Countries.* Dept. of Social Affairs, 1954.

———: *Probation and Related Measures.* Dept. of Social Affairs, 1951.

———: *International Review of Criminal Policy.* (periodical), *(ex-tensive bibliographies in most issues).*

United States, Attorney General: *Survey of Release Procedures. (Vol. 2. Probation, vol. 3. Pardons, vol. 4. Parole)* U. S. Govt. Printing Office, 1939–1940.

United States, Board of Parole: *Annual Reports.*

Van Waters, M.: The tapering-off process from institution to com-munity living. *APA:* 134–137, 1950.

Vaught, B.: Probation and parole from the judge's point of view. *Fed. Prob.,* Dec., 1954.

Vold, G. B.: *Prediction Methods and Parole.* Sociological Press, 1931.

Vogt, H.: Group counseling in probation. *Fed. Prob.,* Sept., 1961.

Wallace, J.: The casework approach to rules. *JNPPA,* Jan., 1956.

Weinberg, S. K.: Theories of criminality and problems of prediction. *JCLC, 45:412–424,* Nov., 1954.

Williams, M. E.: Developing employment opportunities for parolees. *Focus,* Mar., 1952.

Wilson, D. J.: Should we employ ex-prisoners? *Canadian Business,* Apr., 1952.

Wood, A. L.: The alternatives to the death penalty. *Annals,* Nov., 1952.

Yablonsky, L.: The structure and control of gang violence. *Int. Crim. Pol. Review, 17*:138–144 and 178–184, 1962.

Young, P. V.: *Social Treatment in Probation and Delinquency.* McGraw-Hill, 1952.

Younghusband, E.: Report on a survey of social work in the field of corrections. *Social Work Education,* August, 1960.

Yount, P. D.: A compilation of criteria for parole selection. *APA:* 280–286, 1948.

Note: The following abbreviations were used:

ACA, APA Proceedings of the Annual Congress of Corrections (by year) formerly American Prison Association

JNPPA Journal of the National Probation and Parole Association (discontinued)

Focus Journal of the National Probation and Parole Association (discontinued)

JCLC Journal of Criminal Law, Criminology, and Police Science

Fed. Prob. Federal Probation Quarterly

NPPA Yearbook of the National Probation and Parole Association. (discontinued)

INDEX

S

Salvation Army, 124, 317
Schuessler, Karl F., 237
Scott, Austin W., Jr., 42
Sentencing practices, 114
Sexual deviations
  aggressive psychopath, 147
  homosexuality, 144
  most common, 143
Sexual offenses
  delinquents and, 175
  practices, 170
  problems, 171
Social group work agencies, 160
  see also: Community resources
Social Service Exchange, 111
Social Workers
  use of, 97
Social work and corrections, 84
Solitary confinement, 35
Statute of Artifices, 6, 9
Statute of limitations, 35
Stays of execution, 4, 5
  see also: Clemency, Reprieve
Stroup, Herbert, 155
Studt, Elliot, 87
"Sundown paroles," 210
Supervision, 23, 277, 316, 324
  see also: Authority, Casework, Probation, Parole, Treatment
Survey of Release Procedures, 50, 54
Swift, Jonathan, 71

T

Tappan, Paul W., 26
Ticket-of-Leave, 4, 8, 11, 12, 200, 317
  criticism of, 13
  Inspector of Released Prisoners, 17
  Irish System, 15

supervision by the police, 15
  see also: Parole
Time for good behavior, 23
Transportation
  fee, 5
  of criminals, 4
  termination of, 7
Travers, Paul, 290
Treatment, 27, 275
  responsibility for own decisions, 125
  therapeutic approach, 172
  therapeutic community, 85
  see also: Authority, Casework, Group treatment, Probation, Parole, Supervision

U

United Nations, 61, 322
United States
  Board of Parole, 195, 228
  Employment Service, 271

V

Virginia Company, 4
  see also: Transportation
Vocational guidance agencies, 160
Vold, George B., 238
Volunteers, use of
  see: Parole advisers

W

Warrant to detainer, 196
  see also: Detainer, Interstate parole and probation compact
Wilson, Everett E., 155
Women offenders, 85
  see also: Sexual offenses

Y

Younghusband, Eileen L., 84